The
English
Language

The English Language

Its Origin & History

By Rudolph C. Bambas

UNIVERSITY OF OKLAHOMA PRESS: NORMAN

Library of Congress Cataloging in Publication Data

Bambas, Rudolph C   1915–
 The English language.
 Bibliography: p.
 Includes index.
 1. English language—History. I. Title.
PE1075.B26   420'.9   80-5237

MY 18'82

Contents

Preface   *Page* ix

1. English as a World Language   1
2. The Origin of English   14
3. The Sounds of English   37
4. Old English   56
5. Middle English   92
6. Early Modern English, 1500–1700   130
7. Later Modern English, 1700 to the Present   162
8. American English   206
   Bibliography   231
   Index   235

Maps and Illustrations

1. Distribution of the Indo-European Languages
   in Europe and Western Asia   *Page* 18
2. Diagram of the Organs of Speech   42
3. England and the Middle English Dialect Boundaries   120
4. Dialects of American English   221

vii

Preface

Fifteen hundred years ago the English language was a Low West Germanic dialect spoken by a small number of unimportant people who were in the process of overrunning the island of Britain. Now, as a consequence of fifteen centuries of changes and happenstances of various kinds, the English language is used around the world as a mother tongue and as a second language by more people than have ever used any language in the history of man. The story of this rise to linguistic preeminence is inevitably important.

This study of the evolution of English is a linguistic history, a consideration of change in the form, content, and structure of a particular language, but it is connected with the political, social, and literary history of the English-speaking people, because a language, as the vehicle of thought, necessarily responds to all the significant changes that affect the people who speak it.

Considerable attention is paid in this study to the sounds of English, past and present. Language is more often spoken than written, and how it is pronounced is consequently a matter that needs to be understood in as exact a manner as is possible in print. Phonemic transcription, except where otherwise stated, is in the North Central United States dialect, as a matter of convenience. All other regional dialects of

English as it is spoken around the world are, of course, just as "good."

A study of this kind owes much to the work of many able scholars who have published their findings before. Indebtedness is great to the incomparable *Oxford English Dictionary* and to that similar work in progress, the *Middle English Dictionary*, being published at the University of Michigan. Although obligation is felt to many, special mention is owed to the enlightened good sense of Otto Jespersen, John S. Kenyon, and Albert C. Baugh. Uncounted thousands of books, monographs, and articles exist on topics pertinent to the history of the English language, but the bibliographies that follow the chapters are limited to a few books that are fairly accessible and that may interest the nonspecialist reader.

Obligation is gratefully acknowledged to colleagues: to Victor A. Elconin, who read Chapter 8; to Paul G. Ruggiers for his generous aid in matters Italian; to Bruce I. Granger for information on early American; to Frieda Derdeyn Bambas, whose expertise in French and as a critical reader was invaluable; to Roy J. Pearcy for information on British dialects; and to Alphonse J. Fritz, David P. French, and David S. Gross.

The spelling of quotations from older English has sometimes been modernized, without comment, for the convenience of the reader.

Abbreviations
and Symbols

A:	Accusative
AN:	Anglo-Norman
AS:	Anglo-Saxon
CF:	Central French
D:	Dative
G:	Germanic; Genitive
I:	Instrumental
IE:	Indo-European
IPA:	International Phonetic Alphabet
ME:	Middle English
ModE:	Modern English
N:	Nominative
OE:	Old English
OED:	*Oxford English Dictionary*
OF:	Old French
ON:	Old Norse
Pl:	Plural
Sg:	Singular
SVO:	Subject, verb, object
>:	Changed to
*:	A hypothetical form, one not found in records
´ ‿:	Stress marks, ´ indicating primary stress and ‿ secondary stress, as in *nécessàry*.

Glossary of
Linguistic Terms

Case: the form or position of a word that indicates its grammatical relationship to other words in the sentence. In Old English there were five cases: the *nominative*, expressing the subject function; the *genitive*, in the possessive function; the *dative* and *accusative*, in the object function; the *instrumental*, expressing the means by which action was carried out. The genitive case of nouns survives, as in *"day's* work" and in pronouns like *my, our, his*; the pronoun forms *me, us, him, her, them* are surviving examples of the dative case.

Diphthong: a speech sound that begins with one vowel and moves to another in the same syllable, like the vowel sound in *out*.

Fortis: a relatively forceful sound, as *t* in contrast with lenis *d*.

Grammar: the analysis of language.

Inflection: variation in form to indicate grammatical function.

Lenis: a "soft" sound, produced with little aspiration, as *d* in contrast with fortis *t*.

Linguistics: the precisely factual, "scientific" study of language.

Morphology: the study of variant forms of words.

Paradigm: a pattern or set of the forms of a word.

Phoneme: a minimal meaningful speech sound; *p* and *b* in *pit* and *bit* are different phonemes, distinguishing one word from the other.

Phonetics: the analysis and description of the sounds of speech.

Phonology: the broad study of the sounds of language in their various combinations and historical changes.

Semantics: the study of the meaning of words.

Syntax: the combining of words into phrases and sentences; the study of word order.

Voice: the vibration of the vocal cords that makes speech audible above the whisper level.

The
English
Language

1

English as a
World Language

English is only one of some three thousand languages now spoken on the planet Earth. Each of these three thousand languages is important to the people who speak it, for it is a human characteristic to have a deep emotional attachment to one's "mother tongue," which is felt to be faultlessly functional and incomparably "beautiful," whereas all foreigners speak some sort of hideous gibberish. To the Greek ear in the classical period foreign speech sounded like "bar-bar," from which noise is presumably derived the word "barbarian." A complacent approval of the mother tongue is not limited to the Greeks or to the French or Americans, but is universal.

The degree of importance of a language to speakers of other languages varies considerably, however. It depends on the number of speakers of that language and on their economic, political, military, and cultural prestige and authority. English has more than three hundred million native speakers, who collectively have great influence on the conduct of the world's affairs. Consequently, English is widely used as a second language in parts of the world where it is not the mother tongue. This is a convenience to English speakers, who can travel to the seaports and great cities of the world and reasonably expect to find hotel, restaurant, and other business personnel who can understand them. English-speaking tourists seldom need to resort to the language of the country they are in.

As an international language English is not without rivals. Russian has become prominent as one of the consequences of shifts in the world's power balance. Chinese is obviously important because of the influence, actual and potential, of its more than 950 million speakers, who occupy a large and fertile landmass. Spanish is important because of its use from the Río Grande to Patagonia. French is still the diplomatic and commercial language of those states that were part of the French Empire. The five languages named are the five official languages used in conducting the business of the United Nations; a speaker addressing this body must use one of them. His remarks are simultaneously translated into the other four, for the benefit of listeners who are not adept in the language used by the speaker. A speaker whose mother tongue is something else—Danish, Bantu, Turkish—is put at a disadvantage. He must use an internationally functional second language.

There are other important languages besides these five. Arabic is used over a large part of the world's area, from Iraq to Morocco. German, Italian, and Portuguese are widely used, too. Hindi may some day be the language of a half billion people. But most of the world's three thousand languages have limited use and are rarely learned by speakers of other languages.

International languages are not a new phenomenon. The New Testament was composed and distributed not in the language of Christ and the disciples of his lifetime but in Greek, which was the international language of the Mediterranean world in the early Christian era. Greek had become the general commercial and political language of various communities during the development of the Athenian Empire in the fifth century B.C. The use of Greek as the official language in the Macedonian Empire in the following century confirmed and widened its use. Then, long after Greek had ceased to be the voice of actual power, its use continued, since the language was known to many as the means of communication among the schooled whose mother tongues were of various and mutually unintelligible kinds. Once a language is established as a lingua franca, its use as such continues long after the power that established it has disappeared. The reason for this is not hard to find: linguistic habits are hard to acquire and slow to change, and it is convenient to teachers of foreign language to teach the language that they know.

In time, of course, Greek gave way to Latin, the language of a Roman Empire that endured five hundred years. The power and prestige of Rome—and of Latin—were so penetrating that in some sections of the empire, Iberia and Gaul and "Romania," the indigenous populations came to adopt Latin as the mother tongue.

After the Fall of Rome, Latin remained the established language of intercommunication for peoples who spoke a variety of vernaculars. The propagation of Christianity carried Latin into northern Europe as the language of the church. Latin was also the lingua franca of politics and commerce, and state papers intended for distribution as propaganda abroad had to be couched in proper Latin. The position of John Milton as Latin secretary to the Cromwell government illustrates this point. Milton's ability to compose impeccable Latin was necessary to support the prestige of the government.

Latin was the language of learning, too. Sir Thomas More, Erasmus of Rotterdam, Sir Francis Bacon wrote their serious works in Latin in order to reach the widest possible audience of the learned. No Renaissance Englishman could expect to be read on the Continent if he wrote in English, a language then confined to its tight little island.

Not until the late seventeenth century did a living vernacular begin to challenge the position of Latin. The military and commercial power of France in the time of Louis Quatorze gave the language of the country a prestige that began to attract to its use speakers of neighboring vernaculars. We see the effect of this prestige in the practice of that notable eighteenth-century personage Frederick the Great, King of Prussia, who named his palace Sans Souci, wrote French verses badly, and sought the company of Monsieur Voltaire. And it seems curious to us now that the Russian nobility of the nineteenth century spoke French in preference to Russian, a language they regarded as good enough for peasants but not fit for the polite.

English began slowly to rival French with the emergence of the British Empire during the eighteenth and nineteenth centuries. That empire planted its language in the colonies of the Western Hemisphere and then in South Africa, Australia, and New Zealand. Victory over France in Canada and India naturally gave English superiority over French in those areas. Power made the English language attractive everywhere in Europe and made Shakespeare more interesting. By the late nineteenth century, English was just as important internationally as French. And by that time another rival had appeared. The shift of events in the nineteenth century had gradually made German an attractive language. The German universities played an important role in this, leading the world in such energetic intellectual activity that others were forced to imitate it in an effort to catch up. The stunningly quick defeat of France in the Franco-Prussian War, the unification of Germany in 1871 and the phenomenal industrial growth that followed, combined to give the German language great prestige and to make it attractive for international use. On the eve of World War I, English, French, and German seemed to have equal shares of eminence.

Events since 1914 have changed the relative positions of the old rivals. The two world wars damaged Europe catastrophically. The empires formed by Britain, France, and Germany have vanished, and the wealth, power, influence, and prestige of these nations have been sorely diminished. All three languages are still in prominent international use, but English is now more widely used than the other two because, although Britain lost power, the United States gained more power than Britain lost. The later twentieth century has witnessed the use of the English language rise to an unprecedented peak. English is now established as the mother tongue of millions of persons in various parts of the world: Britain and Ireland, South Africa, Australia and New Zealand, the United States and Canada. As a second language English has wider use by more people than has ever been true of any other language in the world's history. Many of the schooled citizens of India are sometimes obliged to communicate with one another in English because they speak languages that are not intelligible to many of their compatriots. Air-traffic controllers use English to guide planes in and out of airports everywhere in the world. A single language is an absolute necessity for this purpose, and English was the only reasonable choice.

Since English is in such wide use, the learning of it as a second language is an important activity in many parts of the world. At any moment of the day thousands of students are earnestly endeavoring to master the intricacies and curious ways of the English language.

It is useful for native speakers of English to attempt to see the language as others see it. As observers we may wonder at the strange pronunciations and odd syntactic patterns that "foreigners" produce as they struggle with English, but anyone who has made a serious effort to learn any second language is aware of the sometimes appalling difficulties that lie in his way. All languages are intricate and difficult to learn; English is no exception.

The foreign student of English finds much to please him at the beginning of his labors. Morphology is hardly a problem: nouns form their plural by affixing *s*: *book*, *books*; *table*, *tables*. The list of exceptions to this rule is so small that it is easily learned: invariable plurals, like *sheep*, *deer*, *swine*, are limited to words for some animals; there are only seven surviving "umlaut" plurals: *men*, *women*, *feet*, *teeth*, *geese*, *mice*, *lice*; of a once-numerous class of *n* plurals only two survive: *oxen* and *children*. The eager student masters this information immediately and goes on to discover that the inflection of the verb for person, number, and tense is also simple. He observes the paradigm of the present tense forms:

I work	we work
you work	you work
he works	they work

The simple base form *work* is used in five of the situations. The only exception occurs in the third person singular: *works*. In the preterit a single form, *worked*, suffices for the three persons and two numbers. The preterit of most verbs is formed by simply adding *t*, *d*, or *ed* to the base, for example, *sleep*, *slept*; *work*, *worked*; *learn*, *learned*. There are exceptions to this rule that must be learned, like *bring*, *brought*; *sing*, *sang*; but the morphology of the verb in English puts a far smaller burden on the memory of the student than it does in languages like French or Spanish. The adjective in English is not inflected for case, number, or gender, and thus the speaker need not bother to make adjectives agree grammatically with the noun they modify; the base agrees perfectly, no matter what the noun does. And in English, grammatical gender does not exist. The learner of French and German must remember that the word for "sun" is masculine in French (*le soleil*) but feminine in German (*die Sonne*). There is none of this to bother with in English.

Thus, in the area of morphology, the labor of the student of English is light. But other matters are far from simple. Syntax, idiom, and spelling are maddeningly irrational. A reasonable working definition of language could be: *Language is an arbitrary system of sounds in certain combinations that members of a social group use in communicating with one another.* Language is indeed a system. If it were not systematic, it could not be learned. But this system has some arbitrary, capricious facets. In a perfectly rational system analogy would always operate, but in actual language analogy sometimes breaks down. The student may observe that in English the following sentences are equivalent:

> It started raining.
> It started to rain.

If, however, the finite verb is changed to *stopped*, then analogy will not work:

> It stopped raining.
> *It stopped to rain.

The last sentence is not real. (* indicates hypothetical form.) The native speaker of English avoids unreal sentences as though by instinct, but the nonnative has to acquire an awareness of what is not real by slow and sometimes painful degrees. The sentences:

> He stopped talking.
> He stopped to talk.

are both real, but they have opposed meanings. This fact has to be learned.

Word order is not a linguistic universal but is arbitrary in all languages. The question "What is your father's name?" in Hindi is "Tumhara bap ka nam kya hai?" Word for word in English that is, "Your father of name what is?" and would be understood only with difficulty, if at all, by an English speaker. The speaker of either language learning the other has to accustom himself to a word order that is not "natural" to him.

English grammar has many delicate points that are difficult to define and explain simply. For example, the infinitive is sometimes marked by the meaningless particle *to* and sometimes not. We say, "They asked him *to* come in early" or "They wanted him *to* come in early," but in "They had him come in early" or "They made him come in early," the particle is omitted. Native speakers learn such nuances without effort as children, but foreign adults need "rules," which are sometimes hard to come by. A grammar popular in Europe by the Hollander R. W. Zandvoort (*A Handbook of English Grammar*), takes twenty pages to explain and illustrate the English infinitive with and without *to*.

The English use and omission of the definite article *the* is another nicety. We omit the article before the names of countries but include it before the names of rivers: England and France, but *the* Thames, *the* Mississippi. We say, "He has a house in town and one in *the* country," a difference that does not seem reasonable to one not to the language born. The British spend time "in hospital," but Americans do so "in *the* hospital." Zandvoort devotes a chapter to "Use of the Definite

Article," in the last section of which he says: "It is impossible to mention here all the cases in which English dispenses with the definite article. Many of them belong to idiom rather than to grammar." He means that some matters in English cannot be captured by a "rule."

Words can be capricious, too. There is a story about two Frenchmen visiting in America. They are asked if they have any children. One says he doesn't because his wife is impregnable. The second Frenchman says, "You mean she's inconceivable." The first replies, "No, I mean she's unbearable." These word choices are not unreasonable, but they are unidiomatic. The large group of verb-adverb combinations can puzzle the mind of the nonnative: houses can indifferently *burn up* or *burn down*; we *put up* tomatoes and *put up* visitors; we *make up* our minds, *make up* for lost time, and *make up* after quarrels; we *put out* cats, effort, and fires, and are *put out* by something that displeases us; if we are *held up*, we have been either "delayed" or "robbed."

The spelling of English is a thing of horror to the student with an orderly mind. The frequent gap between spelling and pronunciation requires that both be memorized. The student thinks it odd that *vestige* and *prestige* do not rhyme. Neither do *break* and *speak*, or *Yeats* and *Keats*. *Heard*, *word*, and *bird* do, however. Words that contain the spelling *-ough* have a remarkable range of pronunciations:

cough (off)	bought (aw)
rough (uff)	though (o)
bough (ow)	through (oo)

The pronunciation of *read* depends on whether the verb is functioning in the present tense or in the preterit. *Lead* has one pronunciation as a noun, but another as a verb. *Close* and *lose* look similar but do not sound that way. *Close* has different pronunciations as adjective and verb.

These discrepancies between sight and sound put a heavy burden on the student who wishes to speak English as well as to read it. As he adds to his vocabulary, he must remember not only the meaning of words but also spellings and pronunciations that all too often are not in harmony. Some schools that teach English as a foreign language refrain from exposing students to the spelling "unsystem" until they have attained some degree of skill in speaking and hearing English. It is hoped that in this way the shock when it comes will be less severe. It has been often argued that the international use of English would be much facilitated if the spelling were reformed so that there would be more coherence in sight and sound. A number of spelling reform systems have been devised and vigorously promoted, but as yet without success. Linguistic habit is too deeply ingrained to be deliberately changed, and inertia is a powerful social force. As long as native speakers of English insist on retaining their traditional spellings, so long will foreign students have to learn them in order to read and write the language. And English is so powerful an international tool that foreign students are obliged to keep on learning the language despite difficulties that sometimes seem unreasonable.

There is one aspect of the English vocabulary that is a convenience to students whose mother tongue is either Germanic or Italic. English belongs to the Germanic group of languages, along with German, Dutch, Flemish, Frisian, Danish, Swedish, Norwegian, and Icelandic, and consequently shares a core vocabulary of thousands of words with these languages, whose native speakers can quickly recognize the English forms of words that have cognates in their mother tongues, words like *mother*, *father*, *water*, *land*, *house*, for example. The English vocabulary also has thousands of words that have been borrowed from Latin or French, and consequently speakers of an Italic language like French, Spanish, Italian or Portuguese can recognize those words that have cognate forms in their own languages, words like *theater*, *part*, *flower*, *age*, and *face*. Of course, this advantage does not exist for students of English who don't know an Italic or another Germanic language. But, nevertheless, the numbers of students around the world who struggle bravely and successfully with English are legion. We can only wish the task were easier.

The future of English is a topic that has drawn some speculation. English is the world's leading means of intercommunication now, and it would seem a matter of mere extension to make it everybody's language. A single universal language would facilitate international understanding and cooperation. Some dream that universal peace might bloom among the peoples if only they could understand one another. This is a naïve view, of course, for civil wars have been notably bloody ones. But a single language used around the world would indeed make commerce, travel, and diplomacy easier to manage. That English or any other language will become a universal tongue is, however, unlikely in the extreme. More than half of the world's population is illiterate in whatever mother tongue. Schools that teach literacy to all, and then English, do not exist in anything like sufficient numbers. Furthermore, political obstacles to promoting English as the one international language are great. Linguistic chauvinism shows no signs of diminishing, and asking lovers of their own mother tongue to give preference to a foreign lingo is to invite a rush to the barricades.

The political and emotional resistance to promoting any living language as the world's sole vehicle led to the invention of artificial languages, such as Esperanto, Ido, Volapük and Interlingua. Such languages are not only emotionally unobjectionable but structurally superior to real languages. They are simple, consistent, and free from baffling idioms. They are consequently much easier to learn. But the world has shown small inclination to interest itself in such invented languages. The lure to do so is not great. After all, there is no *Faust* or *Oedipus* in Esperanto, so why bother? The learning of real languages, if more difficult, is much more rewarding.

Although we cannot expect that there will come a time when everybody in the world speaks English, the future of the language has a favorable look in the last quarter of the twentieth century. Numbers and collective power are the telling factors here. What changes in these factors time will bring we cannot know, but English is in as good a position as its principal rivals of the moment, Russian, Chinese, and Spanish. Terrain and climate limit the possibilities of population expansion for all the rivals. All four languages are spoken by communities that control large landmasses, but there is a limit to the ultimate population that any landmass can support. Food and water shortages are already obvious. The map would seem to indicate that Canada gives English an enormous area for expansion, but, of course, the climate of most of that area inhibits its occupation by any appreciable number. The same limitation holds for most of frigid Siberia, too, so it is not expected that Siberia will some day hold a billion energetic speakers of Russian. The capacity of South America to sustain huge masses of Spanish speakers is limited by terrain that is mountainous or torrid. Man does not thrive on bare peaks or in jungles.

English speakers are thus in a fortunate position in the world today. It should be borne in mind, however, that the eminence of this language is the consequence of a series of fortunate accidents, not of superior virtue either in the language or in its speakers. We should avoid the linguistic complacency that seemed natural to the Greeks and Romans, but should apply ourselves to the assiduous study of as many foreign languages as we can. Other languages are noble, too, and deserve our learning them, to our own advantage. As Goethe put it, "Who is not acquainted with another language doesn't know his own."

2

The Origin of English

It is natural for anyone to be curious about his mother tongue. He is at least occasionally aware of it as an important part of himself, and consequently questions like "Where did the English language come from?" and "How old is the English language?" do not uncommonly cross the speculative mind. Unfortunately, much as we would like to answer these questions, we cannot. The origin of English lies somewhere in remote antiquity, certainly more than five thousand years ago, but precisely how many more no one can say. So, too, the question of what point in the world marks the cradle of the language is not answerable with precision. The educated guess would place this point somewhere in Europe between the Ukraine and the Baltic.

The questions have no certain answer because all languages had their origin in prehistory, before the use of writing, and consequently there are no records before the relatively recent invention of writing systems. English had a life of thousands of years before any of it was recorded, but what its prehistoric life was like we have no certain way of knowing.

English belongs to a "family" of languages called the Indo-European family. There are other families: the Semitic, the Finno-Ugric, the Tibeto-Chinese, for example. What "family" means is that at some time and in some place a community of people invented and developed, over thousands of years, a language that each generation passed on to the next. When the community outgrew its living space, part of it moved out to find and settle in another living space. Then there were two groups who no longer intercommunicated, and in the course of time linguistic changes affecting each group independently became so great that intercommunication was no longer possible. This splitting and diversifying process could be repeated until there were many different living descendants of the parent language.

The ancestral form of the language family that includes English is called proto-Indo-European. What the people who spoke this original form called their language we have no way of knowing, since they left no records. They probably lived in southeastern Europe more than five thousand years ago. Eventually groups of proto-Indo-European speakers broke off from the main community in repeated migrations, gradually spreading over the landmass of Europe and western Asia from India to Scandinavia and Britain.

It would be fascinating to know what the adventures of these migrating Indo-European speakers were. What strange peoples did they encounter in their wanderings? What mighty battles were fought for territorial control? Who were the heroes on either side? Unfortunately we will never know, for nations that have no writing leave no history. What is obvious is that migrating Indo-European communities, separated from one another by space through accumulating centuries, developed mutually unintelligible varieties of the original tongue. English, French, and German are varieties of Indo-European, as are Latin, Greek, Sanskrit, and Russian. All these varieties are unintelligible to one another because although the languages may be related, the changes that take place in them are quite different.

It surprises us to realize that English and Latin are related languages, and it is surprising to understand that they must be coeval since both derive from a common ancestor. Latin is "older" only in the sense that it was committed to writing earlier than English was, but the written history of a language is only a part of its total life.

That some languages might be related to others was discerned on occasion in the ancient past. The Greeks seem not to have suspected that their language was related to the language of their enemies, the Persians, but the Romans perceived enough similarities between Latin and Greek to suppose that Latin was a form of Greek that had somehow "degenerated." Comparative linguistic discovery was inhibited in classical times because the noble Greeks and Romans were snobs who took no interest in the languages of "barbarians," an attitude that is by no means unknown today.

It was also supposed that all men once spoke one language, a notion that is conveyed by the story of the Tower of Babel in Genesis: "And in the earth there was one language and one speech." The bewildering multiplicity of tongues that prevents nations from understanding one another and thus being able to cooperate easily was visited on presumptuous man by an angry God. Men wondered, too, what the original language was. Adam and Eve must have spoken Hebrew, but finding a relationship between Hebrew and other languages, such as Latin, proved baffling. It turned out to be of no help to hold up a passage in Hebrew to a mirror in order to read it from left to right.

Specimens from various European languages were occasionally collected and compared in the Renaissance, but without much result. It was not until the end of the eighteenth century that systematic comparative linguistic study began. The stimulus for this study was provided by the European interest in Sanskrit, the ancient language of India. French and British penetration of India during the eighteenth century brought Sanskrit to the attention of men with an intellectual turn of mind. The idea of the wisdom of the East was a lure here. Sanskrit might hold secrets that men of old understood but that had been lost in the whirl of time. Whatever the motives of the students, Sanskrit writings were studied and brought to the knowledge of Europeans, with the consequence that the relationship of Sanskrit to Latin and Greek was a stunning fact that could not be denied. Many cognates were obvious: the form meaning "father" was *pater* in Latin and Greek, *pitar* in Sanskrit; "is" had the form *esti* in Greek, *asti* in Sanskrit; "they are" is *sunt* in Latin, *santi* in Sanskrit. Lists of similar cognates were easy to compile. It was soon discerned that Sanskrit and Greek had to derive from a common ancestral language. Migrants using this language must have penetrated northern India at some time in the distant past and remained as the conquering society, eventually acquiring a writing system and leaving records of language older than Homeric Greek. In the early nineteenth century, chairs in Sanskrit study were established in European universities and attracted a number of notable scholars. The study of other languages, with comparative linguistic discovery in mind, proceeded with intelligence and zeal, and it was eventually determined that most of the languages in Europe and some in Asia were related and necessarily derived from a common source. Thus we have the concept of a family of languages to which English belongs.

Finding a name for this family proved something of a problem. The term "Aryan" was proposed but it was rejected on the grounds that Aryan implied an ethnic unity that was not necessarily shared by all the people who at one time or another may have spoken the language. German scholars liked "Indo-Germanic," but this term gave invidious emphasis to the Germanic branch of the family. "Indo-European" offended no one, although the compound neglects the inclusion of the western Asian languages, Iranian and Armenian.

Continued study determined that the Indo-European family was divided into a number of branches, of which the principal ones are as follows:

1. Indian	6. Italic
2. Iranian	7. Balto-Slavonic
3. Armenian	8. Celtic
4. Greek	9. Germanic
5. Albanian	

**Distribution of the Indo-European Languages in Europe
Western Asia**

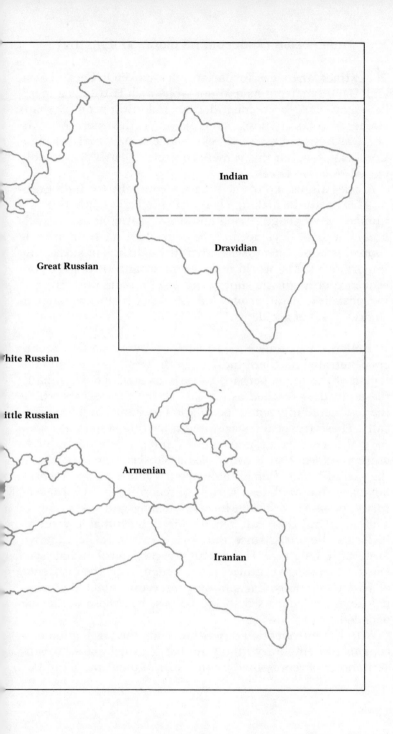

Great Russian

White Russian

Little Russian

Indian

Dravidian

Armenian

Iranian

The extinct languages Tocharian, once spoken in Central Asia, and Anatolian, from Asia Minor—of which Hittite is a member—have also been identified as Indo-European. Perhaps Homer's Trojans (whose city Troja, in northwestern Asia Minor, was besieged by his Greeks) spoke some variety of Indo-European, too, but this is mere conjecture. Paris presumably wooed Helen in Greek.

A brief discussion of the principal branches of Indo-European is useful in making clear that English is only one of a number of languages living and dead, scattered over a wide area, that have developed in the course of time from a single source. It is pertinent to see that, if English is of surpassing importance to the world now, its importance is not the consequence of linguistic superiority or of remarkable virtue in its speakers but rather of a long series of historical happenstances, a set of accidents.

1. Indian.   It is understood that Indo-European (IE) speakers penetrated northern India from the west, moving into the region of the Indus perhaps as early as 2000 B.C. Eventually these invaders reached as far east as the Ganges, absorbing the conquered indigenous population societally and linguistically. These IE speakers acquired a writing system at about the eighth century B.C. and recorded important religious literature in a form that is called Vedic Sanskrit, the language of the sacred Vedas. Remarkable about Vedic is that it records language that predates the time of recording by several centuries, preserving spoken forms that may go back as far as 1500 B.C. Thus the Vedic records are of inestimable value to historical linguists, since they preserve the earliest known forms of IE language. The careful preservation of archaic spoken forms through centuries is accounted for by the insistence of Hindu religious teachers on preserving intact the original language addressed to the deities, lest those deities be offended.

With the introduction of writing came the production of a copious contemporary literature that is called Classical Sanskrit, notably represented by the epics *Mahabharata* and *Ra-*

mayana, and by drama such as Kalidasa's *Sakuntala*. Indian IE flourishes today in dialects called Prakrits, as distinguished from the earlier form we call Sanskrit. The official dialect of India is Hindi, which is native to the north-central area of the subcontinent. Other important dialects are Bengali, with millions of speakers in northeastern India; Punjabi, spoken west of the Hindi area; and Mahratti, spoken on the west coast in the Bombay area.

Indian IE did not prevail in South India, and as a consequence the languages spoken in that area are not IE but of a group called Dravidian, which include Tamil, Telugu, and Malayalam. India thus has a serious communication problem. Officially, all the citizens of the nation are to learn and use Hindi, but there is considerable resistance to this demand in the south. Dravidian speakers are unwilling to lose their mother tongue or even to be effectively bilingual, and consequently communication on the national level is difficult.

As a minor sidelight to Indian, linguists discovered in the nineteenth century that those curious vagrants, the Gypsies, spoke a variety of Indian. Their ancestors migrated west from northwestern India to the Byzantine Empire and from there into central and western Europe, where they were first noticed in the fifteenth century, presumably having fled there from the Turks.

The IE branches vary considerably in their relative international importance. Indian is an important branch not only historically but also because of the great number of people who speak it today. It is important also because of its literature in Sanskrit and in the living dialects, as the stature of the early twentieth-century Bengali poet and playwright Rabindranath Tagore, a Nobel Prize winner, attests.

2. Iranian. Iranian is spoken in Iran, formerly Persia. Similarities between Iranian and Indian suggest that IE speakers, moving eastward, occupied the Iranian plain for some time before a group of them moved farther east into the valley of the Indus. The earliest records in Iranian show a division into an eastern language, called Avestan, and a western language, called Old Persian, the language of Cyrus the Great and his successors Darius and Xerxes. Persian became the dominant language and survives today, with an admixture of (mostly Arabic) foreign words. Avestan was the language of the practitioners of the Zoroastrian religion, some of whom fled before the Moslems to India, where their descendants, known as Parsis, still reside, chiefly in the Bombay area. Europeans became aware of Avestan in India in the later eighteenth century and around the turn of the nineteenth century brought knowledge of the language to Europe, which led to an intensive study of Iranian along with the study of Sanskrit. There in an extensive literature in Middle Persian and Modern Persian, which was brought to the general attention of English speakers by Fitzgerald's translation (1859–79) of *The Rubaiyat* of Omar Khayyam (eleventh century) and by Matthew Arnold's poem *Sohrab and Rustum*, drawn from an episode in the eleventh-century epic *Shahnamah*.

3. Armenian.   The Armenian branch of IE has been spoken in the Caucasus Mountains, in eastern Turkey, and in southern Russia since prehistoric time. Since Armenia is a geographical rather than a political expression, Armenian speakers have for centuries been subject to polities whose dominant language is Turkish or Russian. Isolation in rugged mountain country has helped Armenian communities retain their ancestral tongue, but improved communication and schooling may yet lead their descendants to forgo Armenian in favor of the dominant language on either side of the Turko-Russian border. Under certain conditions communities cling hard to peculiar features of a minority culture, but it is not uncommon for this clinging to cease eventually. To join a dominant culture and assume its language has its advantages. Thus Armenian may perish in a century or so unless its speakers form an autonomous state, which does not seem likely under foreseeable circumstances.

Conversion to Christianity brought literacy to Armenians at about the fifth century, and there is a considerable literature in the language, but it has not attracted much international notice.

4. Greek. Indo-European speakers moved into the area of the Aegean probably around 2000 B.C., acquired a writing system in about the eighth century B.C., and formed a society that was brilliant at its zenith, the fifth and fourth centuries B.C. A great literature survives as its memorial, a literature that will continue to be read in its original language. In the classical period Greek separated into a number of dialects: West Greek, or Doric, East Greek, or Ionian, Aeolic in the north, and a southern variety called Arcadian-Cyprian. Ionian, in the variety called Attic, that had Athens as its focal point, became the dominant dialect, to which other Greek speakers eventually conformed. Attic Greek became a lingua franca in the east Mediterranean area during the time of the Athenian and Macedonian empires, and remained so for long after, which accounts for its use as the vehicle of the New Testament. Greek was the language of the Byzantine Empire, which endured until its destruction by the Turks in the fifteenth century. For nearly four hundred years thereafter, the Greek language, the tongue of a subject people, was culturally submerged. When Greece again became an independent polity, Greek speakers had the problem of refurbishing their language with a vocabulary suited to the purposes of learned and literary use, a vocabulary they preferred to find chiefly in the classical past. This refurbished Greek was a partly artificial language not readily intelligible to the unschooled speakers of "demotic" Greek. The relative propriety of the two kinds of Greek has been a matter of sometimes heated debate among Greeks.

5. Albanian. Albanian is spoken in a limited area northwest of Greece on the eastern Adriatic shore. The territory has been dominated at various times by speakers of Greek, Latin, Turkish, and Slavonic, and the Albanian vocabulary has been added to by these other languages. There is some literature in Albanian, but it has attracted less attention than the literature of other languages.

6. Italic.   Italic IE takes its name from the Italian peninsula, where IE speakers penetrated at some time in prehistory, ultimately displacing other languages spoken in the peninsula, such as Etruscan. The Italian area was large enough that in the course of time Italic consisted of a number of dialects, of which Latin was one. Neighbors of Rome in early history, like the Volscians and the Sabines, spoke some variety of Italic other than Latin, as did speakers of Oscan and Umbrian. When Rome came to dominate Italy, so did Latin; rival dialects perished when all Italians grew eager to be Roman. The expansion of the Roman Empire planted Latin in Iberia, in Gaul, and, as Romanian, in the Balkan area. Latin survives today in many forms over large areas of the world: as Portuguese and Spanish in the Iberian peninsula and in Central and South America; as French in France and Canada and as a culture language in those sections of the Near East, Asia, and Africa that were parts of the French Empire; as Italian, the Latin that stayed home; and as Romanian. These forms of Latin are different languages now because they have become mutually unintelligible, but all can be traced back to varieties of Vulgar Latin as it was spoken at various times during the existence of the Roman Republic and Empire. In addition to these major forms of living Italic, there are minor forms: Catalan is spoken in northeastern Spain, Barcelona being the focal point of this dialect; Romansch is a minority language used by about 50,000 speakers in eastern Switzerland; Walloon, spoken in Belgium, is a variety of French, as are "Cajun" in Louisiana and Canadian French in Quebec and the Maritime Provinces. The spread of Latin and its survival in so many important forms are matters of great historical interest. Because surviving examples of written Latin are more than two thousand years old, the study of linguistic change in Latin forms is richly rewarding.

7. Balto-Slavonic.   This branch of IE is divided in turn into

Baltic and Slavonic. Baltic has two living forms, Lettish and Lithuanian. A third variety, Prussian, perished in the seventeenth century, its last speakers coming to prefer the dominant language of their area, German, to their inherited Baltic tongue. A similar fate may overtake Lettish, the language of Latvia, and Lithuanian, since these are again minority languages dominated by Russian. Between the two world wars speakers of these languages lived in briefly autonomous states, but without autonomy the continued existence of minority languages becomes precarious. A point of special interest in Lithuanian is its conservatism. Some of the forms of the language resemble forms in Sanskrit. This linguistic archaism is a curiosity, since it is usually geographic isolation, such as Iceland's, that encourages linguistic conservatism, but the Lithuanian territory is open and has been overrun many times by speakers of German, Swedish, Polish, and Russian.

The other subbranch, Slavonic, is much larger. It has East, West, and South divisions. East Slavonic is subdivided into Great Russian and Little Russian. Great Russian is the official language of Russia, with Moscow as its focal point, but Little Russian is the language of many millions of speakers in the Ukraine, a large and populous landmass that has the important city Kiev as its political and cultural center. A minor variety of East Slavonic is White Russian, spoken in west-central Russia, against the Polish border. Balto-Slavonic speakers acquired literacy relatively late and consequently were not much noticed in Western Europe until fairly recently, but the steady growth in power of Russia since the time of Peter the Great (1672–1725) has enabled the Russian language to reach a position of world prominence. Russian as a second language is now taught in many more universities in the West than was true before World War II.

West Slavonic is represented by Polish, Czecho-Slovak, and Sorbian. Polish is spoken in a large landmass by perhaps as many as forty million speakers. Czech and Slovak are similar enough to be compounded, Czech being spoken in the western, more populous, part of Czechoslovakia, with the capital, Prague, as its focal point. Slovak is spoken in the largely agricultural eastern part of the country. Sorbian exists in the vicinity of Dresden, as a linguistic island in a German sea, and can be expected to disappear eventually.

South Slavonic consists of Bulgarian, Serbo-Croat, and Slovenian. Bulgarian, because of its proximity to Greece and Christian missionary efforts, was the first Slavonic language to be recorded, in the ninth century. The earliest written form of Slavonic is called Old Church Bulgarian. Serb, Croat, and Slovenian are spoken in Yugoslavia, Serb having the largest number of speakers. Croat has Zagreb as its focal point, northwest of the Serb area. Farther north, bordering on German- and Italian-speaking areas, is Slovenian, a minority language that is threatened with absorption into Serbo-Croat from the south and by German and Italian.

8. Celtic. Celtic IE once covered western Europe from the Elbe to Gibraltar and Ireland, but has been retreating before Italic and Germanic for two thousand years and may perish utterly in the near future. In the days of the Roman Republic, Gaulish speakers were numerous in northern Italy as well as in Gaul. Caesar's conquest of Gaul eventually doomed Gaulish Celtic, as its speakers found it convenient to adopt Latin during the centuries of empire, as did the Iberians south of the Pyrenees. Celtic survives in dwindling numbers of speakers in Britain, Ireland, and Brittany in two principal dialectal varieties, called Britannic and Gaelic.

Britannic Celtic has two surviving forms: Welsh and Breton. Welsh is the language indigenous to Wales, the only area left to a language known as Britannic, which was spoken in all of Britain when the English began to overrun the island in the fifth century. The word *Welsh*, ironically, is an English word meaning "foreigner." A knowledge of English is general in Wales, and a drift away from the preservation of Welsh exists, although there is some pro-Welsh, anti-English sentiment still. The survival of Welsh is doubtful, however, since the convenience of the use of dominant English is clear to those Welsh who want to do more than mine coal or keep sheep or catch fish for a living. The situation of Breton in

France is similar. Breton was planted in the Brittany peninsula by migrants from Britain during the time of the Roman occupation. Why the Gaulish province was more attractive than the home island is not clear, since there were Roman taskmasters and tax collectors in both areas. More migrants seem to have followed during the fifth and sixth centuries, when Germanic speakers were overrunning both Gaul and Britain. Breton is still a living language, and some of its speakers are clinging fiercely to it in defiance of the dominant French. But both Welsh and Breton seem doomed. Political autonomy, a dream of some militants in both areas, would give them renewed hope for life, but such autonomy seems out of reach for either. A third variety of Britannic, Cornish, perished in 1777 with the death of its last speaker, Dolly Pentreath, at the age of 102. Cornish survived for so long because the English did not settle in Cornwall as early and as thickly as they did in the more easterly shires of southern England. Distance allowed Cornish to survive a while, as distance and rugged terrain preserved Welsh from English for fifteen centuries.

Gaelic, the other branch of Celtic, has three living dialects, Irish, Scots, and Manx. Manx is spoken on the Isle of Man, in the Irish Channel, where Manx cats originated. Manx appears to be drifting toward extinction, since its few speakers see little reason to keep the ancestral tongue alive. Tourism is important to the islanders, and the tourists speak English. Scots Gaelic also appears to be dwindling, as improved communications make the Highlands more readily accessible than they once were and Scots Gaels have more opportunity to learn and to use English. Gaelic survives best in Ireland, especially after it ceased to be John Bull's Other Island. In the nineteenth century Gaelic appeared to be on its way to replacement by English, which was penetrating the western counties as well as being dominant in the Dublin area. But a singularly fierce strain of nationalism has promoted a Gaelic revival in the past century, and it is difficult to foresee the fate of the language. Irish writers like Joyce, Yeats, and Shaw wrote in English, of course. An appreciative audience for

Gaelic would be too small, and Gaelic is little studied as a second language. Not all the citizens of Ireland know much Gaelic and not all of them by any means are in sympathy with the idea of a Gaelic "revival." To a disinterested observer Welsh and Gaelic and Breton look like lost causes, but lost causes often find forlorn-hope defenders who enjoy holding up their heroism for the world to wonder at.

9. Germanic.   Germanic IE is the branch of which English is a member. When the Roman Empire reached the Rhine, it impinged upon an area the Romans called Germania. By the time of the historian Tacitus, around 90 A.D., Roman commercial travelers had identified a number of Germanic-speaking "nations," enumerated by Tacitus in his account of them in the short work *Germania*. By that time Germanic speakers were numerous east of the Rhine, in the Baltic islands, and in Scandinavia. Their history before recorded notice by the Romans is unknown, but linguistic evidence makes it clear that Germanic had been a distinct branch of IE for centuries before the beginning of the Christian Era. Certainly Germanic speakers existed as a distinct linguistic aggregation as early as 500 B.C. Their numbers and the territory they controlled continued to increase, and in the fifth century they spilled over the Rhine and wrecked the empire. Ostro-Goths, Visi-Goths, Vandals, Franks, Lombards, and Burgundians engaged for decades in the pillaging of Gaul, Iberia, Africa, and Italy, eventually establishing new nations out of the wreckage of Rome. Some of them, called Angles, Saxons, and Jutes, crossed the English Channel and fell on Britain.

Forms of Germanic came in time to be recorded, and from these records we divide Germanic into three varieties in the early historic era, called East, North, and West. East Germanic is Gothic, spoken for a time in the area of the Black Sea, brought there by far-ranging migrants from the Baltic. In the fourth century a Christian missionary named Ulfilas translated parts of the New Testament into Gothic, and by great good fortune an ornamental manuscript, called the Silver Manuscript, survived as a copy of Ulfilas's work. This copy was made in Italy around the year 500 and was discovered in the sixteenth century in the Abbey of Werden, in Germany, where it was examined by several men of scholarly bent, among them the learned Hollander Goropius Becanus. Thereafter the manuscript had a curious history, shifting to Prague, to Sweden, to Holland, and back to Sweden, where it now reposes in the library of the University of Upsala. The miraculous preservation of this manuscript is important because it provides the earliest extensive record of Germanic and gives us facts about early Germanic that we would not otherwise have. Gothic does not survive, although a variety of it was spoken as late as the sixteenth century in the Crimea, where some records of it were made by a Flemish traveler named Augier Ghislain de Busbecq. A century later another traveler was unable to find any speakers of Krim-Gothic.

The first sentence of the Lord's Prayer in Gothic, compared with English, illustrates both the Germanic character of Gothic and the nature of linguistic change, given differences in time and place:

Atta usar þu in himinam weihnai namo þein.

Father our thou in heavens be hallowed name thine.

North Germanic is the name given to four Scandinavian languages: Swedish and Danish, forming an eastern subgroup, and Norwegian and Icelandic, comprising a western subgroup. Icelandic was simply Norwegian in the Viking Age, the island being occupied by Norwegian migrants, beginning in the last quarter of the ninth century. In the course of a thousand years, however, Norwegian and Icelandic have drifted apart and are not now mutually intelligible. Christian missionary effort and literacy came late to North Germanic speakers, in the eleventh century, and thus surviving records date no earlier than the twelfth century. The Icelanders produced a remarkable literature in verse and prose in the twelfth and thirteenth centuries, mostly in the form of prose sagas that are read with admiration today. Norway was a Danish possession for some centuries, during which time the language of the urban communities was affected by Danish, producing a language called Dano-Norwegian, or *Riksmål* (government language), as distinguished from *Landsmål* (country language). In the nineteenth century, Scandinavian literature, in the work of writers like Henrik Ibsen, August Strindberg, and Hans Christian Andersen, received considerable international attention.

West Germanic has two subdivisions, High and Low, these being topographical terms. High West Germanic covers the mountain area of southern Germany, Switzerland, and Austria, and since the seventeenth century has been the literary language of northern Germany as well. It is called *Hochdeutsch* (High German) as distinguished from *Plattdeutsch* (Low German). Old High German (before 1100) has some written records that are not literarily of much interest, but Middle High German, of the thirteenth and fourteenth centuries, has poetry of a very high order, notably in the work of Gottfried von Strassburg, Wolfram von Eschenbach, and Walter von der Vogelweide. Modern High German is, of course, a language of very great international importance.

Low West Germanic in the early historic era had four distinguishable varieties: Old Low Franconian, Old Saxon, Old Frisian, and Old English. "Franconian" contains the tribal name of the Franks, who overran Roman Gaul and gave their name to France, and, as a misnomer, to the language, French, which is Italic, not "Frankish." Low Franconian survives today as Dutch and Flemish and as Afrikaans, a variety of Dutch spoken by the Boers in South Africa.

Old Saxon was spoken on the Continent by those members of the numerous tribe of Saxons who did not migrate to Britain. The islanders came in time to be called Anglo-Saxons to distinguish them from their continental kinfolk. Old Saxon survives in the various *Plattdeutsch* dialects in North Germany, but these lack prestige in Germany and can be expected to perish eventually.

Old Frisian was the variety of Low West Germanic spoken in the Frisian Islands and the adjoining coastal areas of Holland and Germany. Frisian is still spoken, but it is a minority language, existing in the shadow of Dutch or German, and will presumably perish not long hence.

Old English is the term given to the language spoken by migrant Angles, Saxons, and Jutes on the island of Britain when the speakers of this variety of Low West Germanic acquired writing in the seventh century and began leaving records of the language. Passing through many changes since that time, the language survives as the prime international language whose history is the subject of this study. Thus English is more closely related to *Plattdeutsch*, Dutch, and Frisian than it is to other members of the IE family, but linguistic change over the last millennium has made these four near-kin languages mutually unintelligible. For example, a sentence meaning "Among these children was also a widow's son" reads, in Frisian, "Mank dizze bern wie ek in widdousoan," which would not be readily understood by a current English speaker, although in 893 A.D. King Alfred was able to communicate with the Frisian sailors whom he brought in to help fight off the Danes.

At one time in prehistory, perhaps earlier than 500 B.C., Germanic had become a distinct branch of IE that was spoken by a community small enough to share a common language. This common language is called proto-Germanic, spoken before the proliferation of the population and the division of the community into widely separated groups that in the course of time developed the varieties of Germanic that have been named. Proto-Germanic speakers induced a number of changes in their language that distinguished Germanic from other IE languages and that are still characteristic of all historic and living forms of Germanic. These changes consisted of

1. A simplification of the morphology of the verb system
2. The provision of a "weak" adjective declension
3. Fixing the IE stress on the base syllable of a word
4. A consonant shift known as Grimm's Law

These changes are discussed below.

1. IE had developed a complex system of verb forms to express varieties of tense and mood, a system that is familiar to anyone who has memorized pages of verb paradigms in French or Spanish. Proto-Germanic speakers, for reasons unknown, stripped their inherited tongue of much of its structural machinery, reducing tenses to only two, present and past. Future time was expressed in the present tense or with auxiliaries like *will* or *shall*. Proto-Germanic speakers also invented a simpler inflection for the preterit and past participle, adding a dental stop, *t* or *d*, to the base verb as in *work*, *worked*, *worked*. This is called the "weak" verb inflection.

2. IE required a full inflection of the adjective for case, number, and gender in agreement with the noun it qualified. Proto-Germanic speakers simplified this requirement when a third defining element, usually a definite article, accompanied the adjective. In this circumstance they reduced the number of variant forms, affixing *-an* to the base in most members of the adjective paradigm. This system is illustrated in Chapter 4.

3. In IE the stress shifted from syllable to syllable, as is illustrated in the transliteration of Greek, which marks the stress. Without marking, it is difficult to know which syllable is stressed, as in Greek proper names like Brásidas or Lysístrata. Speakers of proto-Germanic fixed the stress on the base syllable, a characteristic that is still exhibited by all living varieties of Germanic. This fact can be used in distinguishing words of Germanic origin from words borrowed from Latin or Greek. Thus a Germanic word like *fáther* keeps its stress on the first syllable even when syllables are added to the base: *fátherly*, *fátherliness*. In words borrowed from Latin or Greek, the stress still shifts with the addition of syllables, as in *fámily*, *famíliar*, *familiárity*; *ámiable*, *amiabílity*.

4. Proto-Germanic underwent a shift in its system of consonants. The similarities in pairs of Latin and Germanic words—words like *pater* and *father*—had long struck observers as interesting but puzzling. The possibility that such pairs were cognate, that is, of a common origin, was a tantalizing but unaccepted idea until Jacob Grimm, of Grimm Brothers

folk-tale fame, offered a satisfactory explanation in his *Deutsche Grammatik* (1822). As Grimm explained it, the IE voiced stops, *b*, *d*, *g*, shifted in Germanic to their voiceless equivalents, *p*, *t*, *k*, respectively. IE *p*, *t*, *k* shifted in turn in Germanic to *f*, *th*, *h*, the corresponding voiceless spirants:

	labials	dentals	velars	
IE	b	d	g	voiced stops
G	p	t	k	voiceless stops
IE	p	t	k	voiceless stops
G	f	th	h	voiceless spirants

Thus the idea of a systematic sound change explained that words that were semantically similar were indeed cognate, despite some difference in the consonants. The shift described by Grimm's Law does not, of course, affect non-Germanic IE and makes clear the relationship of Germanic to other IE languages like Latin or Greek. *Pater* and *father* are clearly cognate, proto-Germanic speakers having shifted the initial *p* to *f*. Latin *cannabis* and English *hemp* are cognate, *k* (spelled *c*) shifting to *h* and *b* to *p*. Latin *duo* and English *two* are cognate, *d* > *t*. It is thus clear that words in the current English vocabulary like *dual*, *duel*, *duet*, *double*, which convey the idea of "two," are words borrowed from non-Germanic in the literary period, since the Germanic shift from *d* to *t* is not in evidence. When English speakers borrowed a word like *duel*, they pronounced it as they heard it in the speech of their donors. Grimm's Law had long since run its course and had ceased to operate. Words with -*gno*- in them, like *agnostic*, *cognomen*, *cognoscenti*, are borrowed; the English cognate is *know* (even though *k* before *n* ceased being sounded in the fifteenth century). *Agri*-(culture) is the IE cognate of Germanic *acre*. Latin *pisc*-(atorial) is cognate with *fish*; *ped*-(estrian) with *foot*; *dent*-(al) with *tooth*; *tri*- with *three*; *cord*-(ial) with *heart*; *corn*-(et) with *horn*.

Germanic words with *b*, *d*, *g*, like *beer*, *do*, *go*, show the effect of another shift, from IE aspirated voiced stops, *bh*, *dh*, *gh*, as shown in the Sanskrit form for "brother," *bhratar*, to the corresponding nonaspirated voiced stops.

Grimm's Law illustrates the instability of language, and it is by no means a unique illustration. The sound system of any language is subject to change in the mouths of each generation of living speakers. The essential reason for sound change is that language is learned by imitation. Skill in repeating sounds depends on the speaker's acuity of hearing and his ability to mimic, powers that are limited in man. Speakers, children and adults, can be understood if they utter sounds that are similar to, if not identical with, the sounds they hear. Sometimes, in a mysterious social way, a speech sound different from the traditional one is imitated by widening circles of speakers until it becomes universal. Probably at some stages of the Grimm's Law consonant shift, older speakers must have wondered at the strange speech of younger ones, but ultimately the new consonants became universal, and there was no one left to wonder or to object.

Similar sound changes have occurred in other languages. IE *bh* became *f* in Latin and Greek, accounting for the form *bhratar* in Sanskrit but *frater* in Latin and Greek. This change explains the cognates *bear* (to carry) in English and *fer* in Latin and Greek. Another consonant difference in IE that drew much discussion is known as *centum-satem*, *centum* being the word for "hundred" in Latin and *satem* its cognate in Avestan. It was noted that the principal branches of IE fall into two groups, a western, *centum* group consisting of Greek, Italic, Celtic, and Germanic and an eastern, *satem* group made up of Indian, Iranian, Armenian, Albanian, and Balto-Slavonic. The assumptions are that the velar stop *k* was the original sound and that the eastern speakers palatalized *k* to *s*, bringing the tongue farther forward. A line drawn west of Lithuanian and east of Greek perhaps runs through the original home of IE and provides the starting point for migrants east and migrants west. This interesting theory has difficulties, though, for Albanian has its source west of Greek, and Tocharian, spoken in Central Asia, was a *centum* language. This palatalization of *k* to *s*, incidentally, occurred again in historic time in *cent* in French, accounting for the initial consonant in the pronunciation of that word ie French and English.

Surveying the Indo-European family of languages has served to put English into historic context with related languages and gives us an idea of English origins. We may stand bemused in considering the vast spread of IE during the past four thousand years. In the Renaissance and after, the European colonial era planted IE languages in the Western Hemisphere, in South Africa, in Australia and New Zealand, and on the Pacific shore of Siberia, through ancient Mongolian territory. European colonialism is in retreat now, and the complacency over it expressed by Samuel Johnson two hundred years ago is no longer fashionable: in *Rasselas*, Johnson had Imlac say of Europeans: "They are more powerful, sir, than we because they are wiser." Wiser or not, IE speakers now flourish over much of the world, threatening to displace some of the many non-IE languages in areas dominated by IE, among them Amerindian in the Western Hemisphere. In passing, it is of interest to note that not all the languages in Europe are IE: Finnish, Estonian, Hungarian, and Turkish are related Mongolian languages, and in the Pyrenees Basque is a unique language, not discernibly related to any other.

NOTES AND BIBLIOGRAPHY

Pedersen, Holger. *Linguistic Science in the Nineteenth Century*. (Originally published as *Sprogvidenskaben i det Nittende Aarhundrede: Metoder og Resultater*. Copenhagen: Gyldendalske Boghandel, 1924). Translated from the Danish by John Webster Spargo. Cambridge: Harvard University Press, 1931. Pedersen's is a readable account of the remarkable advances made in language study during the nineteenth century.

Prokosch, Eduard. *A Comparative Germanic Grammar*. Philadelphia: Linguistic Society of America, University of Pennsylvania, 1939. Prokosch discusses the characteristics of the various Germanic languages in great detail.

Zandvoort, Reinard Willem. *A Handbook of English Grammar*. 3d ed. Englewood Cliffs, N.J.: Prentice-Hall, 1966.

3

The Sounds of English

Language is essentially a matter of speech, not writing. The illiterate many who inhabit the earth know this, but the literate are not always sure of it. Schooling, learning to read and write, is a remarkable experience, one that makes a lasting impression, for good or ill, on all who undergo it. How many of the world's inhabitants are literate at all is unknown, but certainly fewer than half could be so described with the utmost charity, and the truly literate, those who can read without moving their lips and who not only can read books but do so, are a minority, probably a quite small one. It is reasonable that those who learn to read and write should come to think of "real" language as that of the written word, but this view of language is a mistaken one. If we reflect on it, we realize that we speak much more than we write, however little we may talk and however much we may read. Talking comes so "naturally" to some people that they never seem to stop; indeed, if nobody listens, they talk to themselves. We realize, too, that talking is usually effortless, but that writing, especially writing well, is a difficult process, engaged in as rarely as possible.

Reflection will also inform us that speaking must have preceded writing by untold millennia, before human inventiveness developed methods of recording speech. Writing enabled human beings to make a permanent record, one that the mature could pass on to the young. The evolution of our species from nomads and simple agriculturalists to urbanized technologists depended on the preservation in written form of our gradually increasing knowledge.

But the fact remains that everyone learns his mother tongue in a preliterate stage of life and continues to use it in practical, everyday fashion without reference to letters. The invention of writing is a great event in human history, but the invention of language is a greater one. A tantalizing mystery is the story of how it all began. In the nineteenth century, speculative theories as to the origin of language were spun in numbers, but were finally banned from linguistic conferences as an unrewarding game. All that can be known is that somehow, at various times and places, man realized that he could make a variety of sounds with his vocal organs. He then made combinations of sounds and assigned meanings to various combinations. Eventually, combinations were strung together into sentences, and man was able to communicate complex messages to his fellows by means of speech. He increased his stock of meaningful sound-combinations, or "words," as he found necessary. These developments all occurred in prehistoric time, were not recorded in process, and can consequently not be analyzed now. That the process of inventing language occurred independently is evident from the fact that many of the world's known languages are unrelated to each other; and no society has been discovered, however dismal its condition might otherwise be, that does not, or did not, have a language.

Another feature of language that arouses wonder is the acquisition of a mother tongue by the child, who moves from the meaningless babbling stage to the intelligible forming of isolated words to the formation of sentences by apparently easy steps. No one remembers what he was "thinking" when he went through the stages of learning to speak and understand what was said to him, but by the time the child is six or seven years old he has a considerable vocabulary and has learned the grammatical structure of his mother tongue, meaning that he has learned how to put sentences together in correct word order. Ahead of him lies literacy and, for some, learning huge technical, scientific, and literary vocabularies. Some individuals, despite schooling, proceed very little beyond the six-year-old level. They do not learn the niceties of standard language and are not sensitive to nuance in the selection of words. Others, like Shakespeare, wield their mother tongue with incredible power. To use language with skill is obviously to anyone's advantage, and it is one of the frustrations of education that no method has been devised to assure that all diploma-holders have a fair share of such skill. Let teachers try as they may to prevent it, it would appear that some students' linguistic talents are limited.

To undertake the acquisition of a second language, one other than the mother tongue, is a memorable experience. It is then that a realization of the intricacy and difficulty of language is grasped, and it seems a wonder that children learn their mother tongue at all. Indeed, it has been said that man's hardest work occurs in learning his native language, and it is curious that no memory remains of this early effort. Another linguistic curiosity is the observation that one can learn to read, write, speak, and understand a second language at any age, but to learn to pronounce the sounds of a second language without a "foreign accent" requires a learner who has not yet reached his sixteenth year. After early adolescence the ability to hear and mimic the sounds of foreign speech with native exactness is no longer present. This accounts for the "broken English" of otherwise nimble-witted foreign adults.

Human speech is the product of psychological and physiological phenomena. Physiologically the organs of speech have primary, nonlinguistic functions. The oral cavity and its parts —lips, teeth, tongue, palate—are primarily necessary for the ingestion of food and were only secondarily adapted to the purpose of producing speech sounds, which depend for their force on the expulsion of air from the lungs, but the primary function of the lungs is to inhale oxygen and exhale carbon dioxide through the oral and nasal cavities, which in turn are only secondarily resonance chambers for speech sounds. The larynx is essential to human speech, but its primary function is to retain air in the lungs to enable the chest muscles to work against the expanded rib cage in strenuous effort, like lifting heavy weights or pushing a spade into hard soil.

The importance of that agile set of muscles, the tongue, in producing speech sounds was long ago obvious, which accounts for the use of "tongue" as a metaphor for language; Latin *lingua*, as in "linguistics" and French *langue*, as in "language," also mean "tongue." The tongue is involved in the production of so many speech sounds that someone who loses his tongue cannot speak intelligibly. He can still sound *f*, *v*, and *m*, but many other essential sounds, including *t*, *d*, *s*, and *z*, are beyond his ability. The tongue is quite nimble, shifting positions at great speed without the speaker's needing to be aware of what that appendage is doing in his mouth. It may seem curious, too, that the tongue is a muscle that never tires, even though it may be heavily exercised during sixteen or more consecutive waking hours.

The function of the larynx in speech production is less obvious to casual observation than that of the tongue, but it is the larynx that allows speech to be audible at a distance through the phenomenon called "voicing." Unvoiced speech is a whisper, which is barely audible even at the shortest possible distance from the hearer. "Voice" is caused by the vibration of the vocal cords, membranous bands in the larynx. The fact of voice can be perceived by sounding a vowel, like *a*, and then whispering it, or by sounding *f* and *v* alternately, or *s* and *z*. All vowels are voiced sounds; *f* and *s* are voiceless consonants, but their otherwise homorganic companions, *v* and *z*, respectively, are voiced. Some consonants are voiceless, but their audibility above the whisper level depends on their being combined with voiced sounds in the words in which they occur. The larynx is also called the "voice box" and the "Adam's apple," the last term being jocular, occasioned by the greater size and easier visibility of the larynx at the front of the male throat. Eve also has an apple, but presumably, on the occasion of the fatal sharing of the apple in the Garden of Eden, conscience made Adam's piece stick in his throat. The larger size of the male larynx is a secondary sex characteristic, like facial hair, and accounts for the lower pitch of the male voice. Boys and *castrati* have soprano voices, but during adolescence the male larynx grows larger, the process occasioning that comic "breaking" from soprano to baritone and back again.

Another physiological factor in speech is the function of the velum. The roof of the mouth has distinct parts: the alveolar ridge, a slight protuberance behind the upper teeth, the palate, and the "soft palate," or velum. The alveolar ridge is a point of articulation for the apex of the tongue in forming sounds like *t*, *d*, and *s*, *z*. The palate is a point of articulation for the blade of the tongue for sounds like the medial sibilants in *pressure* and *pleasure*. The velum is a point of articulation for the back (dorsum) of the tongue in producing sounds like *k* and *g*. The velum ends in a bit of flesh called the uvula, which French speakers vibrate in producing the sound *r*. The velum, being soft, is flexible and moves to block off the passage of air through the nasal cavity in producing oral sounds. English has three nasal consonants: bilabial *m*, apico-alveolar *n*, and a dorso-velar nasal conventionally spelled with the digraph *ng*, as in *sing*. When these nasal sounds are produced, the velum relaxes to allow the passage of air through the nasal cavity in order to produce the characteristic sounds. A speaker who is suffering from a severe head cold has his velum swollen shut, so that air cannot proceed through the nasal cavity. In such a circumstance the speaker must inadvertently replace the nasal consonants with corresponding oral ones, and he makes "spring has come" sound like "sprig has cub" and "man" sound like "bad."

Speakers of English produce a great variety of sounds, but some of the sounds are unimportant because they do not affect the meaning of the words in which they occur. An example of an unimportant sound is the puff of air, or aspiration, that follows the initial voiceless stops *p*, *t*, *k*, as in *pick*, *tick*, *kick*. If one holds a lighted match before his lips while saying these words, the aspiration will blow the match out. When *p*, *t*, *k* follow *s*, as in *speak*, *stick*, *ski*, aspiration does not occur,

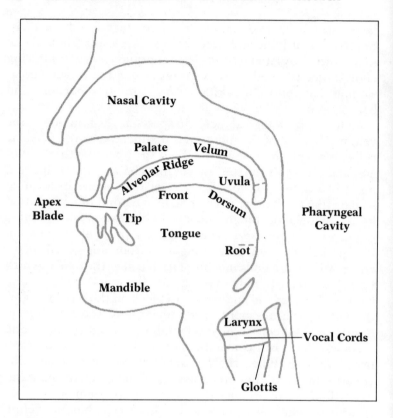

Diagram of the Organs of Speech

and the match will not blow out. But neither aspiration nor its absence is noticed by the native English speaker. Both aspirated and nonaspirated *p* belong to the same *phoneme*, or minimal meaningful speech sound. French speakers do not aspirate initial *p, t, k* and consequently discern something foreign in the French of a native English speaker who aspirates these consonants out of habit and does not realize he is speaking "bad French." Initial *b, d, g* are not aspirated in English, but are so in some other languages, as in Hindi, in which the word for "brother" is *bhai*, the *h* representing the necessary aspiration to make the word intelligible. Another example of an unimportant variation is the presence in English of two varieties of *l*, called "clear *l*" as in *let*, and "dark *l*" as in *well* or *milk*. In producing clear *l* the apex of the tongue is articulated against the alveolar ridge; in dark *l* the dorsum of the tongue moves toward the velum. If these varieties of *l* are interchanged, as it sometimes happens in the pronunciation of English by foreign speakers, the word in which the interchange occurs "sounds funny," but it is still understood. Both varieties of *l* belong to the same phoneme because they are varieties of the same minimal meaningful speech sound.

The study of all the varieties of speech sound is called "phonetics," and its notation involves the use of many symbols and diacritics that are enclosed in square brackets. In this book a simpler, grosser system of phonemic notation, enclosed in what are called slash marks or slant lines (/ /), will be used as sufficient for the purpose of describing meaningful speech sounds in English. To describe the phonemes of English requires some special symbols that are not part of the Roman alphabet of conventional writing. The Roman is not sufficient because it does not have as many symbols as there are phonemes in any English dialect. Leonard Bloomfield, in *Language*, described thirty-two simple phonemes in the Chicago dialect as he heard it in 1933, and any dialect would have about that number. Since the roman alphabet has only twenty-six symbols, it is obviously insufficient to describe the phonemes of any dialect, to say nothing of describing several dialects and those phonemes in past use that are no longer part of the English system. Moreover, the Roman alphabet has some symbols that merely duplicate the functions of other symbols: *q* represents no sound that is not represented by *k*; *c* is the equivalent of *k* in *cut* and *s* in *city*. Consequently, *q* and *c* are discarded in phonemic notation. A one-to-one consistent system of sound and symbol is required. Each symbol must be represented by only one symbol. Conventional spelling is inept in some ways: the initial sound in *shop* is a single phoneme, but is represented by two symbols, *sh*. In phonemic notation this phoneme is represented by the symbol /š/; the word is transcribed /šap/. *Chop* also has three phonemes and is transcribed /čap/. In conventional spelling the combination *th* represents one or the other of two phonemes, /ө/ or /ð/, which distinguish *thigh* from *thy*—/ѳаɪ/ and /ðаɪ/. Conversely, the symbol *x* represents two phonemes, /k/ and /s/; *fix* has four phonemes /fɪks/. The symbols that are added to the Roman alphabet to supply the needs of phonemic notation are drawn from the International Phonetic Alphabet, a notation system developed at the turn of the twentieth century and still being tinkered with. The initials IPA are used as a convenience in referring to this system of phonetic or phonemic notation. Observing the use of the IPA in recording the sounds of English makes clear the inadequacies of Roman notation and the gap between the sounds of words and the various ways in which they are conventionally spelled.

Vowels. The Roman alphabet provides five vowel symbols, *a*, *e*, *i*, *o*, *u*. In addition, *y* is sometimes used, as in *many*, although that word could just as well be spelled *mani*. English, however, has more than five vowels, each of which must have its own symbol in phonemic notation:

1. /a/ as in German *Mann* /man/ or French *la* /la/
2. /ɑ/ as in *father* /faðɚ/
3. /æ/ as in *mat* /mæt/
4. /ɛ/ as in *met* /mɛt/
5. /e/ as in *mate* /met/
6. /ɪ/ as in *sit* /sɪt/
7. /i/ as in *seat* /sit/
8. /ɫ/ as in *merry* /mɛrɫ/
9. /o/ as in *boat* /bot/
10. /ɒ/ as in British *not* /nɒt/
11. /ɔ/ as in *law* /lɔ/
12. /ʊ/ as in *pull* /pʊl/
13. /u/ as in *pool* /pul/
14. /y/ as in German *kühn* /kyn/ or French *rue* /ry/
15. /œ/ as in German *schön* /šœn/

16. /ʌ/ as in *but* /bʌt/
17. /ə/ as in *again* /əgɛn/
18. /ʒ/ as in British or Southern American *bird* /bʒd/

No single dialect, past or present, has all these vowel phonemes. /a/, no. 1, does not occur as a simple phoneme in most current dialects, but in Old English /a/ was in phonemic contrast with /ɑ/: /man/ meant "man" and /mɑn/ meant "crime." /ɒ/, no. 10, occurs in British and eastern New England dialects, but is absent from the other varieties of American English. /y/, no. 14, was common in Old English and early Middle English, but was later unrounded to /i/. /œ/, no. 15, appears from spelling evidence to have occurred for a time in the southwestern dialects of Middle English, but then to have been unrounded to /ɛ/ or /e/.

Speakers produce the repertoire of vowels by varying the shape of the oral cavity. This is done by raising or lowering the mandible and by moving the tongue forward or retracting it. The relative positions of jaw and tongue in producing the various vowel phonemes can be indicated by placing the vowels in nine segments of a quadrangle that represents the oral cavity:

	Front	Central	Back
High	i y ɪ	ɨ	u ʊ
Mid	e œ ɛ	ʒ ʌ ə	o ɔ
Low	æ a	ɑ	ɒ

Thus vowels can be described as high front, mid-central, low back, and so forth, depending on the jaw position as high, mid, or low, and the tongue position as front, central, or back.

Vowels are also rounded or unrounded with reference to the shape of the lips. The back vowels are rounded, and the front vowels in current use are unrounded. /y/ and /œ/ are rounded front vowels, but are not in use in current English. Vowels in the same segment of the quadrangle are described as either tense or lax, depending on the relative tenseness of the muscles of the tongue. Thus in the high front segment /i/ is a tense vowel, and /ɪ/ is a lax one, the difference being sufficient to distinguish them as different phonemes, as in *sit* and *seat*, or *bit* and *beet*. So, too, in the mid-front segment, /e/ is tense and /ɛ/ is lax, distinguishing *fade* from *fed* to the ear of a speaker accustomed to the contrast. In the high back segment, /u/ is tense and /ʊ/ is lax, distinguishing *fool* from *full*.

The mid-central vowels /ʒ/, /ʌ/, and /ə/ did not occur in Old and Middle English, as far as we can now determine, and probably were added to the English repertoire four or five hundred years ago. The vowel /ə/, sometimes called "schwa *e*" or "the neutral vowel," occurs frequently in unstressed syllables, although sometimes /ɪ/ or /ɪ̵/ occurs, as in *frantic* /fræntɪk/ or *many* /mɛnɪ̵/. The phoneme /ʒ/ is used by a speaker of the "*r*-less" dialects who does not curl up the tip of the tongue for *r* when it is preconsonantal or final, as in *third* /θʒd/ or *fur* /fʒ/. American dialects west of the Atlantic coast use the *r*-curl, which is represented by the symbol /ɚ/—/əɚd/, /fɚ/. *Further* in the *r*-less dialects is /fʒðə/; in *r*-curl dialects it is /fɚðɚ/.

Diphthongs.   Vowel phonemes combine in forms called *diphthongs*, or compound phonemes. There are several of these in English: /aɪ/ as in *ice* /aɪs/; /aʊ/ as in *out* /aʊt/; /ɔɪ/ as in *boy* /bɔɪ/.

In producing these sounds the speaker brings the mandible up rapidly from the low position for /a/ or /ɔ/ to the high position for /ɪ/ or /ʊ/. English diphthongs are "falling" ones, the first element being stressed, or "syllabic," the second element, or "off-glide," having less stress and probably slightly less duration. Another diphthong used in some dialects is /ɪu/, as in *new* /nɪu/ or *Tuesday* /tɪuzdɪ̵/, and a distinct off-glide can be heard in the practice of some speakers in sounding /o/ or /e/, as in *go* /gou/ or *day* /deɪ/. There is considerable dialectal variety in diphthongs. Some dialects have /ɑɪ/ in *ice* or /oɪ/ in *boy*. Eastern Virginia and Eastern Carolina speakers have /ʌu/ in words like *out* /ʌut/ or *house* /hʌus/, and Southern Mountain speakers have /æu/, as in *out* /æut/ or *house* /hæus/. Regional dialects differ from each other most noticeably in their selection of vowels and diphthongs.

Consonants. Consonants differ from vowels in that there is some physical articulation or tactile sense involved in producing consonant sounds. Some consonants are *stops*, meaning that the passage of air through the oral cavity is stopped momentarily by the articulation of speech organs and then released. Thus /p/ and /b/ are bilabial stops, the lips being firmly pressed together to stop the puff of air and then released to produce the characteristic sound. For /t/ and /d/ the stop is produced by the articulation of the apex of the tongue and the alveolar ridge. For /k/ and /g/ the articulation is that of the dorsum of the tongue against the velum. The stops are paired with reference to articulation, and the members of each pair are distinguished by voice: /p/, /t/, /k/ are voiceless and /b/, /d/, /g/ are voiced.

Other than the six stops, consonants are *continuants*, meaning that the breath is not momentarily stopped and then released but flows through some variety of constriction by the vocal organs, producing audibility through friction. One group of continuants is called *spirants*, including /f/, /v/, /ə/, /ð/, /s/, /z/, /š/, /ž/. /f/ and /v/ are labio-dental spirants, the breath passing between the lower lip and the upper teeth. These sounds are homorganic except for voice, /f/ being voiceless and /v/ voiced, this difference being sufficient to put the sounds in phonemic contrast, distinguishing *file* from *vile* as different words. /ə/ and /ð/ are paired as apico-dental spirants, the apex or tip of the tongue being placed at the upper teeth, /ə/ being voiceless, /ð/ voiced, distinguishing *ether* from *either*, or *thigh* from *thy*. /s/ and /z/ are apico-alveolar spirants, /s/ voiceless, /z/ voiced, distinguishing *sip* from *zip*.

Speakers who lisp, usually young children, place the tongue slightly too far forward, substituting /ө/ for /s/ and pronouncing *sister* /өɪөtɚ/. Some children are a bit slow in hearing and mimicking the full repertoire of consonants. Another subsitution that occurs occasionally in child speech is /v/ for /ð/, sounding *mother* as *muvver*. Foreign speakers of English whose native languages, like German, French, Italian, do not have /ө/ and /ð/ in their consonant repertoire, have difficulty learning the unfamiliar phonemes and will substitute nearby phonemes, as in "foreignized" *dese* and *dose* for *these* and *those*, or *sink* for *think*, *zis* for *this*, or *tick* and *tin* for *thick* and *thin*. /š/ and /ž/ are fronto-palatal spirants, the blade or front of the tongue, to the rear of the apex, making near contact with the palate, as in *pressure* /prɛšɚ/ and *pleasure* /plɛžɚ/.

Another pair of consonant phonemes is /č/ and /ǰ/, called affricates, a combination of stop and spirant. /č/ could be written /tš/ and /ǰ/ as /dž/, but the single symbols will do just as well. *Church*, with its six conventional symbols, has only three phonemes /čɚč/, as does *judge* /ǰʌǰ/. The spirants /s/, /z/, /š/, /ž/ and the affricates /č/ and /ǰ/ are also called sibilants, from their hissing sound.

The phoneme /h/, the aspirate or "breathy" sound, is a voiceless glottal spirant; it is produced by constricting the glottis, which is the opening to the larynx. It is a barely audible sound, uncertainty as to its presence accounting for the use of "an" before words beginning with *h* in unstressed syllables, as in "an historical novel" or "an hotel." *Hotel* is of French origin, and has no audible /h/ in French speech, the French having disused the phoneme a thousand years ago, although they retain the "silent" symbol in conventional spelling. English speakers tend to restore the phoneme so that the sound conforms to the spelling. French words with an initial *h* that were borrowed in the medieval era, like *honor*, *hour*, *heir* are still pronounced in English as they were in French, but there is currently some uncertainty as to whether or not to sound the /h/ in *humble* and *herb*. The /h/ in the pronouns *he*, *his*, *him*, *her* is sounded when the forms are stressed, but omitted in unstressed position, as in "what's his name" /watsɪznem/. The presence or absence of /h/ in *wh*-words like *where* and *which* is a matter of regional dialect; some dialects sound the phoneme (/hwɛɚ/, /hwɪč/), and other dialects omit it (/wɛɚ/, /wɪč/).

Another group of continuants is called the *sonorants*, including the nasals /m/, /n/, and /ŋ/. The lateral /l/, so called because air flows around the sides of the tongue when the sound is produced, is also a sonorant. In the production of nasal sounds air must flow through the nasal passage; distinction among the three varieties is managed by varying the oral articulation, /m/ being bilabial, /n/ being apico-alveolar, and /ŋ/ being dorso-velar. /ŋ/ is conventionally spelled with the digraph *ng*, as in *sing* (pronounced /sɪŋ/). The idea of "dropping the *g*" in the forms like *huntin'* and *fishin'* betrays a familiar misunderstanding about language. No *g* is "dropped" because there is not one. Speakers who replace /hʌntɪŋ/ with /hʌntən/ are substituting a front consonant for a back one in the unstressed syllable because tongue-front sounds are easier to produce than tongue-back ones. This substitution does not occur in stressed syllables; no native speaker of English would say /sɪn/ for /sɪŋ/.

The consonant phonemes /w/, /j/, and /r/ are called *glides* or *semi-vowels*. /w/ involves lip-rounding and movement of the dorsum of the tongue toward the velum and can be described as a voiced labiovelar semi-vowel. When /w/ is not initial it has dropped out in some instances, as in *sword*, *answer*, *Greenwich*, the conservative spelling preserving the memory of the departed. Among Germanic languages English has been conservative in retaining the phoneme: German shifted from /w/ to /v/, and Scandinavian either shifted to /v/ or simply dropped the phoneme. The word *wolf*, for example, is recorded as *ulf* in Old Norse. The difficulty adult German speakers have with English /w/ is generally familiar, (/vi/ for *we* and /vʒək/ or /wuək/ for *work*). /w/ is not part of the phoneme system of Hindi, whose speakers tend to omit it in speaking English, pronouncing *woman* /umən/.

The phoneme /j/ is the voiced fronto-palatal semi-vowel, the tongue gliding in the palatal area to the position for the following vowel, as in *youth* /juə/, *beyond* /bɪjɑnd/, *inure* /ɪnjuɚ/.

The phoneme /r/ is the voiced apico-alveolar retroflex semi-vowel, the apex of the tongue retroflexing, curling up toward the alveolar ridge. This retroflexive action occurs in all English dialects when /r/ precedes a vowel, as in *run*, *rabbit* /rʌn ræbɪt/, but when *r* precedes a consonant or is final in the word, the retroflexive action does not occur in some dialects, such as standard British and most varieties of Atlantic-seaboard (American) English. These dialects lack the *r*-curl and are called "*r*-less." In such dialects final and preconsonantal *r* is represented by /ʒ/ in stressed syllables and /ə/ in unstressed syllables, as in *murder* /mʒdə/. In those dialects, including "General American," that use the *r*-curl in all positions, the phoneme is /ɚ/, as in /fɚðɚ/ and /mɚdɚ/. /ɚ/ serves as the off-glide of diphthongs in forms like *far* /faɚ/, *fare* /fɛɚ/, *fear* /fɪɚ/, where it can be considered more vowel than consonant. /r/ was a trilled sound in older English, but it has lost much of its consonantal force in recent centuries. Ben Jonson, in an English grammar he wrote in the 1630s "For the benefit of all Strangers," described the sound: "*R* is the Dogs letter, and hurreth in the sound; the tongue striking the inner palate, with a trembling about the teeth. It is sounded firm in the beginning of the words, and more *liquid* in the middle, and ends: as in *rarer, riper*. And so in the *Latin*." Trilled *r* is still heard in some varieties of Scots English and is referred to as a "burr," but it is otherwise currently rare.

An occasional and not important phoneme in English is the glottal stop, a momentary audible "catch" of air in the glottis, represented by the symbol /ʔ/. It tends to occur before an initial vowel but usually goes unremarked. Its presence is noticed when it replaces another phoneme like /t/ before /l/, as in *little* /lɪʔəl/, a phenomenon that occurs in some dialects like London Cockney and in some varieties of New York City speech.

Two phonemes /x/ and /ɣ/ occurred in Old English, the language as it was spoken before 1100, but dropped out of the consonant repertoire in the course of the following centuries.

These were dorso-velar spirants, /x/ voiceless and /ɤ/ voiced. /x/ is a common phoneme in German, in words like *ich* and *nacht*, and is preserved in the Scots *loch* and in forms like *nicht* for "night." /x/ either simply disappeared, as in *bough* and *through* (its ancient presence being suggested by the spelling of silent *gh*), or it was fronted to /f/, as in *rough* and *laugh*. /ɤ/ was replaced by /g/, the voiced stop apparently being more convenient to speakers than the voiced spirant.

In summary, the consonant phonemes are listed below for convenient reference:

1. /p/ as in *pit* /pɪt/
2. /b/ as in *bit* /bɪt/
3. /t/ as in *tip* /tɪp/
4. /d/ as in *dip* /dɪp/
5. /k/ as in *kick* /kɪk/
6. /g/ as in *gig* /gɪg/
7. /f/ as in *fail* /fel/
8. /v/ as in *veil* /vel/
9. /θ/ as in *thigh* /θaɪ/
10. /ð/ as in *thy* /ðaɪ/
11. /s/ as in *sip* /sɪp/
12. /z/ as in *zip* /zɪp/
13. /š/ as in *shape* /šep/
14. /ž/ as in *measure* /mɛžɚ/
15. /č/ as in *chip* /čɪp/
16. /ǰ/ as in *gyp* /ǰɪp/
17. /m/ as in *me* /mi/
18. /n/ as in *knee* /ni/
19. /ŋ/ as in *fling* /flɪŋ/
20. /w/ as in *woman* /wʊmən/
21. /j/ as in *you* /ju/
22. /r/ as in *rue* /ru/
23. /ʔ/ as in *bottle* /baʔəl/
24. /x/ as in Scots *loch* /lɒx/
25. /ɤ/ as in North German *sagen* /zaɤən/

By including several dialects, past and present, we find eighteen simple vowel phonemes and twenty-five consonants, for a total of forty-three, that have been, or are, in use in English. Phonemes occur arbitrarily in some combinations but not in others. The stops /p/, /b/, /k/, /g/ occur in initial position with /l/, as in *plow*, *blow*, *clown*, *glow*, but initial /tl/ and /dl/ do not occur, although there is no reason, except chance, why they should not. Initial /ps/ and /pn/ occurred in Greek but not in English. In the borrowed Greek words *psyche* and *pneumonia*, the Greek spelling is followed, but English speakers have not assumed the sound combination. French speakers are more faithful to the Greek and pronounce both sounds in initial /ps/ and /pn/.

Assimilation. Attending to the mechanics of speech production allows us to understand why some words are pronounced differently from the way they are spelled. The /d/ fell out of *Wednesday* a long time ago because /d/ and /n/ are both apico-alveolar in their articulation, and sounding the cluster /dnz/ without an intervening vowel was too troublesome; /d/ was consequently assimilated by the following /n/. Etymologically, the nonphonemic spelling recalls the name *Woden*, the god after whom that day of the week is named, and the spelling can thus be defended on historic-cultural grounds, although *Woden* is not clearly conveyed by *Wedn-*. In *raspberry* and *cupboard*, /p/ is assimilated by the following /b/, because both sounds are bilabial stops. In /ræzbɛrɫ/, voiceless /s/ is voiced to /z/ by assimilation to the voiced sounds that, after the loss of /p/, precede and follow it. *Pumpkin* is commonly pronounced /pʌŋkən/ for the same reason: /m/ and /p/ are both bilabial; /p/ is dropped and /m/, drawn to the dorso-velar position of /k/, is replaced by /ŋ/.

Other assimilations are commonplace. Cartoonists and fiction writers spell *going to* as *gonna* to suggest a subliterate practice, but "everybody" says /gʌnə/ when they speak in a relaxed, colloquial style as opposed to a formal and public one. So, too, "everybody" says /hæftə/ for *have to* when the phrase is not stressed—"I have to go now"—and /justə/ for *used to*—"We used to think so."

Transposition. Another speech phenomenon is the occasional transposition of sounds. One variety is the transposing of the initial sounds of consecutive words, as in the "Spoonerisms" "sin twisters" for "twin sisters" or "Is the bean dizzy?" for "dean busy." Internal transpositions occur also. *Bird* and *grass* were "brid" and "gærs" in Old English, but later speakers transposed the *r* and the vowel. Similar transpositions occur in "larnyx" for *larynx*, "arnachist" for *anarchist*, "lazy-on" for *liaison*, "nucular" for *nuclear*, "modren" for *modern*—

transpositions which careful speakers take pains not to imitate, since they are considered illiteracies.

Spelling reform.   Observing the gap between pronunciation and spelling has led to the repeated suggestion that spelling should be reformed to agree with some phonemic system, but the suggestion has been vigorously opposed. In the 1580s, Richard Mulcaster preferred comfortable custom to unfamiliar respellings. In 1712, Jonathan Swift spoke out vigorously against

> ... a foolish opinion, advanced of late years, that we ought to spell exactly as we speak; which beside the obvious inconvenience of utterly destroying our etymology, would be a thing we should never see an end of. Not only the several towns and counties of England, have a different way of pronouncing; but even here in London, they clip their words after one manner about the court, another in the city, and a third in the suburbs; and in a few years, it is probable, will all differ from themselves, as fancy or fashion shall direct: All which reduced to writing, would entirely confound orthography. It would be just as wise as to shape our bodies to our clothes and not our clothes to our bodies. Yet many people are so fond of this conceit, that it is sometimes a difficult matter to read modern books and pamphlets; where the words are so curtailed, and varied from their original spelling, that whoever hath been used to plain English, will hardly know them by sight.

Later in the eighteenth century, Samuel Johnson remarked that to spell words as they are pronounced would be to measure by a shadow which is constantly changing.

It is true that phonemic spelling would vary according to dialect and sometimes according to individual practice, leaving readers sometimes uncertain as to a word's identity. The relationship of semantically connected words would occasionally be obscured, as when *heal* and *health* would be spelled *hil* and *hɛlθ*, or *zeal* and *zealous* as *zil* and *zɛləs*. The grand objection to a thoroughgoing spelling reform is that books in libraries would have to be reprinted in reformed spelling, a colossal undertaking in itself, and for several generations the young would have to learn to read the established spelling as well as the reformed kind.

In the twentieth century various plans for reforming English spelling have been advanced, like the "Anglic" system of the Swedish professor, Robert Zachrisson, but without success. Modest suggestions like *tho*, *thru*, *nite* have won tepid approval. For a while the Chicago *Tribune* printed some words in a sensible reformed manner, like *sheriff* with one *f*, but dropped the idea when it became obvious that the literate preferred established spellings to reforms, however sensible. Moderate improvement could be achieved if all publishers of printed matter would agree on the detail, but publishers are reluctant to risk offending the potential buyers of their product. In general it is social inertia that blocks "progress" in spelling reform.

NOTES AND BIBLIOGRAPHY

Bloomfield, Leonard. *Language*. New York: Henry Holt, 1933.
A clear and stimulating discussion of phoneme theory in English and other languages.

Kenyon, John S. *American Pronunciation*. 10th ed. Ann Arbor: George Wahr, 1951. Highly recommended for its good sense and clarity.

George Bernard Shaw treats phonetics with great respect in his play *Pygmalion*. He equips his heroic phonetician, Professor Higgins, with the ability to distinguish one hundred and thirty vowels. Undoubtedly there are that many in human speech, but hearing more than eighteen or so would be remarkable.

Swift, Jonathan. *The Prose Work of Jonathan Swift*. Edited by Herbert Davis. 14 vols. Oxford: At the University Press, 1939.

Swift's remarks on spelling reform in *A Proposal for Correcting, Improving and Ascertaining the English Tongue* (1712), is found in volume 4 of this edition.

4

Old English

Old English is the term given to the language in its earliest written stage, for round-number convenience from 700 to 1100. The whole life of English reaches back through the mists of time to that moment when someone uttered the first sound in Indo-European, but what that sound was we do not know, because nobody wrote it down. A nineteenth-century linguist said, "Give me the texts, and I'll trace language back to Adam." True, but before the existence of the texts our tracing is only conjectural. Knowledge of the facts of English begins with the surviving records, and these date to not much earlier than 700.

We do know that English was spoken in Britain for 250 years before the time of the early records. The traditional date for the arrival in Britain of the first English speakers is 449, a date supplied by the first English historian, the Venerable Bede. Of course Bede, who died in 735, was not an eyewitness of the memorable event, and his assigned date may not be accurate, but 449 is certainly close to the mark.

There is British history before the coming of the English. Celtic speakers had been settled in the island, and in Ireland, some centuries before the Romans found them. What kind of people were in Britain when the Celts arrived there is uncertain. The early Celts made no records, nor did the people in the island before them. If those who built the formation at Stonehenge meant it as a memorial of themselves, they did not leave the means of identifying them. When the Roman legions were moving up through Gaul they were aware of Britain, just across the channel, and in 55 B.C. and again in the following year Julius Caesar made brief excursions on British soil, presumably hoping to deter the British from assisting their Gaulish kinfolk against Rome. In the next century, beginning in the year 43, Rome added Britain to her growing empire. Tacitus's biography of his father-in-law, the *Agricola*, provides a record of the Roman occupation of Britain in the later first century, for Agricola was the governor of Britain shortly after the reign of Nero.

Romans remained in Britain for nearly four centuries, exploiting the country for lead and tin and for agricultural products, building towns and their famous roads, but staying out of Ireland and the hill country of Wales and Scotland. They built and manned a wall in the north to keep out the unconquered Picts and Scots, and then withdrew from Britain in 410, when the Italian homeland was being threatened by the Germanic barbarians. For reasons not now understood, the British, though pacified and Romanized, retained their Celtic speech, unlike the Gauls and Iberians, who had become Latin speakers. The withdrawal of the Roman military left the British unable to protect their towns and their herds from the warlike Picts and Scots. According to tradition, this situation led the South Britons to invite mercenary help from across the sea. As one version of the *Anglo-Saxon Chronicle*, written long after the event, puts it, for the year 449:

Vortigern invited the English here, and they then came in three ships to Britain at the place Ebbsfleet. King Vortigern gave them land in the southeast of this land on condition that they should fight against the Picts. They then fought against the Picts and had the victory wherever they came. They then sent to Angeln [in what is now Denmark], asking them to send more help, and told them of the cowardice of the Britons and the excellence of the land. They then immediately sent here a greater force to help the others. Those men came from three tribes of Germany, from the Old Saxons, from the Angles, from the Jutes.

The fifth century was a time when Germanic speakers were more numerous than the land they occupied could comfortably support. They were turbulent and land-hungry. English speakers, who assumed various tribal names for convenience of identification, were living in Denmark and down the North Sea coast through the Low Countries when the word spread that land was to be had for the taking in that large, ill-defended island that was easily reached by sea. For more than a century the English swept in waves over the Celts, who defended their territory but died in vain. The survivors fled west to Cornwall and Wales and north to the Scottish Highlands. War between Celt and Saxon has remained a constant feature of British history and has not ceased yet. The English settled in great numbers as farmers in the land, absorbing those Celts who survived among them. Intermarriage, of course, occurred. As A. E. Housman put it: "Couched upon her father's grave, / The Saxon got me on the slave." But the Celtic language, for good or ill, died out wherever the English were dominant.

Jutes appear to have been the first to come to Britain, settling in Kent and on the Isle of Wight. Angles occupied the midlands and the area north of the Humber River, forming the kingdoms of Mercia, East Anglia, and Northumbria. Saxons seized the south, establishing a kingdom long called Wessex, meaning "West Saxons." North of the Thames was Essex, the country of the East Saxons, and south of the Thames was Sussex, "South Saxons." In between was Middlesex, "Middle Saxons." Everybody spoke the same language, however, and felt enough identity to disuse the other tribal names in favor of that of the Angles. Thus England is *Anglaland*, the land of the Angles, and the language is "Angle-ish." The spelling and pronunciation of the initial vowel in "Ingland" and "Inglish" reflect stages of assimilation by the high jaw position of the consonant that follows:/ŋ/. The spelling remains fixed at an intermediate stage (/ɑ/ > /ɛ/ > /ɪ/). The Italians, by spelling the name of the language "Inglese," are more accurate. English speakers throughout the island began calling themselves "English" fairly early. Alfred was king of Wessex, but called himself English. The Welsh, curiously, call the English *Sassenach*, a form of "Saxon."

The English were civilized in the sense that they grew crops and raised cattle, but they were poor engineers, and they were illiterate. They were content with farm and village life in smoky wooden houses, chimney-building an art they had not mastered. They seem to have got their pleasure from hunting, fighting, and drinking. The privileged warriors gathered in the mead-hall, where they caroused and listened to the music of the harp and to heroic poems that celebrated the deeds of brave men. They made pets of horses, hawks, and hounds, but had little to say about women. To this rough society literacy was brought with its conversion to Christianity during the seventh century, when Latin-speaking missionaries lived among the English, learned their language, and taught them the use of the Roman alphabet. And thus we have the beginning of the era of records, records that slowly increase in quantity, until now, when printed matter is commonplace.

Records of the language from the eighth century through the eleventh are referred to as Old English, as a matter of convenience. English from the twelfth century through the fifteenth is Middle English, and from 1500 to the present it is Modern English, providing us with three approximately even divisions of time and change.

Eighth-century English had not yet diverged much from the Low West Germanic dialects spoken on the Continent. English missionaries to Germany, some of whom were killed there, conversed readily with the natives, and Alcuin of York presumably had small trouble with Frankish when he took office at the court of Charlemagne. To English speakers now, however, Old English is, at first encounter, an unintelligible form of the language. The opening lines of *Beowulf*, for example, with a literal version in current English, read:

Oft Scyld Scēfing Often Shield Sheaf's son	*sceapena prēatum* (of) scathers (from) troops
monegum mǣgþum (from) many nations	*meodosetla oftēah,* mead-seats took away,
egsode eorlas, overawed earls,	*syððan ǣrest wearð* after first was
fēasceaft funden; destitute found;	*hē pæs frōfre gebād,* he (for) this consolation abided,
wēox under wolcnum waxed under welkin	*weorðmyndum pāh,* (in) honors throve,
oð pæt him ǣghwylc until that him each	*ymbsittendra* (of) around-sitters
ofer hronrāde over whale-road	*hȳran scolde,* obey should,
gomban gyldan; tribute yield;	*pæt wæs gōd cyning!* that was good king!

This passage is difficult for the modern eye and ear because
of the cumulative linguistic changes that have occurred generation after generation since this eighth-century poem was
written. An English speaker living before 1100 would have
spoken the lines approximately this way:

/ɒft šyld šefiŋg šɛaðɛna ɵreatum mɒnɛɤum mæjðum mɛo-
dosɛtla ɒftɛax ɛjzɒdɛ ɛorlas syɵan ærɛst wɛarɵ feašɛaft
fundɛn he ɵæs frovrɛ jɛbɑd weoxs ʊndɛr wɒlknum wɛorð-
myndum ɵɑx pɵ ɵæt him æjhwylč ymbsɪtɛndra pvɛr hrɒn-
rɑdɛ hyran šɒldɛ ɤɒmban jyldan ɵæt wæs ɤod kyniŋ/.

Differences in spelling conventions add to our difficulty.
Two Old English symbols are unfamiliar: þ (called "thorn")
and ð (called "eth"). These symbols were adopted by the early
transliterators of English to represent sounds that did not ex-

ist in their native Latin, the dental spirants /ə/ and /ð/. After we grow used to the phonology and spelling of Old English, we can easily perceive the still living forms of the early language, but vocabulary differences remain as an obstacle to ready comprehension. We can see the current word *threat* in *preatum*, but the meaning in context, though related, is not the same. Some words, like *egsode*, *fēasceaft*, *frōfre*, *gomban*, disappeared centuries ago from the vocabulary, often to be replaced by Latin or French words like *terrified*, *destitute*, *consolation*, *tribute*.

The morphology of the noun, adjective, and verb was more complex in Old English than it has since become. The noun, as in other Indo-European languages, had three genders, masculine, feminine, and neuter. Modern German, in general more conservative than English, retains these genders, but English speakers dispensed with gender in the early Middle English period (1100–1300). The OE noun had four cases: nominative, genitive, dative, and accusative. Of these cases only the genitive survives, as in "*Man's* life is brief," where the base form, *man*, still is inflected to indicate the genitive function of the word in the sentence. The other case forms have disappeared, their function as subject or object being indicated by word order or by prepositions. In the sentence, "The dog bit the man," the word order is necessarily fixed; we cannot interchange the positions of the nouns "dog" and "man" and retain the meaning of the sentence. In "The man gave the dog a bone," "dog" and "bone" are both objective in function, but only word order tells us this, not inflectional affixes. Inflection of the OE noun was not as elaborate as in Latin or Greek, but some objective case inflection, in the dative, was still retained, as in the paradigm for the masculine noun *eorl* (earl):

	Singular	Plural
Nominative	eorl	eorlas
Genitive	eorles	eorla
Dative	eorle	eorlum
Accusative	eorl	eorlas

In this paradigm the distinctive accusative inflection had been lost in both numbers, and consequently the nominative and accusative functions must already be determined by word order.

There were a number of other noun patterns in OE. Some neuter nouns, like *horse*, had an uninflected nominative plural:

	Sg.	*Pl.*
N.	hors	hors
G.	horses	horsa
D.	horse	horsum
A.	hors	hors

In the nominative or accusative case the number of this noun would have to be indicated by the corresponding number of the verb or by the situation. In Chaucer's portrait of the Knight, in the General Prologue of *The Canterbury Tales*, we read: "His hors were good." Here we must know that "hors" is plural, as the plural verb indicates. Analogy drew the word into the dominant paradigm, exemplified by *eorl*, *eorlas*, giving us "horses." But some of the original uninflected neuter plurals remain so, as *sheep*, *swine*, *deer*, and a few others. Some neuter nouns, like *scip* (ship) were inflected in *-u* in the N. and A. plural, *scipu*. These, too were drawn ultimately into the dominant declension.

Another prominent declension was the weak or *n* declension, as represented by the paradigm for "ox":

	Sg.	*Pl.*
N.	oxa	oxan
G.	oxan	oxena
D.	oxan	oxum
A.	oxan	oxan

This declension is called "weak" because there are fewer variants through the paradigm; the single form *oxan* has five functions. The weak declension had many representatives in

OE, *eye*, *ear*, *heart* among them, but today only *oxen* and *children* survive as part of the live language. Forms like *kine* and *brethren* are obsolete.

Another declension that had more members than survive today is the "umlaut" declension. An example is *fōt* (foot):

	Sg.	Pl.
N.	fōt	fēt
G.	fōtes	fōta
D.	fēt	fōtum
A.	fōt	fēt

The front vowel /e/ in some members of the paradigm is accounted for by an instance of phonological assimilation called by the German term "umlaut," which literally means merely "sound change." Another term sometimes used for this particular assimilation is "mutation," which is no more specific than "umlaut"and is consequently no improvement. The principle of "umlaut" is simple: English speakers at one stage of the language fronted back vowels when the front vowel /ɪ/ or the semi-vowel /j/ occurred in the second syllable of a disyllabic form. This sound change seems to have occurred as speakers unconsciously simplified their speech forms: anticipating the front tongue position for /ɪ/ or /j/, they found it more comfortable to place the tongue forward early and to keep it there. The pre-umlaut form of the D. Sg. must have been *fōti*, which speakers then pronounced *fēti*. The /ɪ/ which was the cause of umlaut then dropped off, leaving the recorded form *fēt*. In the N. and A. Pl. the pre-umlaut form is reconstructed as *fōtiz*, which umlauted to *fētiz*. Speakers sensed that the front vowel distinguished those members of the paradigm sufficiently and then dropped the suffix, leaving *fēt* as N. and A. Pl. Like *fōt*, *fēt*, are *gōs*, *gēs* (goose, geese) and *tōð*, *tēð* (tooth, teeth). Some members of the declension, like "book" (OE *bōc*, *bēc*) were later leveled by analogy, so that today the plural of "book" is "books," not "beek," although *feet*, *geese* and *teeth* have survived.

Other vowels were similarly affected, /a/ being fronted and

raised to /ɛ/. In the paradigm for "man," the N. and A. Pl. changed from *manniz to menn. The back vowel /u/ was fronted to /y/: the pre-umlaut plural of mūs (mouse) was *mūsiz, which changed to mȳs, accounting for the surviving forms mouse, mice, and so with louse, lice.

The umlauted plurals brethren and kine survived into Modern English, but have been leveled to brothers and cows. That seven noun plurals—men, women, feet, teeth, geese, mice, and lice—have resisted analogical leveling to *mans, *foots, *mouses is one of the many mysteries of language. Frequency of use and euphony have been offered as reasons for survival, but brethren and kine were certainly frequently spoken, and if forms like booths and houses don't repel speakers as uneuphonious, then neither should *tooths and *mouses.

Umlaut caused the fronting of vowels in other parts of speech, too. The pre-umlaut infinitive "to feed" was *fōdjan. The /j/ fronted /o/ to /e/, producing the recorded form fēdan. Umlaut thus accounts for the variant vowels in a number of noun and verb pairs: food, feed; blood, bleed; brood, breed; moot, meet. The noun forms in the pairs strong, strength; long, length show an umlauted vowel, as do the comparative and superlative forms of the adjective old: elder, eldest. We can see analogical leveling in the process that shows a growing preference for older, oldest ("He is older than his sister"), but eldest (in, for example, "He is the eldest of seven children"), would probably not strike many living speakers as "odd," and the language has yet to produce an analogical *olderly alongside elderly.

Adjectives. In OE the adjective, as in all IE languages, agreed with the noun it modified in case, number, and gender. That adjectival inflection is not necessary in order to understand a message is obvious, since English speakers dispensed with it long ago. But those who developed IE felt that repeating grammatical signals in the adjective helped assure understanding. In OE the phrase "the good earl's land" was "gōdes eorles land," the form gōdes giving the signals genitive, singular, masculine just as the following form, *eorles*, did. Repeating the signals drove the function home to the listener.

The full adjectival system, the "strong" system, for the word *good* was as follows:

		Masc.	*Fem.*	*Neut.*
Sg.	N.	gōd	gōd	gōd
	G.	gōdes	gōdre	gōdes
	D.	gōdum	gōdre	gōdum
	A.	gōdne	gōde	gōd
	I.	gōde		gōde
Pl.	N.	gōde	gōda	gōd
	G.	gōdra	gōdra	gōdra
	D.	gōdum	gōdum	gōdum
	A.	gōde	gōda	gōd

Forms for a fifth case, the instrumental, survive as curious fossils in the masculine and neuter singular.

One of the characteristics that distinguish Germanic from other IE languages is the presence of a "weak" adjective declension, used when another element, such as a definite article, already provided the grammatical signals. Unlike the modern *the*, which tells us nothing of case or number, the OE definite article was extensively inflected.

		Masc.	*Fem.*	*Neut.*
Sg.	N.	sē	sēo	ðæt
	G.	ðæs	ðǣre	ðæs
	D.	ðǣm	ðǣre	ðǣm
	A.	ðone	ðā	ðæt
	I.	ðȳ, ðon		ðȳ, ðon

		all genders
Pl.	N.	ðā
	G.	ðāra
	D.	ðǣm
	A.	ðā

If, in the phrase "the good earl's land," the definite article was included, then the adjective assumed the weak form: "ðæs gōdan eorles land." Germanic speakers apparently felt that providing grammatical signals three times was excessive. In the weak declension the paradigm for "good" is:

		Masc.	*Fem.*	*Neut.*
Sg.	N.	gōda	gōde	gōde
	G.	gōdan	gōdan	gōdan
	D.	gōdan	gōdan	gōdan
	A.	gōdan	gōdan	gōde

		all genders
Pl.	N.	gōdan
	G.	gōdena, gōdra
	D.	gōdum
	A.	gōdan

Variation for case, number, and gender is much diminished in the weak declension, the single form *gōdan* carrying ten of the sixteen functions. This reduction of formal variation perhaps prepared the way for discontinuing the adjectival inflection altogether, although it is interesting to note that modern German, as conservative structurally as English is not, retains the two-fold adjectival declension system.

The personal pronoun. The forms of the personal pronoun have changed less in the last thousand years than the forms of the English noun and adjective. The adjective lost all inflection, except for comparison (big, bigger, biggest), and the noun has retained inflection only for the genitive singular and the plural. The pronoun has retained not only the genitive form but also the dative case objective form. In OE the paradigm for the first person singular was:

N.	ic
G.	mīn
D.	mē
A.	mē, mec

In Modern English the paradigm is:

N.   I
G.   my, mine
D.   me

The nominative form lost its consonant in Middle English, the lax vowel /ɪ/ undergoing a change to /i/, later to be dipthongized to /aɪ/. The modern genitive is more complex than it was, in that it has two forms: *my* and *mine*, their choice being determined by syntactic practice. *My* is used in juxtaposition with the noun it modifies: "That is my book." *Mine* occurs when it stands alone: "That book is mine." "Whose book is that?" "Mine." English speakers had tended to drop the *n*, retaining it only when the form was syntactically independent. In Early Modern English, speakers retained the *n* before vowels: "Mine eyes dazzle"; "Upon mine honor," but eventually *n* was dropped before all nouns.

The Old English first person had not only a plural but also a dual number. The dual paradigm was:

N.   wit (we two)
G.   uncer (our two)
D.   unc (us two)
A.   unc (us two)

Duality was expressed in Indo-European grammar (classical Greek, for example, had dual verb forms), but the dual pronouns in Old English faded out. We know that they were already archaic in literary Old English, since they occur in poetry but not in prose. Nothing was lost to English, however, because it can express the dual idea with words like *two* or *both*: "The two of us worked it out"; "Both of them agreed."

The first person plural forms in Old English were:

N.   wē
G.   ūser, ūre
D.   ūs
A.   ūs, ūsic

Little has changed in this paradigm except pronunciation. The OE variants in the genitive were reduced when ūser was eliminated. So, too, the accusative was simplified when ūsic was dropped, the dative assuming both objective functions. As with *my* and *mine*, the genitive developed two forms—*our* and *ours*. The *s* in *ours* was presumably drawn from the dominant *s*-form of the genitive singular of nouns. By analogy with *mine*, the form *ourn*, though not standard, still occurs as a social dialect variant, as do *yourn*, *theirn*, *hisn*, *hern*.

The second person pronoun forms were:

	Sg.	*Dual*	*Pl.*
N.	ðū	git	gē
G.	ðīn	incer	ēower
D.	ðē	inc	ēow
A.	ðē, ðec	inc	ēow, ēowic

Changes in this person were like those in the first person; the genitive singular assumed two forms, *thy* and *thine*, the older accusative *ðec* was absorbed by the dative *ðē*, and the dual forms disappeared. In the plural the forms became:

N.	ye
G.	your, yours
D.	you

In Early Modern English, speakers confused the functions of *ye* and *you*—sometimes *ye* occurred as object and *you* as subject—until the "problem" was solved by simply eliminating *ye*.

An astonishing and by no means beneficial change in the English pronoun system was the loss of the second person singular forms *thou*, *thy*, *thine*, *thee*. In medieval Europe the practice developed of addressing a respectable person, with whom one was not on intimate terms, with the plural pronoun: in German *Sie* rather than *du*; in French *vous* rather than *tu*. This practice was adopted in English, but unlike the continental vernaculars English dropped the singular forms altogether by the seventeenth century. English speakers are spared the delicate problem of determining when they may safely address someone with the familiar singular, but that they are no longer able to distinguish singular from plural presents a problem of another kind. The solution lay in the invention of a distinctive plural form, and several inventions exist: *you all*, *yous*, and *you uns*. But none of these forms has won general favor. *You all* is limited to the Southern American regional dialect, where it has the approval of the cultivated speakers, but it has not been able to cross the Mason-Dixon line. *You uns* is restricted to Southern Mountain practice, and *yous* is regarded as substandard in those areas where it occurs. (The attitude of the cultivated toward *yous* is illustrated by James Joyce in his *Dubliners* story, "A Mother," when he describes "the son of a hall porter" who is striving to improve his social position: "He said *yous* so softly that it passed unnoticed.") These inventions are all good ones, but they are successfully resisted everywhere outside of the American South, a commentary on the power of social inertia. In the seventeenth century the Quaker sect revived the form *thee* as a singular, using it in the nominative function as well as in the objective, but other speakers had no inclination to imitate this minority practice.

In Old English the paradigms for the third person singular pronoun are:

	Masc.	*Fem.*	*Neut.*
N.	hē	hēo	hit
G.	his	hiere	his
D.	him	hiere	him
A.	hine	hīe	hit

The masculine forms have changed very little, except for the loss of the distinctive accusative case form, which was absorbed by the dative during the Early Middle English era.

The feminine paradigm dropped the accusative form and, beginning in the thirteenth century in the Northern dialect, found a new nominative form, *she*. Finding a clearly distinctive feminine nominative form became a necessity when English speakers "smoothed" the diphthong *ēo* to *ē*, making the feminine form identical with the masculine. Such confusion was intolerable, and in the course of the thirteenth and fourteenth centuries the Northern invention drifted southward, until all English speakers had acquired *she* as the feminine form.

The neuter nominative and accusative lost the aspirate *h*, *hit* becoming *it*. In this instance, the accusative form prevailed over the dative *him*, in order to avoid confusion with a possible masculine antecedent. Confusion as to antecedent also accounts for the replacement of the genitive *his* by the analogical form *its*. This solution to ambiguity was not fully worked out until well into the Renaissance. In Shakespeare's generation, *his*, *it*, and *its* were all in use as competing neuter genitive forms.

The Modern English paradigms for the third person singular forms are:

	Masc.	*Fem.*	*Neut.*
N.	he	she	it
G.	his	her, hers	its
D.	him	her	it

The feminine genitive follows the pattern of *ours* and *yours* in supplying *hers* when the possessive stands alone in the sentence. Analogy breaks down in the absence of **hises* and **itses*, because English speakers tended to shun a combination of sibilants when it was possible to do so.

The Old English plural third person forms were:

N.	hīe
G.	hiera
D.	him
A.	hīe

These forms were replaced in the course of Middle English by the Scandinavian pronouns *they*, *their*, *them*, an extraordinary matter, since pronouns are normally preserved by frequency of use. Borrowing such forms from a foreign language is extraordinary and is accounted for in this instance by growing confusion in reference: by the thirteenth century the form *he* could mean *he, she,* or *they*. Like *she*, the distinctive plural forms *they, their*, and *them* had their first use in the northern dialect and slowly filtered down through the midlands and the south. As late as Chaucer's time (1390) the London dialect had adopted *they*, but the genitive form was still *here* and the dative was *hem*.

It is an inconsistency in the structure of Modern English that, although objective case forms were abandoned in the noun in favor of word order and prepositional function words, objective pronouns—*me, us, him, her, them*—survive through the frequency with which they occur, and their survival presents a problem in usage for many speakers. In compound phrases the nominative pronoun is often used in the objective function: "They invited my wife and I." President Eisenhower created shock waves among the grammatically strict by this solecistic practice. Public figures are thought to be obliged to set a better example to the nation. So, too, the interrogative and relative pronoun *who* retains its objective form *whom*, the proper use of which seems to be a puzzle. Carefully edited print has the *who*'s and *whom*'s regulated by pronoun experts, but in newspaper practice the odds are excellent that *whom* has a subject function: "They nominated the man whom they thought would best serve the party." *Whom* still impresses many as a somehow elegant word, although its use in questions appears to be diminishing except in the formal style. "Who did you talk to?" is said by the nicest people. The demise of *whom* would not injure the language and would reduce anxiety in those who worry about linguistic decorum.

The verb. The morphology of the verb has changed in the last thousand years in some details, but not in its major characteristics. The two major kinds of verb were in OE as they are now—the strong and the weak. The weak verb, a prehistoric Germanic invention, adds a dental consonant—/t/,

/d/, or /əd/—to the base to form the preterit and past participle, as in *walk, walked; fear, feared; fret, fretted*. This category of verb has overwhelmingly the greater number of members and for this reason is called "regular." This method of conjugation must have been in use for centuries before any English was written, for the early recorded language has many more weak than strong verbs. In the strong verb the preterit and past participle are formed by means of an internal vowel change, as in *sing, sang, sung*. OE had about three hundred strong verbs; of these some sixty survive.

Strong verbs are arranged in seven classes, according to the vowels used to distinguish the principal parts. The vowel series is called ablaut, or gradation. An example of a strong verb of Class I is *drive*, which today has three forms: *drive, drove, driven*. In OE there were four principal parts, the ablaut series being /i/, /a/, /ɪ/, /ɪ/:

drīfan   drāf   drifon   drifen

Drīfan was the infinitive and supplied the vowel for the present tense forms: *ic drīfe* (I drive). *Drāf* was the form of the preterit in the first and third persons singular: *ic drāf, he drāf*. *Drifon* was the preterit plural form: *wē, gē, hīe drifon*. The second person singular preterit shared the vowel of the plural: *ðū drife*. *Drifen* was the form of the past participle. English speakers eventually reduced the principal parts to three by combining the preterits into one form, *drove*, which serves both the singular and the plural. A number of Class I verbs survive in current English on the pattern of *drive*: *ride, rode, ridden; write, wrote, written; rise, rose, risen; shine* and *stride* retain the reterits *shone* and *strode*, but have lost the participles **shinnen* and **stridden*. *Bite, bit, bitten*, belongs to this class, but took its preterit vowel from the OE preterit plural rather than from the singular. *Glide* survives as a weak verb, *glide, glided, glided*, rather than *glide, *glode, *glidden*, the pull of analogy into the dominating weak verb category accounting for the change.

Strong verbs of Class II have the ablaut series ēo, ēa, u, o, as in the principal parts of the verb *lose*:

lēosan lēas luron loren

The *r* in the preterit plural and past participle was explained in 1875 by Karl Verner, who gave his name to Verner's Law. Verner hypothesized that in Germanic medial *s* was replaced by *r* when the Indo-European stress did not precede the sibilant. Thus *lusón* and *losén* became *luron* and *loren*. After the sound shift, Germanic speakers moved the stress to the first syllable. Other parts of Verner's Law settled a controversy involving apparent exceptions to Grimm's Law, like the words *centum* > *hundred*; *hund* should be *hunth* according to Grimm's Law, but, according to Verner's stress-pattern theory, *t* became *d* when the IE stress did not precede the consonant in medial position. Another illustration of the *t* > *d* occurs in the Class II verb *seethe*, which in OE has the parts:

sēoðan sēað sudon soden

Seethe is now a weak verb, but the past participle *sodden* survives as an adjective. *Seethe* and *sodden* have drifted apart semantically, however, sodden meaning something wet and cold rather than something wet and hot.

Although *lose* became a weak verb—*lose*, *lost*, *lost*—*lorn* survives in the compounds *forlorn* and *lovelorn*. Verner's Law also explains the *r* in *was*, *were*. *Choose* and *freeze* had the pattern of *lose* in OE, but the participles *coren*, *froren* were leveled to *chosen*, *frozen*. *Frore* and *frorn* survived into the sixteenth century, but thereafter became obsolete. Class II had many more members in OE than it has today. *Fly* and *shoot* are still strong, but *brew*, *chew*, and *creep* survive as weak verbs.

In the strong verbs of Class III the vowel /ɪ/ preceded a nasal in the infinitive. The principal parts of *sing* were:

singan sang sungon sungen

Sing still has three forms—*sing, sang, sung*—as do *drink, begin, shrink, sink, spring, stink* and *swim*. Others were reduced to two forms, like *spin, spun, spun*. Although *span* as the preterit grew obsolete long ago, it is remembered in the medieval jingle: "When Adam delved and Eve span, / Who was then the gentleman?" Other two-form members of the class are *bind, find, grind, sting, swing, wind, win* and *run*, which had *rinnan* as the infinitive in OE.

Examples of strong verbs in the other classes are:

Class IV	beran (bear	bær	bǣron bore	boren borne)
Class V	etan (eat	ǣt	ǣton ate	eten eaten)
Class VI	scacan (shake	scōc	scōcon shook	scacen shaken)
Class VII	grōwan (grow	grēow	grēowon grew	grōwen grown)

Of the roughly three hundred strong verbs in OE, more than two-thirds have perished, either by the disappearance of the word or because the verb joined the weak group. A well-organized "reform" of English would long ago have made all verbs weak. As it is, English speakers feel uncertainty about the forms of some of the surviving strong verbs: *sunk* and *swum* are seen as preterits, and *spit* and *spat* both occur; *trod* is seen in casually edited print as the present tense form of *tread*, and *slank* or *slinked* are sometimes tried. Although morphological change during the past millennium has been generally in the direction of simplification, this change should not be thought of as necessarily an improvement. It is just change, haphazard, and not "planned" by a collective intelligence.

The Old English vocabulary. The English language has changed in every way—in phonology, morphology, spelling, and syntax—since King Alfred spoke and wrote it. The greatest change, however, has been in vocabulary, in the words available to express ideas. In learning to read English as it was written a thousand years ago, the spelling and pronunciation are soon mastered, as is the use of the dative case. Rearranging word order in the sentence is no problem either. It is the difference in the old and the modern vocabulary that burdens the memory of anyone who aims to read early English literature. This difference is far greater in English than in languages like French or German, whose vocabularies have, of course, also changed, but not nearly as much as the vocabulary of English. The principal reason for this greater degree of change in English is to be found in the effects of the Norman Conquest, which brought to England a new landholding, governing aristocracy who spoke French for more than two centuries. As a consequence, several thousand French words were eventually borrowed by English speakers, and many of these words replaced their English equivalents, bringing about a considerable shift in the character of the vocabulary.

In an essay by King Alfred that served as a preface to a translation of Pope Gregory's *Cura Pastoralis*, nearly half of about two hundred base words (omitting the particles) are no longer familiar. Among Alfred's nouns that were replaced by French words are *onwald* (power), *ǣrendwreca* (messenger), *sibb* (peace), *siodo* (morality), *wīg* (war), *ðīowotdōm* (service), *ðēning* (service), *ǣrendgewrit* (message), *onstal* (supply), *wīte* (pain, trouble), *ðēawas* (servants), *māðm* (treasure), *mengeo* (multitude), *geðīod* (language), *stōw* (place), *wealhstōdas* (translators), *spēd* (success), *notu* (use). Not all of Alfred's words that became obsolete were replaced by French, and some would have faded from use without French influence. Alfred's *fultum* is now English "help," as well as the French "aid" or "assistance." *Innanbord* has become "at home," and *utanbord* "abroad"; *rīce* is now "kingdom." Once we account for spelling and pronunciation changes, more than half of Alfred's vocabulary is readily recognizable: *cirice* (church), *gioguð* (youth), *fīfteg* (fifty), *clǣne* (clean), *woruld* (world).

Old English poetic technique required the poet to use as many synonyms for important ideas as he could either remember or invent by compounding, but these synonyms perished in the course of time. The *Beowulf* poet called a king *folctoga*, *folcāgend*, *fruma*, *dryhten*; a warrior was *wiga*, *rinc*, *beorn*, *cempa*, *freca*, *scealc*, *fengel*; the sea was *geofon*, *gārsecg*, *hæf*, *holm*, *lagu*, *mere*.

Foreign words in Old English.   Unlike Modern English, which has a polyglottal vocabulary—words by the countless thousands having been assimilated from more than fifty languages—the vocabulary of OE, while not "pure" Germanic, was almost so. No truly "pure" language is known, since communities trade with their neighbors and in doing so interchange words as well as other negotiable items. English is still hospitable to new foreign words, like *chartreuse* from French, *blitzkrieg* from German, *sputnik* from Russian, and it also exports them: *le weekend* and *rosbif* to French, for example, and the American game which is *beisbol* in Venezuela and *beisboru* in Japan.

Literate English speakers in later eras developed a liking for exotic words—some writers pepper their style with terms like *weltanschauung* and *raison d'être*—but the English in preliterate and early literate times, typical of the non- or barely literate everywhere, were reluctant to assimilate words from strange languages. Inevitably they did borrow words from those foreign communities they encountered in trade and war, but the number of words borrowed is not large. And the number of foreign languages encountered before 1100 is limited to three—the Celtic, the Latin, and the Scandinavian.

Celtic.   Of these three sources of foreign words in early English the Celtic, or *Welsh* (meaning foreign, as the English called it), supplied the fewest words. The conquering newcomers learned a number of place names used by the Welsh, since a need for such names is immediately felt, and borrowing is certainly easier than coining new words for place names, or providing familiar words with a new sense, as in

"New" England or "New" York. The situation is similar in the United States, with its multitude of Indian words as names for rivers and areas: Wisconsin, Potomac, Missouri. In Britain one of the first areas overrun by the English was Kent. It soon lost its Celtic speakers but kept its Celtic name, which survives as the first syllable in Canterbury. English kingdoms north of the Humber were for a while called Deira and Bernicia, which are Celtic tribal names, as are Devon and the Corn- in Cornwall. London and York were already flourishing towns when the English occupied them, and so they kept their original names. Rivers, too, like Thames, Avon, Esk, Wye, had names the English simply fitted into the framework of their language. Celtic place names are more frequent in the west of Britain than in the east, partly because the Welsh refugees crowded there and maintained themselves longer against English encroachment and partly because the English were migrants from flatland and lacked suitable terms for rugged terrain. Welsh elements for "hill," like *torr* and *bre*, as in Bredon in Shropshire, occur in the west; Bryn Mawr means "big hill" in Welsh, and *cumb*, meaning "valley" occurs in Cumberland and a number of other place names (Duncombe, Holcombe). *Crag* and *loch* (lake) are also Celtic terms.

Aside from place names, however, there is a strange paucity of Celtic words in the English vocabulary. A deep and persistent hostility between Celt and Saxon presumably accounts for this; the English rarely had any disposition to learn Welsh or Gaelic or to feel sympathy for whatever is peculiar to Celtic culture. That the current Prince of Wales has learned some Welsh is considered worth mentioning in the public press. King Alfred welcomed the learned Welshman Asser to his court at Winchester and gladly entertained traveling Irishmen, but kindly relations were not common. Some trade relations inevitably existed, attested to by the English borrowing of Welsh *binn* (basket) and *bratt* (coarse cloak). *Brocc*, meaning "badger," was also borrowed, suggesting that the animal was not familiar to the English, who therefore had no name for it.

In more recent times the English reluctance to adopt Celtic

words has persisted. One thoroughly assimilated word is the Gaelic *whiskey*. And the political party terms *Whig* and *Tory*, used originally in scorn by opponents of either party, are Gaelic. Some terms known in English are still associated only with a Celtic context: *clan* is a Highland social organization, and *claymore* is a Highland weapon. The Irish terms *kern* and *gallowglass* referred in Elizabethan English to Irish soldiers, but not to English ones. So, too, *colleen* and *shillelagh* have an exclusively Irish context, just as *squaw* and *tomahawk* are limited to Indian association.

Latin.   Unlike Celtic, Latin was a language that had the attraction of prestige for the English, first the prestige of the Roman Empire, and then that of the Christian church, an international organization. Throughout the era known as the Dark Ages, the centuries that followed the Fall of Rome, Latin was the language in which literacy and learning were preserved, chiefly in the various monasteries of Europe and eventually in the courts of kings like Charlemagne and Alfred.

The English, along with speakers of the other Germanic dialects, began to acquire Latin words long before the migration to Britain. This era can be thought of as the Continental Period in English language history. When Rome overran Gaul in the first century B.C., the Rhine was reached, east of which was a large territory the Romans called Germania. In the year A.D. 9, during the reign of Augustus, a military expedition sent into the area came to a shocking end. The legions, under the command of Varus, were ambushed and destroyed at a place in Westphalia called the Teutoburger Wald. Thereafter Rome practiced caution, although some colonies were eventually planted, such as the one at Cologne (Latin *Colonia*), but Roman merchants moved about freely, doing mutually advantageous business with the barbarians. By the late first century Romans knew quite a bit about the Germanic territory, and Tacitus in *Germania* was able to name a number of tribes, including the Angles and Saxons. *Germania* reflects the admiration and fear Romans felt for the barbarians, but several centuries would elapse before the empire was dismantled by them. Tacitus remarked on the Germanic penchant for drinking and gambling, the strength of monogamy among them, and their ignorance of money. In time the Germanen, the English among them, learned about money and disciplined military tactics from Roman teachers.

Interesting detail concerning Germanic culture can be discerned in considering the character of early borrowings from Latin. The words borrowed are short, simple, and concrete. Germanic speakers were not ready to assimilate the polysyllabic terms of the Roman Forum or the philosophical schools. The fact that *cup* and *dish* are of Latin origin tells us that these manufactured articles were new to the barbarians, who drank from animal horns and ate with their hands out of the cooking pot. *Wine* is another early borrowing. The Germanen had beer and mead, a drink made from fermented honey, but the fermented juice of the grape was new and welcome to them. *Cheese* (from Latin *caseus*) was another article readily bartered for, a means of staving off winter famine, and the word was accepted with the thing. Other food terms are *pepper* and *plum*. Words for the preparation of food are *cook*, *kitchen* (Latin *coquina*), and *mill* (Latin *molina*), the Mediterranean culture being farther advanced in the amenities that the North Sea people were willing to learn. The trade words *cheap* and *monger* were early acquired from Latin, as were the terms of weight and measure, *pound* and *inch*.

Two Christian terms, *church* and *bishop*, were assimilated long before any Germanic speakers were converted to the new religion, leading to a supposition that churches were important to them as objects of pillage during raids on the empire, and that bishops could be negotiated with or held for ransom. During the decline of the empire, Germanen served Rome as mercenary soldiers and consequently adopted some Latin military terms, like *stræt* (street) from Latin *strata via*, the famous level roads that Rome built. Of military use, too, was *mile*, from Latin *mille*, a "thousand" (paces). *Wall* and *pit* were learned from the Roman art of fortification, and although the warrior Germanen had several words for battle, they added the Latin *camp*, which still means battle in German (*Kampf*), but has changed its meaning in English. Latin words in this group that did not survive include *pīl*, a heavy javelin thrown at close quarters, and *myltestre*, "prostitute," a mispronunciation of *meretrix*, which was phonologically too complex for Germanic tongues to manage correctly. Although the barbarians were unapt students of engineering, they did adopt the Latin building terms *pitch*, *tile*, *chalk*.

That these words were in Germanic spoken use before the Germanic dialects could leave written records of them is a conclusion drawn from two factors: (1) their occurrence in various recorded dialects, suggesting acquisition of the words before the dispersal of the Germanic tribes with the fall of Rome, and (2) various sound changes. *Bishop* must have been borrowed early from Latin *episcopus* because in Gallo-Latin of the Rhine area /ɪ/ > /ɛ/ around A.D. 400, and intervocalic /p/ > /v/ in the seventh century, as in the French form *évêque*. So, too, *copper* has a form that precedes the /p/ > /v/ sound change, as seen in the French form *cuivre*. Umlaut is a Germanic vowel shift that occurred in the sixth and seventh centuries and then stopped operating. English records of the late seventh century show umlaut as having run its course. Consequently, a word of Latin origin that shows the effect of umlaut had to be in English mouths before the seventh century. An example is the word *mynet* (mint), meaning coin. The Latin form is *moneta*, which must have had the preumlaut form in Germanic of **munɪt*. The first-syllable back vowel was then fronted, producing the recorded form *mynet*. Later, the unstressed vowel in the second syllable dropped out, leaving the monosyllable *mint*, which survives in the sense of a place where coins are made. *Cheese* also shows umlauting; Latin *caseus* first took the form **/kɑzɪ/*, then **/kezɪ/*, and later sound changes ultimately produced /čiz/.

About fifty Latin words in all can be traced to the Continental Period of English. This is not an impressive number, but communications were slow and difficult then. And it would appear that the barbarians were not only illiterate but also stubborn and slow to change their ways.

A very few Latin words in English can be traced to Welsh

transmission after the English settled in Britain. The long Roman occupation of Britain had, of course, implanted many Latin words in the Celtic language, but for the same reasons that the English learned few Celtic words from the Welsh they also acquired little Latin from them. *Port* (harbor town) and *munt* (mount) as a geographical term have been traced to this source, as have the place-name elements -*caster*, -*chester*, and -*wick*, -*wich*. *Castra* in Latin was the term for a legionary camp around which Romanized towns developed during the imperial occupation of Britain. The different pronunciations that developed in English are matters of dialect. In southern Old English /a/ after /k/ broke into the diphthong /ɛa/, which brought /k/ into juxtaposition with the front vowel /ɛ/ and caused the palatalization, or fronting, of /k/ to /č/, an instance of physiological assimilation. These sound changes did not occur in northern Old English, which accounts for the similarity between -*caster* in Lancaster, Doncaster and the original Latin form, whereas in the southern half of the island, town names have the form Chester, Winchester, Dorchester, Manchester. Latin *vicus*, meaning village, was also used as a place-name element in Roman Britain, and again southern OE palatalized /k/ before or after the front /ɪ/, accounting for /č/ in southern place names like Greenwich, Woolwich, Sandwich. In the north, original /k/ remained, as in the name of the important border town, Berwick, and in names like Warwick and Garrick. Unpalatalized /k/ survives, too, in the northern form *kirk*, as against the southern *church*, from original *cirice* /kɪrɪkɛ/.

A much larger body of Latin words entered the English vocabulary as a consequence of the conversion of the English to Christianity. This was an event of major importance to the study of early English because the Italian missionaries taught the English literacy and thus enabled them, beginning in the seventh century, to record for posterity the earliest literature of a Germanic-speaking nation. Gothic had been recorded in the fourth century, but only in the form of translation of part of the New Testament; Frankish was replaced in Gaul by Latin without leaving any significant records; other continental dialects are written later than English and for a long time leave little that is of historical or literary interest. The Scandinavian dialects remained unwritten until the twelfth century.

The Germanic tribes had been aware of the Christian religion during the latter days of the Roman Empire, but were not disposed to give up the worship of Tiu, Woden, Thor, and Freya (after whom Tuesday, Wednesday, Thursday, and Friday are named), and while the English were occupying Britain the Christian Celts were in no position to convert the fierce marauders who were taking the land. It was a century and a half after the arrival of the English that their conversion began, with the landing in Kent of a band of forty monks under the leadership of Augustine. The year was 597, according to the account given by the Venerable Bede in *The Ecclesiastical History of the English People*. The idea of converting the English was that of Pope Gregory the Great, who had long cherished this ambition. Working to convert the heathen ordinarily took quite a bit of courage, but the work was made easier for Augustine by the marriage of the king of Kent, Æðelbeorht, to a Frankish princess who was a Christian and who was permitted to have a priest and to practice her religion undisturbed. The result of Augustine's mission was the conversion of the king and the people of Kent to the new religion. The introduction of some aspects of Christianity was not easy. It was in the English tradition to raid their neighbors, not to love them, and it was impossible to tell an Englishman to turn the other cheek. Christ was long thought of as an indomitable warrior, for only in this view could he be admired and followed. The missionaries successfully adapted their teachings to the situation and within a century, after some vicissitudes, all the English were, at least formally, Christian. In the seventh century Gaelic missionaries working down from Scotland were successful among the Northumbrians. The Christian organization in Ireland and Scotland was not subordinate to Rome at the time, and the two missionary efforts, the Roman and the Gaelic, collided and fell into dispute, being unable to agree on the tonsure and the manner of determining the date of Easter. In 664, in a council held at Whitby, the king of Northumbria, Oswiu, decided in favor of Rome, and the Celts withdrew from further effort.

A remarkable effect of the conversion was the flourishing of learning in Northumbria. Monastic schools and libraries were established at Wearmouth, Jarrow, and York that produced Bede of Jarrow and Alcuin of York, men famed abroad for learning and skill in Latin. In 782, Charlemagne lured Alcuin to Aachen to head the school in the capital of the Frankish kingdom. In the eighth century the composition and recording of distinguished English poetry, notably the incomparable epic, *Beowulf*, was also possible in the northern kingdom.

The new religion required words for things and functionaries that English could not supply, and consequently Latin words for the purpose were adopted: *altar, mass, minister, temple, shrine, rule, offer, abbot, abbess, monk, nun, priest, pope*. Schooling in literacy was something new, and although *book, read, write, teach, learn* were native English words given new significance, *school, master, grammatic, verse, meter*, and *notary* were adopted from Latin.

A surprising number of Germanic words were adapted to a Christian context: *God*, for example, even though the word had a traditional pagan association. So, too, *Easter* was a word for a pre-Christian spring festival, but now referred to one of the most important Christian holy days. *Angel* and *devil* had no English equivalents and had to be borrowed, but *heaven* and *hell* already existed in English to express the alien *paradise* and *inferno*. *Saint* was conveyed by *hālig* (holy), a variant, *hallow*, surviving in *Halloween*. The term *evangel*, literally meaning "good message," was rendered by the English *gōd-spell* (good story), now *gospel*. The important term *trinity* was translated to *ðrines* (threeness) to make the idea comprehensible to English ears. Scribes and Pharisees, people who could read, were called *bōceras* (bookers). A martyr was a *ðrōwere* (cf. "throes," suffering), a disciple was called *leornung-cniht* (learning boy). The Latin term for library was *bibliotheca*, a formidable word to the English, who preferred a neat compound of familiar elements, *bōchūs* (bookhouse).

The Italians assigned to England brought homely comforts with them, articles new to English life: *cap*, *sock*, *candle*, *cowl*, *tunic*, *chest*, *sack*. Monks were gardeners, that the monastery might be self-sufficient, and introduced a number of plants and words for them: *plant*, the general term, *beet*, *radish*, *lentil*, *millet*, *pear*; tree names *box* and *pine*, and herbs for the medical practice of the time: *fennel*, *lily*, *mallow*, *rue*, *savory* among them.

Looking back on the Old English period from the vantage point of the present, we may wonder at how few the Latin words were that were assimilated in English speech; about 450 such words have been counted. By contrast, the vocabulary since the Renaissance has been stuffed with Latin and Greek. The bookish language now, especially the vocabulary of the sciences and technologies, appears at times to be half classical. The paucity of Latin in Old English can be accounted for by the difficulty of inducing literacy on a grand scale to a society that had not had it. The English were farmers and fighters, not much disposed to using their gross national product for the maintenance of peaceable monks in expensive schools and libraries. The flowering of learning in Northumbria in the eighth century was a wonder, but one of brief duration. In the ninth century the Vikings sacked and burned the schools; the scholars were slain or scattered. It would take centuries for learning to be reestablished in the stricken area. In the south education languished. About 894, King Alfred remarked of learning that:

Swǣ clǣne hīo wæs oðfeallenu on Angelcynne ðæt swīðe fēawa wǣron behionan Humbre ðe hiora ðēninga cūðen understondan on Englisc, oððe furðum ān ǣrendgewrit of Lǣdene on Englisc āreccean; ond ic wēne ðætte nōht monige begiondan Humbre nǣren. Swǣ fēawa hiora wǣron ðæt ic furðum ānne anlēpne ne mæg geðencean be sūðan Temese, ðā ðā ic tō rīce fēng.

So entirely had it fallen away in England that there were very few this side the Humber who could understand their service in English, or translate a passage from Latin to English; and I think there were not many beyond the Humber. There were so few that I cannot think of even a single one south of the Thames, when I came to the throne.

A century later, the learned monk Ælfric said of a teacher he had had that "hē cūðe be dæle Lȳden understandan" (he could understand Latin in part).

Alfred had plans to build schools and increase the number of teachers and scholars, but it was not until after his time that the movement known as the Benedictine Reform succeeded in stimulating learning to a significant degree. Monasticism had lost its fervor everywhere in Europe. The Rule of St. Benedict was hard, and many monks had become like Chaucer's: "A fat swan loved he best of any roast." Monastic reform, successfully carried through on the continent, spread to England and once again produced scholars, notable among them the industrious Ælfric, who wrote homilies and saints' lives in English, for the edification of learned and unlearned alike. The new scholars, like Bede and Alcuin before them, were adept in Latin, and in writing English felt free to add useful Latin words, like *apostle*, *cell*, *cloister*, *creed*, *demon*, *idol*, *prophet*, *sabbath*; medical terms, *cancer*, *scrofula*, *paralysis*; exotic animals, *camel*, *scorpion*, *tiger*. Ælfric preferred *bibliotheca* to *bōchūs* and *columba* to *dove*, although these words and some others like them did not long survive his use. One effect of the revival of learning in the tenth century that is of inestimable value was the copying of poetry in four great manuscripts that miraculously survived: the Exeter Book, the *Beowulf* MS, the Junius MS, and the Vercelli Book. Without the patient labor of monastic copyists obedient to the Rule of Benedict, this brilliant literature would have been lost.

Scandinavian. The third foreign language that contributed words to the Old English word-stock is the Scandinavian, or Old Norse, the language spoken by Danish and Norwegian vikings who first plundered and then settled in northern England. The Viking Age is an era in history that still arouses wonder a thousand years later and supplies material for popular literature in books, cartoons, and movies. For reasons not well understood the Scandinavian countries were for a while "factories of nations" and poured out an endless supply of restless, turbulent men who, from a little before 800 until a little after 1000, were willing to take desperate chances to win wealth and fame. These men were not suicidal, and they mourned slain friends as other people do, but they were indeed daring beyond the usual. They sailed the Atlantic in open, 100-foot boats, without the compass, using celestial navigation, and were able to reach a small target like Iceland from Norway with regularity. Ships foundered and men were lost, but others were not deterred. From Iceland Eric the Red discovered and colonized Greenland, and from Greenland Leif the Lucky and others discovered America five hundred years before Columbus.

Beginning in the late eighth century, roving bands of Scandinavians terrorized Europe in search of plunder and land to settle on. Swedes moved southeast through Russia, established dynasties for a time at Moscow and Kiev, were absorbed by the Slavs, but left a tribal name of theirs, Rus, to serve as the name of the country. Some Vikings practiced piracy at the expense of the Byzantine Empire, but were cleverly lured to serve the empire as mercenaries, being known as a choice group, the Emperor's Varangian Guard. Norsemen enjoyed living in Constantinople, which they called Miklagarð, "big town," as it was a school to them of luxury and manners. Danes and Norwegians looked southwest and raided the areas down the Atlantic coast. Danes, as the English called them all, first appeared in England in 787. The entry in the *Anglo-Saxon Chronicle* for that year records: ". . . there came for the first time three ships of Northmen and then the reeve rode to them and wished to force them to the king's residence, for he did not know what they were; and they slew him. Those were the first ships of Danish men which came to the land of the English." Thereafter ever larger parties of Danes arrived to harry and burn. The English defended themselves and their property vigorously, sometimes beating off the marauders, or trapping and killing them, but there was no end to the supply of Danes. Eventually resistance weakened, and the Danes were able to form "summer armies" and harry as they pleased. In the 860s they seized York and overran Northumbria. Effective resistance ceased, too, in Mercia, and only the southern kingdom, Wessex, was able to survive as an English polity. During the last quarter of the ninth century, King Alfred's skillful defense of Wessex saved the country. He built forts at strategic places, harassed and fought the Danes wherever they appeared, built "long ships," and hired Frisian shipbuilders and sea captains to reduce the Danish superiority at sea. North of the Thames, England was under "Danelaw," various sections being controlled by Viking chiefs, like the formidable Norwegian, Eric Blood-ax, who ruled York as king for a while in the mid-tenth century. During the reigns of Alfred's son and grandson, Edward and Athelstan, Wessex gained control of Mercia, but in the 990s disaster befell the English. Large Norwegian and Danish armies plundered England at will, exacting large sums of money, called "Danegeld" for "peace" that was repeatedly broken. English morale failed under the hapless king, Ethelred the Unready. The able Danish king, Svein Forkbeard, eliminated his Norwegian rival, Olaf Tryggvason, and resolved to make a fief of England. In 1016 Svein's son Cnut was acknowledged king of England, and England remained part of the Danish Empire until 1042. It is this time that is referred to in *Hamlet*, when the king of Denmark could give to officials in England orders that would lead to the execution of Rosencrantz and Guildenstern.

The significant consequence of this long troubled time in English history was the settlement in northern England and Scotland of thousands of Scandinavian speakers, who made themselves at home on the choice farms and in the towns. After doing irreparable damage by the destruction of centers of learning, the Vikings settled down among the English and, as the generations passed, were absorbed societally and linguistically by the greater number of English speakers. In the process of absorbing Danes the English also absorbed several hundred Scandinavian words. Most of these words appear in written records later, in the Middle English period, but they had been part of the spoken language long before. In a way it is surprising that the English should have borrowed words from people who could teach them nothing culturally or technologically. The Danes, of course, had prestige as conquerors and masters of the land. And, unlike Celtic or Latin, Old Norse was so similar to Old English that intercommunication was not difficult. For example, a recurrent phrase in the Old Icelandic sagas meaning "And he fell down dead" reads in the two languages:

> Old Norse: Ok fil hann niðr dauðr.
> Old English: Ac fell hē niðer dēad.

Scandinavian words were not hard to pronounce or remember and had the attraction of fashion about them. Practical ends or necessity were certainly not served by them.

English words assimilated from Scandinavian fall into a number of categories. Place names with Norse elements are numerous in north Britain, over 1400 having been identified by the presence of the suffixes -by, -thorp, -thwaite, and -toft, which meant town, village, or settled place. Thus we find names like Derby, Rugby, Althorp, Applethwaite, and Nortoft. In by-law, meaning town law or local rules, by has the Scandinavian sense, not the English adverbial one. The patronymic -son in personal names is also Norse: Cnut Sveinsson was Cnut the son of Svein. The English patronymic is -ing, as in Browning, but the use of -son was adopted in the north, where names like Johnson, Stevenson, and Thomson are common. The surname in the Burns's song "John Anderson" was familiar, not exotic, in Burns's time.

Aside from names, Norse words borrowed were simple and homely ones, as would be expected, since Viking society was in the preliterate stage. The Old English and Old Norse vocabularies were quite similar, sharing many cognates with slight differences in phonology. For a certain article of cloth-

ing the Norse word was *skirt*, the English, *shirt*, both forms
surviving after a differentiation in meaning. A characteristic
of North Germanic was the preservation of the combination
/sk/, West Germanic having shifted to /š/, as in *fish*, *fisk*. Some
/sk/ words borrowed by the English are *sky*, *skin*, *skill*, *scab*,
score. English had several synonyms for *sky*, among them
rōdor, *welkin*, and *heavens*. *Rōdor* disappeared; *welkin* and
heavens are poetic and rare: "Let the welkin ring"; "The heavens opened and the rain fell." Another phonological clue to
Norse forms can be found in the fact that the velar stop /g/
remained unpalatalized before or after a front vowel in Scandinavian, and thus northern English had *egg*, *give*, *get*, *again*
for southern *ey*, *yive*, *yet*, *ayeyn*. The northern forms became
standard English after a long process of southward drifting.
The publisher Caxton relates in an anecdote that *eggis* was
still unfamiliar in the London area as late as the end of the
fifteenth century. A housewife asked by a northern visitor to
prepare a meal of *eggis* replied that she didn't speak French.
Eyren was the word she knew.

Occasionally, and haphazardly, the Scandinavian pronunciation of cognates replaced the English one. /ɑ/ in English
had the diphthongal form /eɪ/ in Norse; accordingly, *swain*
prevailed over OE *swān*, which would now be pronounced
*swone had the English form survived. *Swain* occurs also in
the compound *boatswain*. The form *sister* is Scandinavian,
the OE cognate being *sweostor*. Sometimes the Norse meaning of a common form prevailed over the English sense, as
with *dream*, which meant "joy" in English, but "vision" in
Norse; and *plough* meant a measure of land in English, not an
implement, which was the Norse sense.

The long rule of Danes over much of England is reflected by
the Norse term *law*, and the compounds *outlaw* and *by-law*.
Ransack had a quasi-legal sense, meaning to search through a
house, as for evidence, or, sometimes, to plunder it.

The intimate intermingling of the two Germanic communities is reflected by the borrowing not only of nouns but also
of other parts of speech from Norse. Among adjectives are
awkward, *ill*, *low*, *meek*, *odd*, *rotten*, *rugged*, *sly*, *tight*, and

weak. Verbs include *call*, *cast*, *crave*, *crawl*, *die*, *egg* (to urge to action), *gape*, *gasp*, *lift*, *raise*, *scare*, *scowl*, *take*, and *thrive*. English had words for these ideas, like *sweltan* and *steorfan* for *die* and *niman* for *take*; *swelter* and *starve* survive with semantic shifts, but *niman* strangely vanished from the language. Adverbs of Scandinavian origin include *till* and *fro*, alongside English *to* and *from*, *aloft*, and *aye* and *nay*. The pronouns *they*, *their*, *them* are Norse, and so is the verb *are*.

In standard English as many as nine hundred words of Scandinavian origin have been counted, an astonishing number, to be attributed not to practical need by English speakers, but to fashion and novelty, a comment on the instability of language and its responsiveness to shifting circumstance. Besides the many words that are familiar ones to standard English speakers, the dialects of northern Britain have additional Norse words that are encountered only in literature. The fourteenth-century poem *Sir Gawain and the Green Knight* has words like *tulk* (man), *carp* (speak), and *cayre* (ride) that did not find their way into the standard dialect. In ballad literature the verbs *busk* and *boun* (get ready) occur. In Robert Burns's Ayrshire-dialect poems we find *gar* (make), *big* (build), *bairn* (child), and *waur* (worse), words that also appear in Sir Walter Scott's novels that have a Scottish setting.

All in all, foreign influence on the English vocabulary had a limited effect through the Old English era. In 1100 the vocabulary was still for the most part a Low West Germanic one. The centuries following would see a far more profound vocabulary shift through the influence of French.

NOTES AND BIBLIOGRAPHY

Blair, Peter Hunter. *An Introduction to Anglo-Saxon England.* Cambridge: At the University Press, 1966. Blair treats the history of early England in an informed and readable way.

Brunner, Karl. *Altenglische Grammatik nach der Angelsächsischen Grammatik von Eduard Sievers.* 3d ed. Tübingen, 1965. This work contains a thorough description of Old English phonology and morphology.

Campbell, Alistair. *Old English Grammar.* Oxford: At the University Press, 1959.

Ekwall, Eilert. *Concise Oxford Dictionary of English Place Names.* 4th ed. Oxford: At the University Press, 1960. This dictionary has interesting information on place names.

5

Middle English

Middle English is a term of convenience that enables us to
distinguish an evolutionary stage that lies chronologically between the old and the modern language. The three stages of
English since the beginning of written records are still in near
balance:

Old English	Middle English	Modern English
700	1100 1500	2000

But Modern English is already a century longer than the
other two stages, and eventually the boundaries must shift. If
English is still spoken in the year 3000, speakers living now
will be thought of by their descendants as having spoken Late
Middle English. The terminal dates for the stages of linguistic
change in English are arbitrarily set. Certainly nothing remarkable happened to the language between 1099 and 1101,
or between 1499 and 1501. Living language changes but almost imperceptibly in so short a span as a generation. Cumulative changes through several generations make an appreciable difference, however, as is obvious when we look back at
the English of Shakespeare, Chaucer, and Alfred. The farther

back we look, the greater the degree of change from the language of the present.

The rate and degree of change is not necessarily constant in eras of comparable length. The language responds to changing circumstances, and the kind of circumstance to which it responds can vary significantly. Middle English was spoken during an era in which the language changed more than it did in the preceding or following eras: there was great change because there were great numbers of foreign conquerors who lived among the English for a long period of time. Between 950 and 1350 the English absorbed thousands of persons whose mother tongue was Danish and then thousands more whose mother tongue was French. During these centuries of bilingualism, morphological simplification in the various parts of speech proceeded farther than it would have without the presence of the foreigner. The disuse of grammatical gender, the loss of objective case forms of the noun, the analogical attraction of noun plurals to the dominant -s pattern, the complete loss of adjectival declension, and the sharp reduction in the number of strong verbs can be accounted for by the willingness of the English to accommodate foreigners who were speaking English with an imperfect grasp of its grammatical niceties. Those to whom a "pidgin" form is spoken tend to respond in kind. Sufficient repetition over a long period of time can make simpler forms the rule. One may wonder that a similar pidginizing of English did not occur in America, where millions of foreign speakers of "broken" English have been absorbed. But the American situation was different because English was at all times the language of prestige and power, and there was small disposition to accommodate those whose grasp of the language was imperfect. In medieval England, by contrast, it was the Danes and then, more especially, the French speakers who held prestige and power. English was for a long time the language of the conquered and the inferior.

The Norman Conquest.   An event that had a very great effect on the English language was the conquest of England by the French duchy of Normandy. After defeating the English at Hastings on October 14, 1066, Duke William was crowned king of England on Christmas Day. The Conqueror, as he was then called, subjugated all the sections of England and brought them under central control, building castles at strategic places to overawe potential rebels. William made great landholders of the barons who followed him, and, of course, thousands of French commoners—soldiers, artisans, clerks, and servants—accompanied the new masters of the land. The effect of the Conquest was revolutionary. Monarchs of England take their names and numbers from William I, and precedent in English law does not precede 1066.

The Conquest is a curious event, seen from the viewpoint of the present, in that Normandy was a smaller polity than England. Many factors contributed to William's success, one of which was geography, the proximity of Normandy to England across the narrowest point of the English Channel. Sea-borne invasions are hazardous, but the risk declines with the distance across the water. Normandy has been called "a pistol pointed at the heart of England," and both Napoleon and Hitler seriously threatened the invasion of England from Normandy. So, too, "D-day" in 1944 had its setting in Normandy because of the peninsula's convenient proximity to England, the base of Allied operations.

Other factors of consequence are the character of William himself, and of the people he commanded. The name Norman takes its origin from Vikings who settled on the peninsula in the ninth and tenth centuries, who called themselves "Northmen," pronounced "Norman" by the French, who made no attempt to sound the unfamiliar /ə/ in the cluster /-rəm/. The Vikings were a menace to the French, swarming up the Seine to lay siege to Paris and harrying at will. To alleviate this distress, the king of France, Charles the Simple, acknowledged in 912 a Danish chief, Hrolfr Gangr, ("Rollo the Rover"), as Duke of Normandy, the province being so named after the foreign settlers, and the new duke swearing fealty to the king. Thereafter the Scandinavians were soon assimilated by the French majority. Danish continued to be spoken for a time at

Bayeux, but by 1066 the Normans were Frenchmen and spoke only French.

William the Conquerer was the sixth duke in descent from Rollo. He began his spectacular career inauspiciously as the illegitimate son of the fifth duke, Robert, and Arletta, the daughter of a humble tanner of the town of Falaise. Robert made the boy his heir and died while William was still a child. The boy-duke grew up in a violent society to which he adapted himself perfectly. He survived being taunted by his enemies as "the bastard" and "the tanner" and made himself into a formidable military leader, dominating the turbulent barons of his duchy and defending his territory against rival dukes and the king of France. Unable to expand his power on the Continent, William looked across the channel to England and planned the conquest of that kingdom.

The internal weakness of England was an important factor in making the Norman plan feasible. When the Danes withdrew in 1042, the English regained control of their own country, but political affairs were chaotic. The king from 1042 to 1066 was Edward the Confessor, the son of Ethelred, but Edward's power was sometimes overmatched by that of the Earl of Wessex, Godwine, and Godwine's son Harold. The earldoms of Mercia and Northumbria were semi-independent, reluctant to submit to rule from London, and internecine warfare went on intermittently during Edward's reign. William was well aware of the disorganization of the English, since information was easy to come by across the narrow channel. Edward had spent his years of exile in Normandy and on his accession had brought Norman associates and advisers with him. William's plans were no secret, since he had to advertise them in order to draw able captains and their followers to his camp from various parts of France, barons lured by the hope of grants of land in the conquered country. Edward died childless in 1066, whereupon Harold was declared king. Harold levied forces to meet the threatened Norman invasion, but the summer passed without action. In September, William was assisted by fortune. The king of Norway, Harald Hardrada, "the last of the Vikings," landed at the Humber, bent on conquest himself. The English Harold marched north, where he defeated and drove off the Norwegians. On September 28, however, while the English were returning home, the Normans landed their forces in the south. On October 14 the decisive battle occurred, stubbornly contested until late in the day, when Harold and his brothers were killed, whereupon the English force dissolved. No further effective resistance was made, and William was able in the time that followed to consolidate his hold on the country. As a minor sidenote to history, the French in 1966 celebrated the 900th anniversary of the Battle of Hastings with considerable fanfare, retaliating for the British celebration the year before of the 150th anniversary of the Battle of Waterloo.

William's stunning triumph had a profound effect on English life. The newly formed landholding aristocracy spoke French. Normans took over all the important functions of government, law, and the economy, and these functions were exercised in French, not English. Unlike the Danes, who were absorbed linguistically with reasonable facility, the French retained their language for a surprisingly long time, and England became a bilingual country, like Quebec or Belgium, for nearly three centuries. French speakers were never more than a small minority, of course, but the governing class had no disposition to learn the language of the governed. Communication was managed through bilingual interpreters—stewards, overseers, clerks, and various members of the petty officialdom of church and state. The continued use of French by the new English aristocracy was encouraged by the retention of landholdings in Normandy. The king of England was also the duke of Normandy. This was an awkward situation, since barons owed fealty to both the king of England and the king of France. This difficulty was removed in 1204 during the reign of King John. France seized Normandy, and double landowners were forced to choose between their holdings in England and those in France. This political break with the Continent was undoubtedly important eventually, but French did not cease to be the official language of England for another century and a half. The Plantagenet kings, including the one romanticists made into an English hero, Richard the Lion-Hearted, spoke no English, and there were occasionally new migrations of French speakers through the reign of Henry III (1216–72).

During the fourteenth century the use of French gradually declined and by 1400 French was heard no more, except as a learned accomplishment of the educated few. A number of events that contributed to the recovery of English occurred during the long reign of Edward III (1327–77). One such event was the Hundred Years' War (1337–1453), in the course of which the French were enemies of the English. Notable victories of the English at Crécy (1346), Poitiers (1356), and Agincourt (1415) were credited to the wielders of the formidable long bow, who were commoners and English speakers. Another event that had a great effect on the use of English was the pestilence known as the Black Death, which broke out in the 1340s and reduced the population of Europe by as much as a third. In England, French speakers who were carried off by the plague—officials, clerks, schoolmasters, and priests —were replaced by drawing on the much larger English-speaking group, who knew little French or none at all, and thus the use of French for official and scholastic purposes necessarily dropped sharply off. In 1385, John of Trevisa complained that boys in school "know no more French than their left heel." The plague made agricultural laborers scarce, enhanced their value, and helped bring about the end of serfdom. The towns grew in size and importance, and the English-speaking middle class had a greater voice in the conduct of affairs. The year 1362 is a clear turning point, for then parliament decreed that the language of legislation and the law courts was to be English, and not French. The language of law is naturally conservative, and the fall of this last stronghold makes it clear that French was no longer being significantly used in England.

Another factor that contributed to the decline of French in England was the growing recognition in France of the superiority of the Parisian, or Central French, dialect. In the days of the Conqueror the Normans could think their French as good as anybody's, but as Paris grew ever more important, provincial dialects came to be scorned as inferior. Parisian linguistic snobbery is notorious and has a history dating from the twelfth century. In the meantime, the Norman French spoken in England became Anglo-Norman, a subdialect. Anglo-Norman speakers traveling in France found their dialect ridiculed. Landed families could hire Parisian tutors to teach their children "good" French, but this method had its limitations, and surely the French dialect problem speeded the day when the Norman aristocracy became English speakers. The attitude toward provincial French is clear in Chaucer's gentle mockery of the airs his character, the Prioress, gave herself:

> And Frenssh she spak ful faire and fetisly,
> After the scole of Stratford atte Bowe,
> For Frenssh of Parys was to hire unknowe.

The career of the poet Chaucer is another clue to the recovery of English on all levels during the later fourteenth century. Chaucer's education was in French, and his early literary models were French ones, but his mother tongue was English, and he sensibly wrote his poetry in his mother tongue. Since he was a court poet, it is clear that his noble patrons expected to be entertained in English. The recovery of English for literary purposes was slow in coming, for through the thirteenth century Norman patrons were not prepared to reward a poet for writing in a language they did not understand. Nothing in English of literary consequence survives from the twelfth century, and important poems written at the turn of the thirteenth century like *The Owl and the Nightingale* and Lawman's *Brut* were composed for a local audience and probably a quite small one. English was not used as a means of communication on the national level until its reestablishment for such purposes in the fourteenth century. This situation contributed heavily to the development of widely divergent regional dialects of English during the Norman era.

The long bilingual phase in English history had a profound effect on the structure of the English language, indirectly in its morphology and syntactic practice, and directly in the vocabulary. Had the Norman era not occurred, English today would be closer to the language of King Alfred than it is and would more nearly resemble German than in fact it does. It would be easier for the modern English speaker to read *Beowulf* and other works composed before 1300 and easier to learn German or Dutch. On the other hand, the enormous influx of French words into the English vocabulary by 1400 facilitates our learning to read French. Consequently, the Norman effect on English is altogether neither "good" nor "bad." Linguistic change in Middle English made English different, but did not necessarily make it better.

The most obvious and spectacular change was the effect on the vocabulary. It is estimated that about 10,000 French words were added to English by 1400, inviting the witticism that English is French—badly pronounced. The witticism has no validity, of course; English is still structurally a Germanic language, not an Italic one. Its word-stock merely has more French words than the other Germanic languages. The centuries-long era during which French was spoken by a prestige class broke down the normal reluctance of a linguistic community to assimilate many alien words. In this sense the English experience differed from that of its continental neighbors. Medieval and Renaissance Italy was occupied here and there by Spanish-, French-, or German-speaking groups, but never in such numbers for so long a time, and Germany, France, or Spain had no foreign influence comparable to that of medieval England.

In the course of assimilating French words English speakers let fall into disuse some Germanic synonyms that might otherwise have survived, and for some of these it is possible to feel nostalgic regret, as, for example, for *swink*, which meant *labor*. *Swink* was still among the living in Chaucer's time. In *The Miller's Tale* Chaucer has the industrious carpenter, John, advise the idle student, Nicholas: "What! thynk on God, as we doon, men that swynke." Words have no guarantee of permanence, and *swink* might have died without French competition, but French *labor* and *toil*, alongside Germanic *work*, may have forced an early death on *swink*.

French words acquired by English fall into various categories, homely and literary, commonplace and learned. They cluster thickly, however, in those areas that had of necessity to be closely controlled by the Normans: government, the law, church affairs, and the military. Terms pertinent to the pleasures of the privileged are also for the most part French.

Government. French speakers managed the affairs of state in England in their own language for so long that when English regained its position as the official language of the country the terms particular to governing it remained largely French, through sheer weight of custom. *Govern* and its derivatives *governor* and *government* are French, as are *state, nation, country, county, city, hamlet,* and *village.* Some English terms for political divisions survived: *kingdom, land* (in the sense of "nation"), *shire, town,* and *borough.*

It may seem a curiosity that William I was crowned *king* of England, not as Norman French *rei,* but the retention of the English title was politically shrewd, designed to assure William's English subjects that nothing vital had been changed. But the attributes of kingship were given French terms: *royal, majesty, reign, sovereign, crown, scepter.* English kings had set on a *gifstōl* (gift stool), but the Norman kings occupied a French *trône* (throne). Besides *king,* several other English titles were adopted by the Normans: *queen, earl, lord, lady, knight, alderman. Lord* and *lady* had originally been simple terms for the managers of a household (*hlāfweard*—loaf keeper; *hlāfdige*—loaf kneader), but French use elevated them to an aristocratic level. *Knight* in Old English meant a young man, not necessarily of any importance, a sense retained in the German cognate, *knecht.* An *alderman* (older man) had held a position of prestige and power as a military and political leader; the term survived in English civil affairs, but with a considerable diminution of its significance. English titles for lesser functionaries that survived were *reeve* and *sheriff* (shire reeve). Other titles are French: *prince, princess, duke, duchess, marquis, baron, noble, peer.* The English had had no title for an earl's wife, so the French *countess* was used for this purpose. French functionary titles on various levels are *chancellor, chamberlain, councilor, minister, warden, mayor, bailiff, marshal, constable, coroner, squire,* and *page.*

Terms of respectful address were French, like *sir, mister, mistress, madame.* The English titles *goodman* and *goodwife* (contracted to *goody*) survived into the seventeenth century, but the urban English had long before that aspired to the prestigious French ones. As Chaucer says of the wives of the lower-middle-class tradesmen of London (General Prologue, *The Canterbury Tales*): "It is ful fair to been ycleped 'madame'." ("It is very nice to be called 'madame'.") *Mister* and *mistress* as titles are written in abbreviated form: *Mr., Mrs.* The abbreviation *Mrs.* retains the /r/ that is, however, not pronounced. Both /t/ and /r/ in *mistress* dropped out; the word as title is pronounced /mɪsəz/. The full form survives, but with a semantic change: a man's mistress is not the same thing as his Mrs. *Miss* is the clipped form of *mistress* and was used in addressing children and servants until the later eighteenth century, when the practice of using *miss* as a title for an unmarried woman began. The form /mɪz/ has long been in use as a regional dialect variant in parts of the United States, and when the speaker leaves the sibilant a little uncertain, it can conveniently be heard as either *Miss* or *Mrs.* Like *mistress, madame* has undergone a number of changes: *mádam,* with the stress on the first syllable, is an Anglicized form of /madámə/. *Ma'am, mum,* and *um* (as in "yessum") are various reduced forms. *Madam* has a specialized pejorative sense (brothel manager) that can cause some uneasiness in using the term.

The various functions of government in Norman England were named in French: the legislative and advisory body was called *parliament,* the body that engaged in parley, or talk. The English equivalent, *witenagemōt* (meeting of wise men), though a more attractive word, fell into disuse. *War* and *peace* are French, as are *alliance, treaty, repeal, tax, revenue, subsidy, rebel, traitor,* and *treason. Freedom* is English, but *liberty* is French.

Law. After 1362 the language used in legal process was again supposed to be English, so that English-speaking defendants and litigants could understand something of the proceedings, but the terminology after three centuries of unbroken use necessarily remained French. *Law* is Danish, but *lawyer* is a hybrid form, the suffix *-yer,* signifying a practitioner, being French. *Court, bar, judge,* and *jury* are French terms, and the two kinds of jury, *grand* and *petty,* have the simple French sense of "large" and "small," not as a modern English speaker might misunderstand them as "sublime" and "mean." The traditional cry announcing the opening of a court session is *oyez,* pronounced /ojés/ in the Old French manner, meaning "hear ye." *Crime* and *punishment* are French, as are *justice, sue, plead, acquit, convict, sentence, prison,* and *pardon. Innocent* is French, but *guilty* is, strangely, English, the Old French synonym, *culpable,* having more limited use. The names of a few crimes remained English, perhaps because the numerous poor committed them often: *murder, theft, stealing;* the other crimes have French names: *assault* and *battery, adultery* (English *spousebreach*), *libel, slander, arson, treason, larceny, misdemeanor,* and *felony. Hang* and *gallows* are English. In "draw and quarter," *draw* is English, *quarter* French. A few property terms remained English: *landlord, goods, own(er), will,* but most are French, such as *property, estate, entail, heir, inheritance, legacy, chattels, tenant, tenement.*

Church. The medieval church was an important institution which the Normans controlled as they did the state. Consequently, a considerable number of French words pertinent to church affairs were absorbed into the English vocabulary. *Faith* (with an Anglicized final consonant) and *religion* replaced *belief* in the theological sense, and *pray* replaced *bid.* French *trinity* replaced the no-longer-fashionable *threeness;* other important borrowed terms are *sermon, sacrament, confession, penance, baptism,* and *passion.* Titles include *clergy,* *clerk*, *prelate*, *chaplain*, *dean*, *parson*, *pastor*, *vicar*, and *friar*. Terms for the virtues are French: *virtue* itself, *piety*, *pity*, *charity*, *mercy*. In the triad *faith*, *hope*, and *charity*, the middle term is English, although its negative, *despair*, was borrowed, replacing the English term *wanhope*.

Military. Control of the military was, of course, essential to the Normans, and consequently the terms in this area, as in the political, are largely French: *arm* (verb), *arms*, *armor*, *armory*, *army*, for example. English words for army, *here* and *fierd*, disappeared. English *weapon* survived, as did *fleet*, but *navy* is French, as are *enemy*, *force*, *battle*, *skirmish*, *ambush*, *siege*, *defense*, and *retreat*, and the titles, *captain*, *lieutenant*, *sergeant*, *soldier*. Terms for obsolete weapons like the *lance*, *gisarm*, and *mace*, and for armor, like *mail*, *hauberk*, *greave*, are themselves obsolete, of course, but *helmet* was reintroduced in World War I. Many other familiar French military terms were borrowed in later eras, but the terms cited here are Middle English adoptions.

The good life. Pleasure and good living were the privilege of the upper class and were matters of great importance to them, so terms in this area that occur in late Middle English are largely of French origin. Some English dress terms survived: *cloth*, *clothes*, *clothing*, *shoe*, *glove*, *shirt*; *skirt* is Danish, and *cap* and *sock* had been acquired earlier from Latin. The Norman upper-class concern with appearance is reflected in the impressive number of French dress terms that were assimilated by English: *apparel*, *attire*, *buckle*, *button*, *coat*, *cloak*, *collar*, *dress* (verb), *garment*, *gown*, *habit*, *mantle*, *pleat*, *robe*, and *veil*. The wearing of fur was an aristocratic mark, so the word *fur* is French, as are *beaver*, *ermine*, and *sable*. An interest in *color* is indicated by the word itself and by *blue*, *crimson*, *russet*, *scarlet*, and *saffron*.

Like good dress, good feeding was important to noble folk. Some English terms in this area survived (*food*, *drink*, *meal*, *meat*, *bread*), but many French terms were acquired by the English, like *appetite*, *taste*, *victuals*, *feast*, *dinner*, *supper*, and *mess.* English *breakfast* survived, obviously because an early meal was needed by those who did the work, but not by their masters. Meat dressed for the table had French names, but the animal on the hoof was still English. Sir Walter Scott called attention to this distinction in *Ivanhoe* (chapter 1), when he had Wamba the jester point out to surly Gurth the swineherd that ". . . when the brute lives, and is in the charge of a Saxon slave, she goes by her Saxon name; but becomes a Norman, and is called pork, when she is carried to the castle hall to feast among the nobles." And indeed the animals are English (*swine, boar, ox, cow, calf, sheep, lamb, deer*) and the meat is French (*pork, brawn, beef, veal, mutton, venison*).

Terms for the process of cooking are also French, except for the English *bake*, which survived presumably because of commoners' dependence on bread, but *boil* replaced *seethe*, and other French terms were introduced: *broil, fry, roast, stew, mince, grate.* French terms for condiments and flavoring include *spice, sauce, season, gravy, clove, mustard, cinnamon,* and *vinegar.* French service terms are *saucer, cruet, goblet, plate, platter.* Fruit names introduced by the Normans include *date, grape, lemon, orange,* and *pomegranate.* A. C. Baugh, in *A History of the English Language* (p. 171), remarks that "It is melancholy to think what the English dinner table would have been like, had there been no Norman Conquest," but travelers in Britain today sometimes conclude that the English forgot what the French taught their ancestors.

Arts and amusements. In this area some English terms survived: *game, play, glee, laugh, mirth, merry, song, harp, hunt,* but many French terms were assimilated in Middle English, among them *leisure, pleasure,* and *joy; art, beauty, paint; music, melody, carol, dance, juggler, jester, fool; cards, suit, partner, trump, ace, deuce, trey, jack* (English *knave*). The French numbers for four, five, six—*cater, sink, size*—dropped out, but were in use in Chaucer's time.

In architecture and household matters French is much in evidence: *castle* was acquired early, before the Conquest; later borrowings include *masonry, palace, mansion, tower, pinna-*

cle, chimney, garret, cellar, dungeon, chamber, parlor, closet, pantry, scullery; chair, table, couch, cushion, blanket, and *towel.*

Hunting and hawking were English sports and words; the French added *chase* and *falconry* and terms for varieties of hawk, *falcon, merlin, tercelet.* Heraldry was an elaborate art form in the Middle Ages with color terms like *gules, sable, verdant,* an animal figure that could be *couchant* or *rampant,* and *sinister* and *dexter* for left and right.

When English recovered its position for literary use, French supplied models and a number of terms: *letters, literature, poet* (replacing English *scop* and *maker*), *rime, romance, lay, story, chronicle,* and *tragedy,* among others.

Improved medical practice for the benefit of the Norman upper class introduced a number of French terms: *medicine, physician, surgeon, apothecary, malady, pain, ague, gout, plague, pestilence, anatomy, remedy, arsenic,* and *poison.* The names of the prominent parts of the body remained English, like *head, hand, heart,* except that *stomach* displaced *womb,* which remained to refer to a different organ.

Commonplace words. The French terms cited above fall into categories of special importance to the French-speaking aristocracy, as do words for refined behavior, like *manners, gentle,* and *courteous,* but the intimate mingling of French and English is indicated by the many commonplace French words that English speakers assimilated. As with the Norse words borrowed earlier, ordinary French words did not have necessity or even convenience to recommend them. No compelling reason forced the English to replace native words like *ansīen, lyft, earm, ieldo, ēam,* and *wiht* for the alien *face, air, poor, age, uncle,* and *person,* but replaced they were. It is likely that English speakers acquired words like these through hearing them during the years 1250–1400, when upper-class speakers were bilingual. A speaker of French, when forming English sentences, would insert French words here and there because he did not know the English equivalents. In this way English speakers grew accustomed to French words by hearing them in English contexts. The evidence of surviving records supports this view, since many more French words appear in English writing after 1250 than they do in the earlier records. French words must often have had the attraction of prestige; it was nicer to be called "madame," for example, than "goodwife."

In a number of instances the English word survived alongside the French borrowing, creating bilingual synonymy, as in the following pairs:

French	English
people	folk
table	board (room and board)
flower	bloom, blossom
flour	meal
language	speech
marriage	bridal, wedding
pain	ache
noise	sound
part	side (take his part, side)
cry	weep

In some of these pairs the French word has become the more commonplace. In other pairs the French word is rather more genteel, elegant, aloof, or bookish:

French	English
mortal	deadly
sanguine	bloody
vivacious	lively
flame	fire
cordial	hearty
desire	wish, want
grant	give
purchase	buy

Students of style have celebrated this synonymy, feeling that the French additions enriched the English vocabulary and made delicate distinctions possible: a barmaid can be lively, but a lady is vivacious; a cordial greeting is cooler than a hearty one. Skilled users of language, however, find the means they need to express nuances without necessarily resorting to foreign sources. Speakers of German and Dutch, for example, manage nuance very well without so many French words, whose large presence in English is after all coincidental, the result of a peculiar political and social circumstance.

The large number of commonplace French words in English makes clear how intimately the French language had penetrated the English consciousness during the long Norman era. The overused intensive adverbs *very*, *just*, and *pretty* are French, as is the ordinal number, *second*. The French *clock* has English *hands* but a French *face* and tells French *hours*, *minutes*, and *seconds*. The names of a number of occupations are French: *grocer*, *haberdasher*, *tailor*, *barber*, *butcher*, and *mason*, as are a great many homely, everyday words: *case*, *chance*, *close*, *cover*, *reason*, *sure* and *certain*, *pure* and *simple*, to cite merely a few.

Anglo-Norman and Central French. French words assimilated in Middle English had two dialect sources. Words borrowed early were in the form of the Norman dialect spoken in England, whereas later French borrowings had the form of Central French (CF), the prestigious dialect of Paris and its environs. Certain sound changes in CF make it possible to determine which dialect is the source of some of the Middle English forms. In CF /ka/ came to be pronounced /ča/. *Cattle* and *chattel* both meant property in general in Old French; *cattle* is the Anglo-Norman form, *chattel* the CF form borrowed later in ME. Both forms survived with a differentiation in meaning. Pairs of this kind are called "doublets." Other doublets are *catch* and *chase*, *carnal* and *charnel*, but most of the borrowed words in ME have a single dialect form: *castle*, *carry*, *carriage*, *carrion*, *capital* from AN, *chapel*, *chaplain*, *charm*, *charter*, *chariot*, *chaste*, *charity* from CF, for example.

Speakers of Central French developed a distaste for the initial semi-vowel /w/, prefixed the velar stop /g/, and dropped the /w/, although paying respects to the departed in the spelling with a *u*. Thus, we have doublets in AN *ward* and CF *guard*, and in *warden*, *guardian* and *warranty*, *guarantee*. We see the same pairing in *war* and *guerre*, but *guerre* did not enter the English vocabulary. Other AN words with initial /w/ are *warrior*, *warren*, *warrant*. As a curiosity, all the words in this group were originally Germanic and were acquired by Gallo-Latin speakers from the language of their Frankish conquerors. English thus acquired some words from another Low West Germanic dialect through the means of two French dialects. Central French dropped /w/ in the combination /kw/ also, and thus *liquor* /lɪkɚ/ has a CF source, but *liquid* /lɪkwɪd/ is an Anglo-Norman form. A third form, *liqueur*, from its spelling, pronunciation, and stress pattern, is obviously a recent acquisition from French. A number of Middle English borrowings have the /kw/ sounds and are thus from the AN source: *quality*, *quart*, *quarter*, *question*, *quit*, *require*.

CF *loyal* and *royal* supplanted AN *leal* and *real* in standard English use, although *leal* survived into modern times in Scottish English.

The Anglicizing process.   When French words are thoroughly assimilated and begin to "feel" less foreign, English speakers make the pronunciation conform to the English way. In nouns and adjectives the stress is shifted to the first syllable, and vowels and consonants turn English by analogy. Thus, /madúmə/ is Englished to /mǽdəm/. This process can be seen at work as early as Chaucer's day. In his line, "It is full fair to been ycleped 'madame,'" *madame* rhymes with *blame* and must be stressed on the second syllable, but in the line in his portrait of the Prioress, "And she was cleped madame Eglentyne," rhythm requires *madame* to have an English first-syllable stress. In the line that follows, "Ful well she soong the service dyvyne," *sérvice* must follow the English stress pattern to allow the line to scan. Chaucer regularly used French stress in rhyme position—a great convenience—but in other positions felt free to stress French words either way to suit the needs of scansion, and there were apparently no purists about who were likely to object.

Anglicizing is an erratic process and does not always take effect. Most of the French words acquired in Middle English have the first-syllable stress, but some do not, as in the phrase cited from Chaucer, *service divine*; *sérvice* is anglicized, but *divíne* retains its French stress position, as it still does. French has continued to lend words to the English vocabulary, and very new acquisitions can be discerned by their pronunciation and stress pattern, like *chartréuse*, *liquéur*, *cuisíne*, *gourmét*, *chapeáu*, *modíste*, *parfúm*, words that indicate continued French dominance in food and fashion. The retention of French stress is no sure clue, however, to newness. *Véstige* is anglicized, but *prestíge* is not, and neither are *ravíne*, *políce*, *hotél*, although these words have been in English use for many generations. *Pólice* and *hótel* are sometimes heard now, but the language of those who anglicize these words is considered substandard. *Chauffeur* and *perfume* vary in their stress pattern. The *Oxford English Dictionary* records that Shakespeare has *pérfume* seven times against three instances of *perfúme*, but the French stress is still not uncommon four hundred years later. *Garbage* is thoroughly anglicized, but *garage* is a twentieth-century borrowing that is hovering on the brink. American speakers vary between strict French /gəražˇ/ and the partly anglicized /gərajˇ/. Later Old French shifted the affricate /jˇ/ to the sibilant /žˇ/, and /čˇ/ was replaced by /šˇ/, but Middle English has the earlier affricates, as in *judge* and *charge*, and these are consequently more familiar to English speakers, accounting for the shift to /gərajˇ/, and to /rujˇ/ for *rouge*. British speakers are less timid than Americans and boldly say /gérɪjˇ/, as they anglicize *bállet* and *cháteau*.

Another phonological clue to early dating of French words is found in the fifteenth-century "breaking" in English of /i/ to /aɪ/. French words used by English speakers at that time underwent the vowel shift, like *nice* and *vine*: /nis/ > /naɪs/. Some words acquired later have resisted this anglicization, like *prestige*, *police*, *ravine*. *Oblige* hesitated to be English for a while. In 1735, Pope rhymed *obliged* with *besieged*: ". . . by flatterers besieged, / And so obliging, that he ne'er obliged." A little later, some who were troubled by hearing both /əblij/

and /əblaɪj/ appealed to the Earl of Chesterfield to decide between the variants, and the Earl, however uncertain he may have felt, declared in favor of the anglicized pronunciation. As late as 1820, however, Byron in *Don Juan* could rhyme "obliging all" with "besieging all."

French dropped /s/ in the cluster /st/, as in *bête, fête*; the English forms *beast, feast*, were acquired before the sound change occurred in French. The French shift from /č/ to /š/ is another clue to newness. The doublets *chief* and *chef* (meaning "head") are old and new, respectively. Charles is old, but Charlotte and Charlemagne (Latin *Carolus Magnus*) use the New French consonant.

English still Germanic.   The mass of French words absorbed into the English vocabulary during the Middle English era is impressive, but its effect on the language should not be misunderstood. English was not converted into a semi-Italic language by French additions to the word-stock. In phonology, morphology, and syntax, English remained Germanic. The hard, inner core of the vocabulary, even though some common, indispensable words have a French source, is still Anglo-Saxon. These are the words that "come home to men's business and bosoms," words like *house, hearth,* and *home;* the familiar parts of the body—*head,* and *heart, eye, ear, nose,* and *throat, hand* and *foot;* the close family terms *father, mother, sister, brother, son, daughter,* the system of particles— and much else. It has long been a rhetoricians' rule that wherever possible the Anglo-Saxon word is to be preferred over its alien synonym, whether Latin or French. Unpretentious prose, and poetry that aims at the emotions, are likely to be more than eighty percent Anglo-Saxon. Tennyson's line, "Tears, idle tears, I know not what they mean," is all AS, and in A. E. Housman's quatrain:

> With rue my heart is laden
> For golden friends I had,
> For many a rose-lipped maiden
> And many a lightfoot lad.

rose is an early loan from Latin, but all else is native English.

The grammatical structure of one language is not seriously affected by the model of another. Morphological simplification went far in Middle English, but the French presence affected this only indirectly, in that the English lost for a while the normal concern for the traditional forms of their language. Possibly the growing preference for the -*s* plural noun form (*book*, *books*) was affected by French, but more likely this bilingual similarity is coincidental, the dominance of the -*s* plural in English being the result of analogy operating without restraint.

In syntax, English adjectives precede the nouns they modify, whereas in French they follow. Late Middle English poets made occasional use of the French pattern to put adjectives in rhyme position. In Chaucer, phrasing like "service divine," "tubs three," "herbs sweet," "pains strong" occurs fairly often. The use of such inversion came to be called "poetic license" and was thought of as unnatural English. A few examples of the French pattern survive: Knights Templar, Lady Fair, Prince Charming, durance vile, body politic, malice aforethought, but these phrases seem "literary," and the pattern has not been adopted as part of the English system. In "court martial" English speakers are fusing the elements into a compound noun and pluralizing as *courtmartials* rather than *courts martial*.

Some phonological changes. The sounds of language are not stable, but shift slightly in each generation, because children learning the phonemes of their mother tongue hear and mimic with less than perfection. Both vowels and consonants change in the course of time, but the consonants are more easily preserved because of the tactile sense involved in producing them. Vowels and diphthongs lack this advantage. The child, in imitating a vowel sound, must shape his oral cavity properly with only his hearing to guide him. Speakers will sometimes produce a vowel adjoining the original one without being aware that they have done so. The new or "incorrect" vowel may be imitated by a widening circle of speakers until it is in general use in a regional dialect. The dialects of a language vary chiefly in the variant vowels and diphthongs uttered by speakers at a given time. For example, the syllabic vowel in *door* varies between /ɔ/ and /o/—/dɔɚ/, /doɚ/—in American dialects now. The vowel in the first syllable of *woman* has American variants among /ʊ/, /o/, /ɔ/, /ʌ/, depending on regional and individual practice. The variants are not a serious impediment to mutual understanding. Speakers of one region may think those of another "talk funny," but with a modicum of good will comprehension is easily managed.

English speakers who lived south of the Humber River shifted the vowel /ɑ/ to the adjoining /ɔ/ in the course of the twelfth century. The word "home," OE /hɑm/, came to be pronounced /hɔm/, and the vowel was then spelled with an *o*— *hom*. The final *e* that was added later was scribal, not representative of a sound. So, too, with words like *go*, *woe*, *stone*: /gɑ/ > /gɔ/, /wɑ/ > /wɔ/, /stɑn/ > /stɔn/. North of the Humber this vowel-change did not occur, which accounts for the ModE forms *gae*, *wae*, *hame*, *stane* in the northern dialect.

After the shift from /ɑ/ to /ɔ/ in midland and southern England was completed, another change involved the lengthening of short vowels in "open" syllables. An open syllable is one in which the vowel is terminal, usually followed by another syllable. In the word *father*, the *a* is in an open syllable. A closed syllable is one that is terminated by a consonant, like ModE *name* /nem/. In early English *name* had two syllables and in OE was pronounced /nama/. The /a/ in the first, stressed, syllable was open and was shifted to /ɑ/ in ME. The vowel in the second, unstressed, syllable was reduced to /ə/, and thus the word was pronounced /nɑmə/. The fact that lengthening of /a/ to /ɑ/ did not occur until after the /ɑ/ > /ɔ/ shift had run its course accounts for *name* not being pronounced /nɔmə/ in ME and not rhyming with *home* in ModE.

Short vowels were also lengthened before certain consonant clusters like /ld/ and /nd/. *Child* was pronounced /čɪld/ in OE and /čild/ in ME. With the "breaking" of /i/ to /aɪ/ we have /čaɪld/ in ModE. The lengthening of /ɪ/ to /i/ did not occur, however, when other sounds followed /ld/, and thus *children* preserves the original /ɪ/. The same phenomena account for the different vowels in *wild*, *wilderness* and *wind* (verb), *windlass*.

Long, tense vowels shifted to short, lax ones before consonant clusters: /i/ > /ɪ/ and /e/ > /ɛ/, which accounts for the variation in vowels in related forms like *five—fifteen*, *fifth*, *fifty*; *wise—wisdom*; *sleep—slept*, *creep—crept*. Long vowels in the first, stressed, syllable in trisyllabic forms were shortened: /u/ > /ʊ/ in *sutherne* (southern), which, after the later vowel shift of /u/ to /aʊ/, explains the variant vowels in ModE *south*, *southern*.

The short vowel /æ/ was lowered to /a/ in ME: *at*, *that*, *was*—/æt/, /θæt/, wæs/ in OE—were pronounced /at/, /θat/, /was/ in ME.

Unstressed vowels were reduced to the mid-central /ə/: *a* in *oxa* (ox), *o* in *nacod* (naked), second-syllable *u* in *wudu* (wood). In late ME unstressed /ə/ began to be dropped, /wʊdə/, for example, becoming the monosyllable /wʊd/. In Chaucer's verse /ə/ is elided before vowels; elsewhere it could be sounded or not for the convenience of scansion. Spoken English in Chaucer's London must have varied in dropping or retaining the unstressed vowel, allowing the poet the liberty of sounding it or not.

Spelling changes. As the sounds of the spoken language changed, no systematic method of representing them in spelling was developed. The traditional spellings of OE had been lost sight of during the Norman era, and, when English came again to be commonly written, scribes spelled words in a variety of ways. The diphthong /ɔu/, for example, was variously spelled as *au*, *aw*, *ag*, *agh*, *ou*, *ow*, *og*, *ogh*. Confusion was increased by adopting some French spelling practices: /u/ was spelled with *o* before *n*, *m*, *v*—*sune* (son) was written as *sone*, and *lufe* as *love*, the French symbol *v* being added to the alphabet; /u/ was spelled in the French fashion with the digraph *ou*—*hūs*, *mūs* being written *hous*, *mous*. The unnecessary symbol *q* was adopted from French and was used to spell *cwic* and *cwēn* as *quick* and *queen*. As an oddity, the combination /hw/ came to be respelled as /wh/: *hwæt* was written *what*, misrepresenting the order of the sounds, an error that is faithfully maintained today.

Morphological simplification.   A reduction in the number of variant forms in the paradigms of the noun, adjective, demonstrative pronoun, and verb proceeded through the Middle English era, until by the end of the fifteenth century the forms of the parts of speech differed very little from those of today. We can read the prose of Caxton and Malory with little sense of encountering English that is morphologically archaic.

In the noun, sound changes and analogy combined to reduce the forms of *earl* from six to two—*earl* and *earls*. In OE the paradigm ran:

	Sg.	*Pl.*
N.	eorl	eorlas
G.	eorles	eorla
D.	eorle	eorlum
A.	eorl	eorlas

The vowels in the unstressed syllables dropped out. In the dative plural the *m* was first replaced by *n* (*eorlen*) in early ME; later the unstressed syllable stopped being sounded, and then the operation of analogy extended the form *earls* to the genitive and dative plural functions, leaving a single form, without case distinction. In the singular paradigm the genitive and dative forms lost the inflectional vowel, although the genitive retained its inflectional consonant. As a consequence of these changes the form *earls* is in itself ambiguous, functioning as a genitive singular, or as nominative, genitive, dative, or accusative plural. The possessive apostrophe that was later added to the writing system—*earl's*, *earls'*— is an aid to the reader's eye, but since it is silent it is not a part of the spoken language. This formal simplification put a greater burden on word order and the use of prepositional function words than

had been present before and made the syntactic pattern—
subject, verb, object (SVO)—very nearly an exclusive one. As
late as Chaucer's time deviations from SVO still occurred, as
in the sentence "It am I," uttered by Pandar in *Troilus and
Criseyde*, but thereafter speakers replaced *am* with *is* because
of the sense that the noun or pronoun preceding the verb was
the subject.

Analogy drew most nouns into the dominant pattern illustrated by the paradigm for *earl*: *scipu* became *ships* and *beek*
became *books*. Analogy stopped short of functioning absolutely, however. Some nouns in the uninflected plural group remained, like *sheep*, *swine*, *deer*. A number of members of the
weak declension were absorbed into the dominant pattern:
eyen became *eyes*, and *earen*, *ears*, but some weak noun plural
forms survived, although the paradigm was simplified. The
OE forms for *ox* had been:

	Sg.	Pl.
N.	oxa	oxan
G.	oxan	oxena
D.	oxan	oxum
A.	oxan	oxan

ME reductions left the surviving forms:

	Sg.	Pl.
N.	ox	oxen
G.	ox's	oxen's
D.	ox	oxen
A.	ox	oxen

Several umlaut paradigms survived also. The OE forms of
man had been:

	Sg.	Pl.
N.	mann	menn
G.	mannes	manna
D.	menn	mannum
A.	mann	menn

and the incomplete operation of analogy left the paradigm partially intact:

	Sg.	*Pl.*
N.	man	men
G.	man's	men's
D.	man	men
A.	man	men

The extension of the *s* inflection from the genitive singular to the genitive plural in *oxen's* and *men's* is another instance of analogy. The dominant *s* plural declension has no distinctive genitive plural form, recalling that the apostrophe in phrases like "friends' invitations" has no oral existence.

The failure of analogy to operate absolutely is one of the mysteries of language. If it were to do so, "irregularities" and "exceptions" would vanish, making language easier for children and foreigners to learn, but this theoretic advantage has yet to be attained. We can only conclude that linguistic change is a fitful phenomenon, one not managed by intelligent design. In the realm of theory, it may be wondered that English speakers disused the dative case but retained the genitive, which can also be expressed by syntactic means and is sometimes so expressed by preference: "Oxen's eyes are brown" is less idiomatic than "The eyes of the oxen are brown"; "That house's paint" is less likely than "The paint on that house." So, too, the retention of inflection for plurality was not determined by necessity. If "a flock of sheep" and "a school of fish" are unambiguous, so would be "a fleet of ship" or "a shelf of book."

By late Middle English the adjective had lost all inflectional forms, except for comparison. For a time the plural adjective was distinguished from the singular by an inflectional *e*: *sweet lady* but *sweete ladies*, but this distinction eventually disappeared, as did occasional fossilized forms like Chaucer's "Up roos oure Hoost, and was oure aller cok," where *aller* is a genitive plural, meaning "of all."

The elaborate paradigms of demonstrative pronouns were

reduced by late ME to five forms: the definite article *the* and four demonstratives, *this*, *that*, *these*, *those*.

In the personal pronoun a number of changes occurred. The first person singular form in OE was pronounced /ič/ in the West Saxon dialect, but /ɪk/ in the northern region. The consonant was lost, and the vowel shifted to the adjoining tense /i/, later to be diphthongized as /aɪ/. In the second person plural, the dative *ēow* came to be pronounced /ju/. By the thirteenth century the third person form /he/ meant *he*, *she*, or *they*, an intolerably ambiguous situation that led to the adoption of the feminine *she* in the northern dialect, the form that all dialects eventually accepted, as were the Danish plural forms *they*, *their*, *them*.

In the verb the inflectional syllable /ən/ fell away in ME in the infinitive, as in *shaken* (to shake) and in the plural forms *we shaken*, *we shooken*, to survive only in the past participle, *shaken*. The survival of the *-en* form of the past participle is useful, since the grammatical function is distinguished by the form, but, of course, most verbs in English are weak, and in this category there is no formal distinction between the preterit and the past participle. The drift of some strong verbs into the dominant weak group proceeded hesitantly in ME. *Weep*, *creep*, *sleep* had analogous weak forms alongside the traditional strong ones. In Chaucer's use the past participle *cropen* survived alongside *crept*, as did *wopen* with *wept*, and he used the older preterit of *walk*—*welk*—alternatively with *walked*. Verbs borrowed from French were put into the weak group with few exceptions, one being *strive*, which was given the parts *strove*, *striven* by analogy with Class I strong verbs like *drive*.

The gross reduction of inflectional variants in the parts of speech during Middle English is a remarkable phenomenon. That the effect was to improve the language is a dubious conclusion, since there had to be a greater dependence on syntactic patterning and on prepositions to avoid ambiguity, and English grammar became a tangle of syntax rather than a tangle of morphology. The cause of inflectional reduction is presumably to be found in the native accommodation of foreigners' English and in the temporary loss of respect for the traditional patterns of the mother tongue. What English would be like today if the Danes and the French had stayed home is, of course, speculation, but it is interesting to observe that standard German, whose medieval speakers had no foreign conquerors to absorb, today has a morphological system almost identical with that of Old English.

The dialect problem.   A language that is distributed over a landmass of appreciable size, like England, will inevitably develop dialectal variations, localized patterns that are not commonly interchanged over great distances. A language such as English today, however, that has a written standard form thus has a literary "dialect" that is universally understood by speakers who have been schooled in the standard. It is remarkable that native English is now spoken in areas as widely separated as Australia, South Africa, Britain, and America by speakers who share an international literary standard and can consequently understand one another. Dialect variations are discernible, but are not so gross as to impede mutual comprehension.

There were dialects of English in the Old English era. Most of the surviving OE written material is in the West Saxon (southern) dialect of OE, but enough evidence survives to identify two Anglian dialects—Northumbrian and Mercian— and a southeastern dialect called Kentish. Whether these dialects were sufficiently different before 1100 to make understanding difficult for travelers north and south and east and west is uncertain. The written form called late West Saxon (900–1100) was presumably understood by the literate everywhere south of the Humber. What matters were like north of the Humber at this time, after the overrunning of the area by the Danes, is not clear.

In the period 1100–1350, English was a culturally submerged language. National written communication was managed more often in French or Latin than in English. No standard dialect was available to English speakers, and local variations developed without restraint. In the fourteenth century, when English was recovering its position as the national language on all levels of communication, the dialect problem was severe. At the end of his long poem *Troilus and Criseyde* Chaucer expressed concern that his work might be miscopied "for there is so great diversity / In English and in writing of our tongue." He went on to pray that "read whereso thou be, or else sung, / That thou be understood, God I beseech!" A contemporary of Chaucer's, John of Trevisa, in a 1385 translation of Higden's *Polychronicon*, comments that English has been impaired by mingling "first with Danes and afterward with Normans" and that some use "strange wlaffyng, chyteryng, harryng and garryng, grisbittyng" (stammering, chattering, snarling and grating, grinding). Trevisa went on to say that the language of the Northumbrians, especially at York, was "so sharp, cutting and rubbing, and shapeless that we Southern men can scarcely understand that language." Trevisa obviously disapproved of the northern dialect, but disapproval of dialects other than one's own is nearly universal. Dante, writing in *De Vulgari Eloquentia*, estimated that there were more than a thousand Italian dialects in his time. He disapproved of all of them, including his own Florentine, but reserved his greatest dispraise for the Roman variety: ". . . the vulgar tongue of the Romans, or rather their hideous jargon, is the ugliest of all the Italian dialects." And in the twentieth century disapproval of other people's "drawl" or "twang" is still very much with us. Language practice is a social matter, and toleration of differences is a rare commodity.

In Middle English, dialect drift had proceeded so far that, had it continued unchecked, mutual intelligibility would have been lost, and the English would have been speaking different "languages." But the drift was checked by the need to have a standard dialect that was nationally understood. The selection of one of the regional dialects as standard was a natural process, not achieved by parliamentary or royal fiat. The dialect selected was the Southeast Midland. The five major dialects of ME are identified as Northern, East Midland, West

Midland, Southern, and Kentish. The map below shows an additional subdivision into Northeast Midland and Southeast Midland:

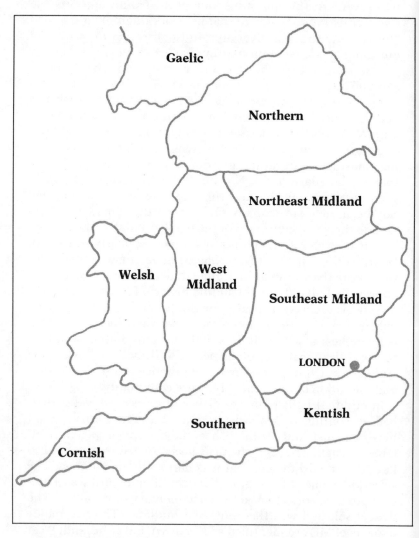

England and the Middle English Dialect Boundaries

All the major dialects had subdivisions, and no dialect is "pure," a tendency toward "contamination" occurring across the boundary lines. Some dialect mixing in manuscripts was undoubtedly occasioned by the carelessness of copyists, especially when their dialect differed from that of the writer whose work they were copying. Identifying all the dialect features of some medieval manuscripts is therefore difficult, but the principal features of the major dialects emerge clearly enough. The Midland dialects agree in important features, and Southern and Kentish share many details, so that it is convenient to reduce the number of major dialects to three: Northern, Midland, and Southern. These dialects have as part of their boundaries the rivers Humber and Thames. Rivers, like mountain ranges, served as barriers. They could be crossed, but with some difficulty, and traffic across them was not common.

Northern.   The dialects were distinguished from one another by phonological and morphological differences. In phonology a significant difference lay in the shift south of the Humber of /a/ to /ɔ/. This shift did not occur in the Northern dialect, and consequently the presence of unshifted /a/ is a ready means of identifying this dialect, as in *Haly Gaste, swa, twa, mar* for *Holy Ghost, so, two, more*. In other details Northern presents more linguistic changes than do Midland or Southern, but in this matter Northern is conservative.

Northern speakers shifted /š/ to /s/ in *shall* and *should*: *sal, suld*.

In the conjugation of the present tense of verbs Northern replaced /ə/ with /s/ as the inflectional element for the present tense third person singular and plural: *he sings, they sings* (OE *hē singeð, hīe singað*). The *s*-form of the third singular slowly drifted south and by 1600 had been accepted in standard English as a variant with *th*: *he has, he hath*, but the *s* inflection in the third plural remained peculiar to English of the north. To illustrate the plural *s*, we find the Yorkshire mystic Richard Rolle writing in *The Form of Living* (1349): "... men and wymmene that ... ledys [leads] theire lyfe," and "Twa lyves thar er that Cristen men lyfes [lives]." The Scot John Barbour in his chronicle poem *The Bruce* (1375) wrote: "And wreik on thame the mekill ill / That thai and tharis has done us till." (And avenge on them the great evil / That they and theirs *has* done to us.)

> For aulde storys that men redys
> Representis to thaim the dedys
> Of stalwart folk that lyvyt ar.

(For old stories that men *reads* / *Represents* to them the deeds / Of stalwart folk that lived before.)

The present participle is inflected in *-and* or *-ande*, a suffix later replaced by *-ing*: "birds are singand(e)" became "birds are singing."

The Northern dialect adopted the pronoun forms *she, they, their, them* and the verb *are*, all of which, like the *s*-form of the third person singular verb, went south and eventually became part of standard English.

Chaucer put the Northern dialect to literary use in *The Reeve's Tale*. The poet had presumably observed the details of the dialect spoken north of the Humber during his travels on official business. In the tale two students at Cambridge, John and Aleyn, whose home is "far in the north" bring grain to a mill in the neighborhood of the university. They converse in their dialect with the miller, who understands them without difficulty, although Cambridge is in the Southeast Midland dialect area. The students' English has unshifted /ɑ/ in *ham, gas, banes, bathe* (home, goes, bones, both); *s* in verb forms *has, werkes, wagges, falles*; *is* in the first and second persons: "I is," "thou is"; *sal* for *shall*; and the Danish adverbs *til* and *fra* (to and fro).

Southern. The Southern dialect is at the other extreme from the Northern in significant phonological and morphological detail. /ɑ/ > /ɔ/, which scribes then spelled with an *o*, as in *home*. Southern was conservative in retaining the high, front, round vowel /y/. Speakers in this area also rounded the mid, front vowel /e/ to /œ/. These lip-round vowels were eventually unrounded to /i/ and /e/ in conformity with practice in the other dialects. Southern speakers voiced initial /s/ and /f/ to /z/ and /v/: *say* > *zay*; *for* > *vor*.

Present tense forms preserved the *-eth* inflection in both singular and plural: "the bird singeth," "birds singeth." The present participle was inflected in *-ind(e)*: *singind(e)*.

A passage in Kentish, or Southeastern, may serve to illustrate characteristics of the Southern dialect of the fourteenth century. The passage is drawn from a book composed at Canterbury in 1340 by a priest, Dan Michel of Northgate, called *Ayenbite of Inwyt* (Prick of Conscience). The place is not far from London, and the time is near the birth of Chaucer, but the dialect differs from that of Chaucer's London in a number of significant details:

> Verst zigge we of þe zenne of glotounye þet is a vice þet
> þe dyevel is moche myde y-payd and moche onpayþ God.
> Be zuych zenne heþ þe dyevel wel grat miȝte in manne.
> Huerof we redeþ ine þe godspelle þet God yaf y-leave þe
> dyevlen to guo into þe zuyn; and þo hi weren ine ham,
> hise adreynten ine þe ze, ine tokninge þet þe glotouns
> ledeþ lif of zuyn and þe dyevel heþ y-leave to guo in ham
> and hise adrenche ine þe ze of helle and ham to do ete zuo
> moche þet hi tocleve an zuo moche drinke þet hy ham
> adrencheþ.

> First say we of the sin of gluttony that it is a vice that the
> devil is much pleased with and that much displeases
> God. By such sin hath the devil very great power in man.
> Whereof *we readeth* in the gospel that God gave leave to
> the devils to go into the swine; and when they were in
> them, they drowned them in the sea, in tokening that the
> *gluttons leadeth* the life of swine and the devil hath leave
> to go in them and drown them in the sea of hell and cause
> them to eat so much that they burst and drink so much
> that *they drowneth* themselves.

The language of Dan Michel illustrates the prominent features of Southern: the voicing of /f/ and /s/, as in *Verst, zigge, zenne, zuyn*; the verb forms in /ə/; the conservative pronouns; and a peculiarity of Kentish, the occasional shift of /ɪ/ to /ɛ/, as in *Verst* (first) and *zenne* (sin).

Midland. The midland dialect shifted /ɑ/ to /ɔ/, inflected the verb in *-eth* in the third person singular (the bird singeth) and in *-en* in the plural (birds singen). The present participle was inflected in *-end(e): singend(e)*. The feature that principally distinguishes West Midland from East Midland is the retracting of /a/ to /ɔ/ before nasals, *man, land* appearing as *mon, lond*. Texts written in Midland are not "pure," Northeast and Northwest Midland showing occasional Northern features and Southeast and Southwest Midland having occasional Southern characteristics. Midland provided a middle position between the extremes, less radical than Northern, less conservative than Southern. As John of Trevisa put it, ". . . men of middle England, as it were partners of the ends, understand better the side languages, Northern and Southern, than Northern and Southern understand each other." This compromise position undoubtedly made easier the acceptance of a variety of Midland as the ultimate standard.

The emergence of a standard dialect. When English was once again the language of everybody for all purposes, the variation of dialects was a problem in communicating in any but local situations, and there was a pressing need to have a standard dialect, one that could be readily understood by all. The choice of dialect for standard purposes fell in the course of time on Southeast Midland. This choice was a natural and inevitable one for a number of reasons. The counties that made up the area were well populated and were prosperous in agriculture and in the industries of the time, notably cloth manufacture. Of major importance was the inclusion of the speech of London in the Southeast Midland dialect area, even though London was on the Thames, the boundary between Midland and Kentish. By the fourteenth century London had assumed a dominating position in the conduct the affairs of England. It was the center of government, where king, court, and parliament sat. London was also the commercial center, the principal port for overseas trade, and a place of manufactures of various kinds. It was a bustling city that attracted migrants from distant shires and foreign lands. London was as important to England as Paris was to France and Madrid to Spain and had a similar effect in establishing a standard dialect.

The universities, Oxford and Cambridge, lay in the Southeast Midland area, and presumably contributed to the prestige of the dialect. The students in Chaucer's *Reeve's Tale*, John and Aleyn, were still speaking Northern unselfconsciously at the time of their encounter with the Cambridge miller, but they might in time have become bidialectal speakers and brought Midland features home with them. How often this may have happened in medieval times is unknown, although dialect shifting by the young at school is not uncommon now. Wycliffe and his associates did Bible translating in the fourteenth century at Oxford, and their work, distributed elsewhere in England, undoubtedly helped make Midland forms familiar in other dialect areas. What weight to give this factor is not possible to determine with precision, however.

The influence of Chaucer and of his contemporary, John Gower, in making London English familiar throughout England and Lowland Scotland, although surely important, has been exaggerated. These poets were read, admired, and imitated by the literate in the fifteenth century, and there was a "School of Scottish Chaucerians," including Dunbar, Henryson, and King James I of Scotland, who used Chaucer as their model, but to assume, as was fashionable not long ago, that Chaucer "invented" modern English is an absurdity, as is the idea long entertained in Italy that Dante "invented" standard Italian. It is obvious that in order to be read Chaucer had to use the English that was understood by the audience he aimed to please, the courtly, cultivated circle in which he moved. Chaucer has been credited with introducing a number of French words into English, but surely those words were already familiar to the educated who read the poet's work.

A prime factor in making Southeast Midland the literary

standard dialect of England was the introduction of printing in 1476. William Caxton learned the printing business on the Continent and set up the first press in London, naturally writing and printing in the dialect of the capital and of his immediate market. Printing made books cheap for the first time and made the written word available to many who would otherwise never have had access to it. It permitted the proliferation of schools and the literacy of a greater proportion of the population than would have been possible without it. The books from Caxton's press and from those of his successors were distributed everywhere in Britain, making all who learned to read familiar with the written standard English. London remained the publishing center, as it is today, and those who learned to read its dialect practiced writing it, too. Sixteenth-century Scots like John Knox and Drummond of Hawthornden, however their spoken English may have sounded, conformed perfectly in their writing to the established standard. It was said of Sir Walter Raleigh that "he spake broade Devonshire to his dyeing day" (according to John Aubrey in *Brief Lives*), but there was no Devonshire in Raleigh's written English.

Thanks to the availability of print and to nearly universal schooling in the English-speaking countries from New York to Melbourne, written standard English is very nearly uniform around the world. Minor variations in vocabulary and spelling are no serious impediment to understanding. Historically the origin of this standard is found in the Southeast Midland of Chaucer's time, which accounts for the fact that Chaucer, although he could not foresee it, is more readily intelligible to readers today than are his contemporaries who wrote in other dialects, the authors of *Piers Plowman* and *Sir Gawain and the Green Knight*, whose dialects present difficulties that inhibit comprehension without close study of the language. It is this relative ease that accounts for the notion that Chaucer "invented" modern English.

Although print and schooling provided English with an international standard form, some details of the dialects that evolved during the Middle English era survived in Britain, still spoken by the unschooled, as records occasionally made by writers attest. Edgar in Shakespeare's *King Lear* pretends to be a southern peasant and talks like one, using forms like *zir, zo, vurther, vortnight* (IV, vi). The eighteenth-century novelist Henry Fielding made some use for purposes of local coloration of the southwestern dialect of Somerset, where he had lived as a boy. In *Joseph Andrews* (1742) the boorish country parson, Trulliber, snatches a cup of ale from a guest, saying, "I caal'd vurst." In *Tom Jones* (1749) peasants voice /f/ fairly consistently, as in *vight, voke, vurst, vamily*. The comic figure, Squire Western, although he has had formal schooling, lapses occasionally into the local dialect: "'And to gu [go]' said the squire, "to zet Allworthy against thee vor it!'" Western's lapses into the local dialect tend to occur when he is angered, not coolly rational—a shrewd observation on Fielding's part, for the dialect Western learned as a child is the form of English he is most comfortable with. His sister and daughter, however, never depart from standard English, nor do the better behaved neighbors of his social class.

A century later, a minor poet, William Barnes, published verse in the southwestern dialect of Dorset, as lines from "A Witch" (1844) may illustrate:

> Vor there, woone day they happened to offend her,
> An' not a little to their sorrow,
> Because they woulden gi'e or lend her
> Zome'hat she come to bag or borrow;
> An' zoo, they soon began to vind
> That she'd a-gone an' left behind
> Her evil wish, that had such pow'r
> That she did meäke their milk an' eäle turn zour,
> An' addle all the aggs their vowls did lay.

In this passage, "sorrow" and "soon" are spelled with *s*, not *z*. Whether the inconsistency is Barnes's or that of his Dorset informants is difficult to determine now.

The fame of Robert Burns as a poet has made familiar his use of the Northern dialect of Ayrshire in the late eighteenth century, as in these lines from "The Holy Fair":

> How monie hearts this day converts
>   O' sinners and o' lasses
> Their hearts o' stane, gin night, are gane
>   As saft as ony flesh is.
> There's some are fou o' love divine,
>   There's some are fou o' brandy;
> An' monie jobs that day begin,
>   May end in houghmagandie
>   Some ither day.

Notable is the consequence of the unshifted Northern /ɑ/ in surviving forms like *stane* and *gane* for *stone* and *gone*. The tendency to drop consonants is illustrated in the elided final *l* in *fou* (full). Burns, as a schooled man, could and did write impeccable standard English, but is better remembered for his poems in dialect, despite the need for considerable glossing of the vocabulary.

Less well known is Tennyson's recording in some half dozen poems of the Northeast Midland dialect of Lincolnshire, as a stanza from "Northern Farmer, Old Style" (1864) may illustrate:

> Wheer 'asta beän saw long and meä liggin' 'ere aloän?
> Noorse? thoort nowt o' a noorse; whoy, Doctor's abeän
>   an'agoän;
> Says that I moänt 'a naw moor aäle, but I beänt a fool;
> Git ma my aäle, fur I beänt a-gawin' to breäk my rule.

The superdotted vowels in the Barnes and Tennyson transcripts are intended to indicate diphthongs, but the exact character of the diphthongs can only be guessed at.

NOTES AND BIBLIOGRAPHY

Moore, Samuel. *Historical Outlines of English Sounds and Inflections*. Revised by Albert H. Marckwardt. Ann Arbor: George Wahr, 1951. A convenient account of Middle English characteristics and dialect matters.

Baugh, Albert C. and Cable, Thomas. *A History of the English Language*. 3d ed. Englewood Cliffs, N.J.: Prentice-Hall, 1978. This book has three informative and interesting chapters on Middle English.

Jespersen, Otto. *Growth and Structure of the English Language*. 9th ed. Oxford: Basil Blackwell, 1948.

McKnight, George H. *English Words and Their Background*. New York and London: D. Appleton-Century, 1923. Vocabulary change in Middle English is well treated in both of these books.

6

Early Modern English, 1500–1700

Modern English is considered, arbitrarily, to begin in 1500. Nothing remarkable, of course, happened to the language just at the turn of the sixteenth century. Written records of the late fifteenth and early sixteenth centuries certainly can not be distinguished from one another by their linguistic forms. As the sixteenth century wore on, however, England and the English language were affected by the Renaissance and the Reformation. The sixteenth century was a time of ferment and excitement in Europe. The discovery and exploration of the New World aroused wonder and the expectation of marvelous things to come, as did the discovery of seaways into the Indian Ocean around the Cape of Good Hope and into the Pacific through the Straits of Magellan.

Of even greater consequence was the use of printing, which made books cheaply available and led to what is called the Revival of Learning. Learning had not perished, of course, but printed books made it accessible to far greater numbers than had been true when only expensive handwritten books had been available to the necessarily privileged few. Common schools multiplied, and many more learned to read the mother tongue than would have been possible without cheap primers. How many of the inhabitants of Shakespeare's London could read is unknown, but an estimated one-third to one-half is probably reasonable, providing a considerable market for printed material. A desire to read and learn was present everywhere in Europe, and the presses labored to supply the demand. Manuscripts in the classical languages were exhumed from dusty libraries, edited and published for the use of the learned in Greek and Latin. The study of Greek was firmly established at the universities, and men like Sir John Cheke at Cambridge were famed and honored for their classical learning in the mid-sixteenth century. Greek studies had been stimulated by the westward flight of Byzantine scholars bearing manuscripts and knowledge after the fall of Constantinople to the Turks in 1453, but it was a while before the desire to study Greek took root in England, since the communication of ideas was a slower process in the Renaissance than it is now.

As more knowledge of the various arts and sciences grew available to the learned, those who could read Latin and Greek, there also grew a desire to make knowledge democratically available to those who had learned to read English, but had "small Latin and less Greek"—those to whom the classical languages were unintelligible. The Reformation contributed to the democratizing of knowledge, especially through the Protestant position that every Christian should read the Bible for himself, without needing the intercession of an educated priesthood to explain the Word of God. This view led to the controversial translation of the Bible by men like Tindale and Coverdale and ultimately to the great King James Version of 1611. The propriety of translating the Bible and thus allowing every man to misunderstand it for himself had been hotly debated for centuries, but the Protestant attitude prevailed. Translations of admired works in logic, rhetoric, mathematics, astronomy, and medicine also appeared. Like the theologians, physicians protested the making of their lore available to the barely educated, but they were reproved by the translators for meanness and avarice. Notable translations of literary works were published, like Sir Thomas North's translation of Plutarch, George Chapman's of Homer, and John Florio's of Montaigne. The market for translations was large and profitable and continued to grow as lower middle-class families strained their resources to provide their offspring with enough schooling to enable them to read competently in English. Education past that level, to the management of Latin and Greek, was beyond the reach of many, but literacy in the mother tongue could be arranged.

The translation of classics into English brought attention to a problem, however, the problem of the inadequacy of the English vocabulary to express ideas that were precisely and eloquently expressible in Latin and Greek. As an anonymous translator put it in 1530, ". . . there ys many wordes in Latyn that we have no propre englyssh accordynge therto." Through the first three-quarters of the sixteenth century English men of learning were embarrassed by what they took to be the unpolished crudity of their language. A favorite word used to describe English was "uneloquent"; other terms used were "barbarous," "rude," "base," "vile," and "indigent." Such a view of the mother tongue seems strange now, and it is a view not expressed in Chaucer's time or at any time earlier. But in 1500 and through the decades that followed, England was struggling to emerge from a long period of cultural stagnation. Perhaps preoccupation with the Hundred Years' War, which came to a dismal end in 1453 and was followed by the dynastic competition called the Wars of the Roses, contributed to England's stagnancy. And through the fifteenth century Italy, the cradle and home of Renaissance ideas and artistic achievement, was a distant place. To Boccaccio England was "that most remote little corner of the world." Eventually the Renaissance penetrated northern Europe and England, but until near the end of the sixteenth century the English suffered from a sense that their language was inferior to the classical languages and to the Mediterranean vernaculars as well. Translators repeatedly encountered situations in which English words were lacking to express ideas that were eloquently expressed in the original. One solution to the difficulty was obviously to transfer the Latin or Greek terms into the English text, to "borrow" necessary words. This tactic was heavily employed and was called "enriching" the English language.

English in the Renaissance shared with the continental vernaculars the problem of being recognized as equivalent to Latin as a vehicle for the communication of serious ideas. Latin was the international language and had the prestige of long and eminent use, against which the living tongues had to struggle to make headway. In Italy, Petrarch's attitude toward the vernacular was condescending. Although he is now best known as a vernacular sonneteer, in his own time his great fame stemmed from his compositions in Latin, and in later years he referred to his Italian poems as "silly, boyish trifles." He left no prose in the vernacular; even his correspondence was done in Latin. In a letter to Boccaccio, written about 1366, he remarked: "To be sure, the Latin, in both prose and poetry, is undoubtedly the nobler language. . . . The vernacular . . . has but recently been discovered, and though it has been ravaged by many, it still remains uncultivated, in spite of a few earnest laborers, and still shows itself capable of much improvement and enrichment." That one of the "earnest laborers" in the vernacular had been Dante Petrarch did not mention here, but elsewhere he referred to Dante as the "prince of the vernacular," with at least a hint of condescension. Ironically, Petrarch's ambitious Latin poem, *Africa*, is now little regarded, whereas the *Divine Comedy* is one of the world's poetic treasures. Dante understood, as Petrarch did not, that great poetry must be written in the poet's mother tongue, where the esthetic qualities remain and defy translation.

The vernacular did not win recognition as a competent means of expression easily. Boccaccio thought Italian "effeminate" compared with Latin. In the fifteenth century the learned Alberti, while admitting the grandeur of Latin, argued that the Tuscan dialect could equal it if scholars would "refine and polish it with zeal and care." The situation was similar in France, where in 1549 Du Bellay felt constrained to argue for the recognition of French in his well-known treatise, *Deffence et Illustration de la Langue Françoyse*. Although progress toward equality with Latin was slow, the vernaculars eventually achieved it, helped by the arrogance of skilled Lat-

inists who scorned any composition written in less than the
Ciceronian high style, snobbishness like that of Browning's
bishop (in "The Bishop Orders his Tomb at Saint Praxed's
Church") who insisted that his epitaph be in:

> Choice Latin, picked phrase, Tully's every word,
> No gaudy ware like Gandolf's second line—
> Tully, my masters? Ulpian serves his need!

Those who were timid about their Latin could find safety in
the vernacular. International communication had, of course,
to be conducted in Latin. English was little known on the
Continent in the Renaissance, for England did not yet carry
much weight in European affairs.

But at home by the end of the sixteenth century Englishmen began to feel less ashamed of their humble vernacular,
and, indeed, boasted of its powers. Richard Mulcaster, the esteemed and influential headmaster of the Merchant Taylors's
School and teacher of Spenser, argued: "I do not think that
any language, be it whatsoever, is better able to utter all argu-
ments, either with more pith, or greater plainness, than our
English tongue is, if the English utterer be as skilfull in the
matter, which he is to utter as the foreign utterer is." Patrio-
tism is evident in Mulcaster's remark that "I love Rome, but
London better, I favor Italy, but England more, I honor the
Latin, but I worship the English." Grounds for praising English had gratefully been found in the admired literary compositions of Sidney and Spenser, and soon other writers,
Shakespeare and Jonson among them, would do gratifying
things with the mother tongue.

The desire to enrich the English vocabulary by adding
words to it from Latin and Greek had a patriotic motivation,
and the enrichment movement proceeded at an accelerated
pace, leading to the addition of perhaps as many as ten thousand words to the literary vocabulary by 1650. Since ade-
quate dictionaries did not exist at this time the burden on the
understanding of the ordinary reader was severe, and com-
plaints against the use of unintelligible terms were soon

heard. Learned writers seemed at times to be competing with one another to see who could do the most to embellish the vocabulary, and affectation, the desire to display one's wit and learning, was obviously the motive of some who took part in the enrichment movement. Quarrels ensued, between Nash and Harvey and between Jonson and Marston, each antagonist accusing the other of affectation. In his play *The Poetaster* Jonson had an emetic administered on stage to Marston, in the character of Crispinus, who disgorged an odd assortment of words, including *retrograde*, *reciprocal*, *lubrical*, *defunct*, *turgidous*, *ventosity*, *oblatrant*, *furibund*, and *fatuate*.

The unintelligibility of "hard" words, as they were called, was a real problem; alarm over it was sounded early and continued long, and there was some fear that English might cease to communicate. As Sir John Cheke put it: "I am of this opinion that our own tongue should be written clean and pure, unmixt and unmangled with borrowing of other tongues, wherein if we take not heed by time, ever borrowing and never paying, she shall be fain to keep her house as bankrupt." Cheke's play on "borrowing," as though words were like money, was a bit strained, of course, but some Renaissance writing indeed made difficult reading. Cheke suggested finding English equivalents for Latin words and supplied examples in a translation he wrote of part of the New Testament, offering *crossed* for *crucified*, *freshman* for *proselyte*, *mooned* for *lunatic*, the technique used by the earliest English Christians when they translated *trinity* into *threeness* and *evangel* into *gospel*, and as Germans did around 1900 who preferred the native compound *Fernsprecher* (distant speaker) to the newly coined Greek compound *telephone*. This device of using compounded English elements in place of foreign words occurred to others: *witcraft* was offered for *logic*, and in a treatise on geometry *tweylike* and *threlike* served as translations of *isosceles* and *equilateral*.

This method attracted few imitators and was little used. Another suggestion was offered by some of an antiquarian bent that antique words be drawn from the "Saxon" and have new life breathed into them. This suggestion, too, met with little favor, for most educated men were under "the spell of the classics" and thought of earlier English as barbarous and crude, unlike the prestigious polysyllables of Greek and Latin. The prominent archaizer was the poet Spenser, who, in his set of pastorals, *The Shepherd's Calendar* (1579), used a number of obsolete words. Spenser's motive was nostalgia for the English past and admiration of his model, Chaucer, whom he called "the well of English undefiled." That Spenser's use of archaic words would meet with disapproval was foreseen: the poems were accompanied by an introduction, written by "E. K.," in which Spenser's intentions and practice were vigorously defended. "E. K." conceded that archaisms were "something hard, and of most men unused, yet both English, and also used of most excellent authors, and most famous poets." Since Spenser was deeply read in his English predecessors, it was inevitable that "having the sound of those ancient poets still ringing in his ears, he must needs in singing hit out some of their tunes." "E. K." went on to say:

In my opinion it is one of especial praise of many, which are due to this poet, that he hath laboured to restore, as to their rightful heritage, such good and natural English words, as have been long time out of use, and almost clean disherited. Which is the only cause, that our mother tongue, which truly of itself is both full enough for prose, and stately enough for verse, hath long time been counted most bare and barren of both. Which default when as some endeavoured to salve and recure, they patched up the holes with pieces of rags of other languages, borrowing here of the French, there of the Italian, every where of the Latin; not weighing how ill those tongues accord with themselves, but much worse with ours; so now they have made our English tongue a gallimaufry, or hodgepodge of all other speeches. Other some not so well seen in the English tongue, as perhaps in other languages, if they happen to hear an old word, albeit very natural and significant, cry out straightway, that we speak no English, but gibberish, or rather such as in old time Evander's mother spake: whose first shame is

that they are not ashamed, in their own mother tongue,
to be counted strangers and aliens.

"E. K." supplied a gloss for each of the twelve poems, with
items like "*her*, their, as useth Chaucer"; "*sparre the yate*, shut
the door." Among the archaisms Spenser used are *wight*
(man) and *swinck* (labor); verb forms like *sayne* (say, infinitive
and present plural), *han* (have), *yode* (went), *hight* (is called).
Besides Chaucerisms he used a number of Northern dialect
terms that "E. K." had to gloss for Londoners: *gars* (makes),
greet (grieve), *warre* (worse), *sike* (such), *siker* (sure), *gang* (go),
thilk (the same).

Spenser's archaisms met with considerable disapproval.
His friend Sidney, in *Defence of Poesie*, wrote: "That same
framing of his style to an old rustic language I do not allow,
since neither Theocritus in Greek, Virgil in Latin, nor San-
nazaro in Italian did affect it." Sidney's argument by analogy
was not very compelling, but at least it provided a "reason"
for his dislike. And Spenser had precedent in the views of
the French poet Ronsard, who advocated reviving medieval
words that had fallen out of use. The formidable critic Ben
Jonson, in putting it that "Spenser in affecting the ancients
writ no language," expressed the general opinion; certainly
Spenser's example was little followed, and "Chaucerisms"
were thought to be quaint, but not useful. In 1662, Thomas
Fuller (in "Fuller's *Worthies*") remarked in an ambiguous
compliment that Spenser's "many Chaucerisms used (for I
will not say affected by him) are thought by the ignorant to be
blemishes, known by the learned to be beauties, to his book,
which notwithstanding had been more saleable, if more conformed to our modern language."

However indisposed the learned were to Chaucerisms,
there was a general impulse to make English eloquent by
adding to it words from Greek and Latin. The reading of
Greek and translation of the historians Herodotus, Thucydi-
des, and Xenophon brought attention to Greek political terms
that had no convenient equivalent in English. It seemed obviously advantageous to take over the Greek words. An early

enricher, Sir Thomas Elyot, in *The Governour* (1531), introduced *aristocracy* and *democracy* by explaining what they meant: "... Aristocratia ... in englisshe, the rule of men of best disposicion"; "Democratia ... in englisshe the rule of the comminaltie." Elyot thought the Greek *encyclopedia* a useful word and introduced it. Some other Greek words that appeared in the Renaissance are *anachronism, anathema, anarchy, oligarchy, enthusiasm, catastrophe, chaos, chasm, criterion, polemic* and literary terms like *drama, scene, climax*, and *theater* (in the sense of a building for the staging of plays). The Latin vocabulary was heavily raided for eloquent words, like *education, dedicate, meditate, benefit, appropriate, expend, expedient*. The words cited are familiar now through long use, but were "hard" words when they were new. They were referred to in derision as "inkhorn" or "inkpot" words, meaning that they were bookish and not part of the ordinary, "real" language.

Those who were opposed to borrowing foreign words were called "purists," but their purism was not absolute. Men like Cheke, Roger Ascham, the tutor of Princess Elizabeth, and Thomas Wilson were ready to accept new words that were "necessary," but were opposed to unrestrained affectation. The poet Samuel Daniel, who was called the "well languaged" for the clarity of his style, in his essay *Defence of Rhyme* stated a preference for plain English over needless foreignisms:

> ... our own accustomed phrase, set in the due place, would express us more familiarly and to better delight than all this idle affectation of antiquity or novelty can ever do. And I cannot but wonder at the strange presumption of some men, that dare so audaciously adventure to introduce any whatsoever foreign words, be they never so strange, and of themselves, as it were, without a Parliament, without any consent or allowance, establish them as Free-denizens in our language.

In his last sentence, suggesting the advisability of approval by a "Parliament," a body of the judicious, Daniel is anticipating the idea of a linguistic academy that was to be vigorously proposed a century later. Controversy over the propriety of introducing obscure words continued through the seventeenth century. Ben Jonson observed ruefully (in *Discoveries*) that "A man coins not a new word without some peril and less fruit; for if it happen to be received, the praise is but moderate; if refused, the scorn is assured." Jonson's use of the metaphor "coin," as though words were like money, is interesting. In 1698, Daniel Defoe in *An Essay on Projects* recommended that without the authority of an academy "it would be as criminal then to coin words as money." In 1697, Dryden defended his own practice with a commercial metaphor: "I trade both with the living and the dead, for the enrichment of our native tongue. We have enough in England to supply our necessity, but if we will have things of magnificence and splendour, we must get them by commerce." By 1697 the English language had been enriched indeed, but Dryden, a skilled Latinist, was still looking for additional ornaments.

The survival of a borrowed word depended on its use by a widening circle of writers, and such use appears to have depended in turn on chance, or whimsy. The Greek *polemic* survived through repetition, but *polemarch* (commander) and *polemy* (strife) died in infancy. Latin *approbation* survived, but the perfectly reasonable corresponding verb, *approbate*, though used in the Renaissance, fell out of the vocabulary. *Impede* survived, but its convenient antonym, *expede*, did not, the longer verb form, *expedite*, being, oddly, preferred. So, too, *expedition* lived, but *impedition* did not, although Renaissance writers tried it repeatedly.

The actual coining of words out of classical elements was sometimes done, as is still the practice in naming chemical compounds, like *trinitrotoluene* (TNT, for short). One bold spirit coined *anacephalize*, meaning "to sum up," a word that would have made Aristotle stare. Coinages out of Latin that failed to attract use include *deruncinate*, which meant "to cut off," according to the seventeenth-century lexicographer Blount, and *desarcinate*, which Blount cited in the sense of "to unload." In 1645, John Milton published a treatise to which he gave the coined title *Tetrachordon* (four-stringed). Milton observed readers stumbling over the unfamiliar word and vented his annoyance at their ignorance in a sonnet, lines 5–11 reading:

Cries the stall-reader, bless us! what a word on
A title page is this! and some in file
Stand spelling false, while one might walk to Mile-
End Green. Why is it harder Sirs than Gordon,
Colkitto, or Macdonnel, or Galasp?
Those rugged names to our like mouths grow sleek
That would have made Quintilian stare and gasp.

The sonnet concludes with a lament that the past hundred years had not raised the cultural level of England:

Thy age, like ours, O Soul of Sir John Cheke,
Hated not Learning worse than Toad or Asp;
When thou taught'st Cambridge and King Edward Greek.

Milton's attitude may seem unconscionably arrogant, but it reflects the freedom the learned felt at that time to coin whatever words they wished to, and hang the ignorant.

There were others than Milton who refused concessions to the less learned. The Renaissance was an age of experimenting with vocabulary, of straining for gorgeous effects with new and startling words. Shakespeare is a familiar member of the group of unrestrained enrichers. He cannot be understood now without extensive glossing and must have often baffled the audiences of his own time, but such was the triumph of the idea of enrichment that Shakespeare was praised and admired without having been always understood. The playwright himself ridiculed affected language as used by the pedantic Holofernes in *Love's Labour's Lost* and by the courtier Osric in *Hamlet*. And in *Hamlet* when the player recites the phrase "the mobled Queen," Hamlet questions it: "The mobled Queen?" and foolish Polonius chimes in, "That's good, 'mobled Queen' is good." (act 2, scene 2, lines 524–526). But hard words abound in Shakespeare, like *romage, precurse, cli-*

matures, and *suspiration* in the first two scenes in *Hamlet*. When Macbeth says that his bloody hand will "The multitudinous seas incarnadine" (2.2.62) and Othello tells Desdemona of "the anthropophagi," Shakespeare is being "eloquent" indeed. The playwright invented forms freely, as when in *Lear* Goneril asks her father "A little to disquantity your train" (1.4.270), and a reading of *Measure for Measure* turns up *extirp*, *prolixious*, *prompture*, and *vastidity*. Not all writers were so difficult. Marlowe wrote gorgeous poetry with a more familiar vocabulary.

After 1700 the flow of classical terms into English diminished but did not cease, and the formal style has continued to make copious use of the polysyllabic Latin and Greek, with variations in degree. In the later eighteenth century the stately style called "Johnsonese" was heavily Latinate, as is the current ponderous manner known as "bureaucratese," which, for "the house burned down" has "the conflagration consumed the edifice," and for "turn out the light" prefers "extinguish the illumination." The impressiveness of "big words" has regularly tempted the half-educated to take dangerous risks with them, and comic fiction has many versions of Mrs. Malaprop. Whether the Latinate vocabulary is on balance an advantage or not is difficult to decide. It has added synonyms for the judicious to choose from, but many classical terms seem to be imperfectly assimilated into the English wordstock. Vocabulary tests prove monotonously that readers with only some education have no idea what certain not uncommon Latin words mean, like *celerity*, *enervate*, *morbidity*, *moribund*, *ambiguous*, to cite only a few. The distinguished Danish linguist, Otto Jespersen, who otherwise thought English to be the most efficient language yet devised, is wittily severe with the prevailing disadvantages of the classical element in English (*Growth and Structure of the English Language*, chapter 6, "Latin and Greek"). Jespersen put it that "The international currency of many words is not a full compensation for their want of harmony with the core of the language and for the undemocratic character they give to the vocabulary." By "undemocratic" he meant that the elitist few who had the advantage of the standard classical education were the only ones who could control the "learned" part of the vocabulary. In recent decades, however, the study of Latin has been declining, with the possible effect that the Latin element will itself decline in nontechnical use during the generations to come. This will probably be a good effect, since the literary vocabulary does seem to be overly "enriched" with synonyms, some of which could be dispensed with to advantage.

Overseas words. Another source for new words, called "overseas words," in Renaissance English was the various Italic vernaculars—French, Italian, Spanish, and Portuguese. French was an intermediary language for English through which classical and Italian words were sometimes filtered. Literary French in the sixteenth century was vigorously engaged in Latinizing and Italianizing; the English were looking to France for literary models and tended to imitate French practices, although some Italian words were being brought back to England from the original source by traveled Englishmen. The idea of the Grand Tour had taken root, and young gentlemen of means were enjoying extended stays in fascinating Italy and returning home with Italian clothes, manners, and words. Some conservative English, especially those of a Puritan disposition, feared that English manners would be corrupted by Italian license. Roger Ascham gave as his opinion that "An Italianate Englishman is a devil incarnate," but Italian travel continued to be fashionable, and many Italian words pertinent to various arts entered the English vocabulary, either directly or through the French.

Italian innovations in music were eagerly adopted in the other European countries, and along with innovation came the terminology that is familiar to students of music. Terms for voice pitch: *soprano, contralto, basso*; instruments: *viola, cello, pianoforte*; rhythms: *allegro, adagio, andante*; miscellaneous: *opera, concerto, sonata, pizzicato, diminuendo, crescendo, fortissimo*. Terms for characteristics of Italian architecture were borrowed: *balcony, portico, piazza, stucco*, *cupola*, *grotto*. Frequent warfare in the Italian peninsula during the Renaissance led to improvements in military organization which were assimilated by others, as the Italian words attest: *infantry* and *cavalry*; through French, which lopped off the final vowel, Italian *battaglione* and *brigata* took the forms *battalion* and *brigade*; *colonnello* and *fregata* were reduced to *colonel* and *frigate*. *Bravo* in the sense of "assassin" retained its final Italian vowel, perhaps to avoid confusion with the adjective *brave*.

The lead taken by Spanish and Portuguese explorers and settlers in Africa and the "New World" brought words from their languages for exotic people, plants, and animals into other vernaculars, such as *cannibal*, *negro* (black), then *mulatto*, and ultimately *quadroon* through the practice of miscegenation, in which the Iberians had precedence over others and consequently provided names for the results. Useful plants found in America were brought to Europe with Spanish names: *banana*, *tomato*, *potato*, *tobacco*. Among words for strange fauna, *mosquito* and *armadillo* are Spanish, as is *alligator*, anglicized from *el lagarto* (the lizard). *Bravado* and *desperado* retain their Spanish final *o*, but *barricado*, *renegado*, and *palisado* eventually took on the French style as *barricade*, *renegade*, *palisade*.

Another source of foreign words was Dutch and Low German. The Low Countries were close neighbors of England, and commerce with them and the Hansa towns was extensive, as was the migration of Flemings and Hollanders to England during the Middle Ages and Renaissance. England supported the Dutch in their wars against Spain, and some English, Sidney and Ben Jonson among them, served in these wars and introduced the military terms *furlough* and *forlorn hope* from Dutch. The age of Rembrandt attracted art terms like *sketch*, *easel*, and *landscape*. Dutch prominence in shipbuilding and the carrying trade introduced sailing terms: *yacht*, *yawl*, *sloop*, *boom*, *deck*.

Early Dictionaries. The difficulty readers were encountering in understanding printed matter made obvious a need for dictionaries that would explain the sense of "hard" words, and from 1604 such dictionaries were published, gradually becoming larger and more informative. The first such book was Robert Cawdrey's *A Table Alphabeticall* (1604). Cawdrey defined about 3,000 words, often with a single synonym, like "*Magistrate*, governour"; "*Mutation*, change." He expressed some diffidence on the title page: his list was "gathered for the benefit and help of Ladies, Gentlewomen, or any other unskilfull persons." Dictionaries that followed Cawdrey's also aimed at "Ladies and Gentlewomen, young scholars, clerks, merchants, and strangers," meaning all those who could read but had not had the advantage of a literary education. The well-schooled had the use of bilingual dictionaries, Latin-English, French-English, Italian-English. Following Cawdrey there appeared John Bullokar's *An English Expositor* (1616), Henry Cockeram's *The English Dictionarie* (1623), Thomas Blount's *Glossographia* (1656), Edward Phillips's *The New World of English Words* (1658) and others, growing fuller and less unsatisfactory, until the eighteenth-century works of Nathaniel Bailey and Samuel Johnson assumed the appearance of current dictionaries, with etymologies and superior definitions. The early dictionary compilers copied liberally from their predecessors and sometimes plucked curious gems from Latin-English glosses that may never have been used in English, like *commotrix, glacitate, concinnate, periclitation*. Despite their limitations and defects, these early dictionaries had a good market, being reissued many times until they were superseded by Bailey and Johnson.

Spelling as a problem. The spelling of English before 1200 was reasonably consistent. Scribes learned and practiced the conventions with few idiosyncratic variations. Furthermore, they tended to adjust spelling to pronunciation changes; when in the late West Saxon dialect speakers unrounded /y/ to /i/, scribes sensibly spelled the sound *i* rather than with traditional *y*. When speakers contracted verb forms like *grētep* to *grēt* and *rǣdep* to *rǣt* (greeteth, readeth) scribes spelled as they spoke. But during the long Norman interval when written English was little used, the conventions were forgotten, and when English recovered its position as the sole language in common use, the spelling of it had become chaotic. The practice of adjusting spelling to pronunciation changes had ceased. Some curious French spelling practices were adopted in English, leading to the spelling of *hūs* as *hous* and *tung* as *tongue*. In the fifteenth and sixteenth centuries individual writers spelled as they pleased, there being no convention, authority, or dictionary to provide restraint on variation. *Where* had other forms, among them *wheer*, *whair*, *weer*, *were*. At least nine spellings of *tongue* can be found in sixteenth-century print: *tung*, *tunge*, *tong*, *tonge*, *toong*, *toonge*, *toung*, *tounge*, *tongue*. (The variant ultimately settled on as "standard" was a poor choice, as it uses the French *o* before a nasal and the silent final *ue*, as in the French equivalent, *langue*.) Readers of early print had to be adroit in recognizing words in their variant spellings. Shakespeare's name had several forms during his lifetime, including Shaksper, Shackspear, Shaxspere. The playwright seems not to have minded, since surviving examples of his signature have variants. Indifference to the desirability of a consistent spelling was obviously general during the Renaissance.

Classical learning added confusion in some instances. *Debt* and *doubt* had been written *dette* and *doute* in Chaucer's time, but the learned added silent *b* to the spelling on the grounds that the Latin forms had *b* in them—*debit* and *dubit* (as in *indubitable*). That some speakers then pronounced the *b* is suggested by Shakespeare's absurd pedant, Holofernes (*Love's Labour's Lost*, 5.1.23), defending the practice. Those who don't sound the *b* Holofernes calls "rackers of orthography," but it would appear that only pedants strained to sound it. Similarly, *p* was inserted in *receipt* and *c* in *indict* without affecting the pronunciation. *Island* had had the form *iland* until the learned inserted the *s* because the Latin equivalent *insula* had one. That *insula* and *iland* had no etymological connection seems not to have mattered to the "improvers" of orthography. The consequence of this misapplied learning was that the literate have been obliged ever since to remember to include symbols that represent no sound. On occasion the pronunciation changed to agree with the respelling, as in the instance of *perfect*, which had earlier been *parfit*. So, too, when *voirdit* was spelled *verdict*, the pronunciation eventually agreed with the new spelling. These examples lead to the conclusion that linguistic phenomena are bewilderingly unpredictable.

Another orthographical oddity, the silent *h* in *ghost*, *ghoul*, *ghastly*, *gherkin*, is attributed to Dutch printers imported in Caxton's time, who followed a practice used in their own language in setting English type. The *h* in *ghospel* and *ghess* fell out eventually, the *h* in *ghess* being replaced by the French silent *u* in *guess*, a change, but not an improvement over Chaucer's *gesse*.

Some of the learned were perturbed by the chaos in spelling and offered solutions which, however, were not adopted by others. Sir John Cheke made a practice of dropping final *e* in words like *giv* and *deceiv*; when *a* represented the sound /e/ he doubled the letter, writing *made* as *maad*; he dropped unpronounced letters like *u* in *would* (wold), *b* in *doubt* (dout), *w* in *whole* (hole); replaced final *y* with *i*, writing *my* and *say* as *mi* and *sai*. Despite Cheke's great prestige, his sensible reforms did not attract imitation. After Cheke, several ambitious systems designed to make English spelling phonetic, so that it might provide an accurate "picture" of speech, were promoted by Sir Thomas Smith in a Latin treatise published in 1568, by John Hart in *An Orthographie* (1569); and by William Bullokar in *A short Introduction or guiding to print, write, and reade Inglish speech* (1580). These reformers observed that English spelling lacked a sufficient number of symbols to provide a one-for-one correspondence and invented various symbols and diacritics to supply the deficiency. Reformed spelling plans aroused heated opposition then, as they do now in the twentieth century, and it was observed that an extensive spelling revision would make existing printed matter unintelligible. The influential scholar Richard Mulcaster in his book, *The First Part of the Elementarie which entreateth chefelie of the right writing of our English tung* (1582), was opposed to making violent changes in spelling, citing custom as a comfortable guide in the matter.

Certainly nothing remarkable came of plans to make English spelling coincide consistently with the sounds of the language, any more than similar plans have won general support in the nineteenth and twentieth centuries. Inertia, or "custom" has always prevailed in this matter. What did happen was that the number of variant spellings of single words was sharply reduced by 1650. *Where*, *tongue*, Shakespeare's name, and most other words settled on a conventional single form, presumably through a gradual process of agreement among the printers of London. That single conventional forms are a convenience is supported by the current practice of "modernizing" the spelling of Renaissance literature, because readers could not now be counted on to know what *whair*, or *toonge*, or Shaxsper mean.

Phonological changes, 1400–1600. The two centuries falling between Chaucer's day and Shakespeare's mark an era of considerable change in the sound system of English. Although consonants are more stable than vowels in the successive stages of language use, speakers sometimes yield to the temptation to drop one of the consonants in a pair or cluster. Initial /k/ and /g/ were dropped before /n/ in words like *knit*, *knot*, *knight*, *knife*, *knurl*, *knock*, *knack*, *knee*, *knuckle*, *know* and in *gnat*, *gnarl*, *gnaw*, *gnash*, *gnome*. The spelling remained fixed and is an anachronistic reminder of sounds that were heard six hundred years ago. The velar spirant /x/ fell out before /t/, in words like *night*, *light*, *flight*, *daughter*, *slaughter*. *Night* had been pronounced /nɪxt/; when /x/ fell out, speakers replaced the vowel with the tense /i/, which was later diphthongized to /aɪ/. These changes produced a considerable difference between Chaucer's /nɪxt/ and the present /naɪt/, and the /k/ loss made *night* and *knight* homophones. /x/ was sometimes fronted to /f/ when final, as in *laugh*, *rough*, and in the derivative *laughter*.

/l/ fell out between /a/ or /ɒ/ and /k/, /f/, and /m/, as in *yolk*, *folk*, *walk*, *talk*, *calf*, *half*, *calm*, *palm*, *psalm*, but remained after other vowels: *ilk, silk, sulk, bulk, self, pelf, elm, helm, whelm.* Holofernes called it "insanie" to pronounce "calf, cauf; half, hauf" (*Love's Labour's Lost*; 5.1.25); pronunciation should conform to the spelling, in his view. It would have been an advantage to have the spelling change to conform to the new pronunciation, but the written forms assumed a stubborn convention divorced from the sound. /w/ before /r/ as in *wring, wrong, wright, wrought,* was sounded before the fifteenth century, but survived only in the spelling.

Initial /θ/ was voiced to /ð/ in the frequently used monosyllables *the, this, that, these, those, thou, thy, thee.* Final /s/ was voiced to /z/ in *is* and *was.*

Before /r/ the various perimeter vowels tended to move into the mid-central segment of the oral cavity, which accounts for the fact that variously spelled vowels plus /r/ have the value /ɚ/ (or /ʒ/ in the "r-less" dialects): *irk, birth, berth, earth, work, world, word, murk, fur, churl.* /ar/ survived as /a/ or /aɚ/ in *hard, card, bard,* and /ɪɚ/ remains in *ear, hear, beard, cheer, weird,* and others; the vowel shifted to /ɚ/ in *heard,* providing the anomaly of different vowels in the paradigm *hear, heard.* /ɛɚ/ or /æɚ/ survived in *where, there, air, hair, merry,* and others. /ɔɚ/ or /oɚ/ remains in *four, more, horse,* and others.

Among the lax vowels, /ɪ/ and /ɛ/ remained unchanged and have been stable since OE. Words like *bid, bed, sit, set* as pronounced today would be intelligible to a pre-Conquest speaker. The adjoining vowels /æ/ and /a/ have sometimes interchanged positions: *that* was pronounced /θæt/ in OE, /θat/ in ME, and is /ðæt/ in ModE; OE /wæs/ is now /waz/ or /wʌz/. /ɒ/ has remained before the voiceless stops /p/, /t/, /k/, as in *top, not, rock* in standard British and in the Eastern New England dialect, but in most American dialects the vowel has been fronted to /a/. /ʊ/ shifted to the mid-central vowel /ʌ/: Chaucer's /bʊt/ is now /bʌt/; in some instances, after the labial consonants /p/, /b/, /f/, the shift did not occur, as in *pull, bull, put, full*; it is an anomaly that *but* and *put* do not rhyme.

A remarkable phenomenon that began its course some time after 1400 is known as the Great Vowel Shift. This change involved all the tense vowels, just as all the stop consonants were involved in Grimm's Law. The tense vowels were raised in the oral cavity, and the high tense vowels /i/ and /u/, which could not be raised, were diphthongized to /aɪ/ and /aʊ/. Both back vowels and front vowels were involved, as may be shown in diagram form:

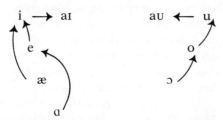

The front series involved a two-step movement of /ɑ/ to /e/ and /æ/ to /i/.

The reason for this systematic shift is unknown. It might seem as though English speakers through several generations were unconsciously unwilling to drop the mandible to the traditional positions and practiced a close-mouthed attitude. This would accord with the "principle of least effort," although, of course, diphthongizing /i/ and /u/ required more effort, not less. But as with linguistic change in general, it is difficult to assign a rationale for this change.

The spelling of the vowels remained unchanged, leading to a difference in the sounds represented by the symbols *a, e, i* that are shared with the continental languages. In German and French *a, e, i* represent /ɑ/, /e/, /i/, not /e/, /i/, /aɪ/, as in English. English speakers learning a continental language must use the "continental vowel system," while continental speakers learning English are bemused to associate new sounds with familiar symbols.

The Great Vowel Shift presumably evolved slowly and in gradual stages. Whether all the vowels began the upward movement simultaneously or some preceded others cannot now be determined, nor can all variations in regional dialect, or between urban and rural speech. While the shift was going on some speakers were probably uneasily aware that the speech of others had odd features, but no orthoepists were on the scene to record impressions of the shifting pronunciation. It is probable that the diphthongization of /i/ and /u/ to /aɪ/ and /aʊ/ had an intermediate /ʌɪ/ and /ʌʊ/, speakers in 1600 pronouncing *like* /lʌɪk/ and *out* /ʌʊt/, the lowering of the mandible to /a/ for the stressed element occurring in later decades. Similarly, the double shift from /ɑ/ to /e/ and /æ/ to /i/ may have reached an intermediate stage by 1600: *name*, pronounced /nɑmə/ in 1400 was likely /næm/ on Shakespeare's stage, to be raised to /nem/ some time later; and *clean*, /klæn/ in 1400, may have reached the /klen/ level in 1600 and /klin/ later. As a rule, words spelled *ea* with the sound /i/ had the vowel /æ/ in 1400, like *sea*, *speak*, *lean*; oddly, the vowel in *break* and *great* remained at the /e/ stage. The vowel in *bread*, *dead*, *death*, *deaf* must have been the lax /ɛ/ in 1400 and was consequently not involved in the shift. The raising of /e/ to /i/, as in *green*, *seem*, *be*, is uncomplicated.

In the back series the shift /ɔ/ > /o/ is also simple, whether words are spelled *oa*, as in *foal*, *foam*, *roam*, *moan* or *o*, as in *so*, *bone*, *home*. The shift /o/ > /u/, however, had further developments: in some words the shift was simple—*soon*, *moon*, *fool*, *food*; with others, like *good*, *book*, *look*, *cook*, speakers shifted /u/ to lax /ʊ/; and in *flood* and *blood* a further shift to the mid-central /ʌ/ occurred. A number of words in the *oo* group now have variant vowels according to regional dialect: /u/ or /ʊ/ in *roof*, *root*, *soot*, *cooper*, *room*, *broom*. Stages in the development of /o/ > /u/ > /ʊ/ > /ʌ/ are difficult to discern. Poets' rhymes are an unreliable clue because of the tendency to use eye-rhyme, as in Pope's couplet: "Pleased to the last, he crops the flowery food, / And licks the hand just raised to shed his blood."

As minor oddities, *Rome* and *gold* were for a time pronounced with /u/, but returned to /o/; *wound* (injure, injury) returned to /u/ from /aʊ/, and *wind* (noun) assumed the lax vowel /ɪ/. The transcription of the Scots dialect pronunciation of *blood* and *good* as *bluid*, *guid* presumably indicates the vowel /u/. The Scots pronunciation of *house* as /hus/ is a conservative feature of that dialect, and *hame* for *home* reflects the retention of /ɑ/ in the Northern dialect in Middle English.

Morphological changes.   The inflectional patterns of English maintained a number of variants in the Renaissance that were slowly reduced through the operation of analogy. A few weak noun plurals survived as occasional variants into the seventeenth century: the plurals of *toe*, *shoe*, *eye*, *cow* could still be *toon*, *shoon*, *eyen*, *kine* until the force of the dominating *s* plural finally swept them away as obsolete. *Oxen*, *children*, and *brethren* endured, however, to demonstrate that analogy does not work with absolute authority.

Among the pronoun paradigms, the second person singular forms *thou*, *thy*, *thine*, *thee* were gradually fading out of use. The King James translation of the Bible (1611) consistently retained the *thou*-forms, but the translators were consciously preserving older forms of the language with stylistic dignity in mind, and these traditional forms still survive in liturgical use. A new seventeenth-century religious sect, the Quakers, used *thee* in all their discourse in the subject function as well as the objective. Lyric poets in the nineteenth century occasionally revived *thou* as a deliberate archaism. In the second-person plural, *ye* as the original subject form eventually disappeared, its function being assumed by the objective *you*, which then served both functions. The genitive case form *mine* preceding the noun it modified persisted when the noun had an initial vowel, as in "Upon mine honour," "Mine eyes dazzle," to avoid consecutive vowels, but this practice faded in the course of the seventeenth century. The neuter genitive singular had three forms—*his*, *it*, and *its*—going into the seventeenth century. Speakers were apparently uneasily aware of possible ambiguity in the use of the original *his*, which might have a masculine antecedent, and were seeking a distinctive neuter form. *Its*, formed on the analogy of the genitive form of nouns, finally prevailed, but around 1600 writers used all three forms without being troubled by the charge of inconsistency. Wilhelm Franz in *Shakespeare-Grammatik* cites several instances of all three forms in Shakespeare's plays, including "It lifted up *it* head" (*Hamlet*; 1.2.216) and the Fool's remark in *King Lear* (1.4.235–36): "The hedge sparrow fed the cuckoo so long / That it had *it* head bit off by *it* young." Several examples of *his* occur, including "How far that little candle throws *his* beams!" (*Merchant of Venice*: 5.1.90). Eighteenth-century editors of Shakespeare, like Rowe and Pope, "corrected" these pronouns to *its*, but modern editions restore the playwright's choices.

A curious change took place in the inflection of the third-person singular present indicative of the verb from -*th* to -*s*, as in *goeth, goes*. The -*s* inflection had been in use in the Northern dialect since the thirteenth century, but didn't appear in London writing until the second half of the sixteenth century. Northern migrants had been bringing this peculiarity of their speech to London ears for three hundred years before the southeasterners inexplicably adopted it as a variant. Around 1550, -*s* began appearing in verse. Poets found it a convenience for meter that *goeth* had two syllables and *goes* only one. Verb forms ending in -*s* rhymed nicely with plural nouns: *goes, foes*. Verbs using -*s* must have been heard often enough to be familiar, since it is most improbable that poets would use a grammatical form that had no currency in the spoken language. Prose style was a little slower to accept the -*s* forms as variants, but by the 1590s -*s* verbs occurred with some frequency. For the next two hundred years -*s* and -*th* alternated without distinction until the -*th* forms began to be considered archaic, although the common verb *hath* still appeared occasionally in the first half of the nineteenth century. Twentieth-century grammarians, among them Franz (*Shakespeare-Grammatik*) and Jespersen (*A Modern English Grammar*), supposed that the Elizabethans regarded forms like *has, does, comes* as colloquialisms tolerable as license in verse and in breezy, informal prose, but not in dignified prose. But such was not the case: in the poet Spenser's serious prose work, *A View of the Present State of Ireland* (1596), of 533 examples of the verb form in question, 94 are in -*s* (18%), and it is clear in context that Spenser used *seemeth* or *seems* and *cometh* or *comes* without considering either form more appropriate than the other. In "well-languaged" Daniel's *The Collection of the History of England* (1612–18), dignified prose indeed, the newly acceptable -*s* forms occur in 94% of the possible instances. Renaissance speakers and writers were more tolerant of variations—in spelling, vocabulary, and grammatical forms—than has been true since the eighteenth century. The seventeenth-century view of variant -*s* and -*th* was clearly put by Ben Jonson in a brief grammar he wrote, probably about 1633 (*The English Grammar*, published posthumously in 1640): "The second and third person singular of the present are made of the first, by adding *est* and *eth*; which last is sometime shortened into *z* or *s*." In writing the grammar Jonson used -*s* forms 20% of the time, indicating a habitual preference for the traditional -*th* forms without regarding the -*s* forms as not proper for serious discourse. The ultimate triumph of -*s* over -*th* can be laid to whimsy, not to the inexorable march of reason; in fact, the shift to -*s* was disadvantageous, since it added another function to the inflection in /s/ or /z/: context must determine the function of words that have several functions, like *dogs* in "dogs bark," "a dog's life," "he dogs our footsteps," and context is needed to indicate whether forms like *rows* or *comforts* are noun or verb. Convenience would be better served by distinctive verb forms— *doggeth, roweth, comforteth*, despite the additional syllable.

The preterit and past participial forms of some of the strong verbs had variants in Renaissance English that were ultimately reduced through arbitrary choice. The preterit of *speak* was indifferently *spoke* or *spake*, of *drive* was *drove* or *drave*, of *write, writ* or *wrote*, the past participle having *writ, written, wrote* as equally acceptable forms. *Strike* was rich in variants, writers using *strake, strook, stroke, struck, striked* in the preterit and *struck, strucken, stricken, striked* in the participle. Had "reason" presided over the choice among forms, *striked* would have prevailed over *struck*, as *helped* did over *holp*. A uniformly weak verb system would make English an easier language to learn and use, but analogy is an erratically operating force in language. Still pending today are choices between *dived* and *dove, strived* and *strove*, and the participles *proved* or *proven*, *showed* or *shown*; respectable writers still vary between preterits like *sang, sung*; *rang, rung*; *sank, sunk*; *sprang, sprung*. A view commonly held since the eighteenth century is that between variants one must be proscribed as "wrong" and the other prescribed as "right," but it is obvious that toleration of variants was general in the Renaissance. In *The English Grammar*, Ben Jonson cited either *lien* or *lain* as the participle of *lie* and used *lien* more often in his own writing, not foreseeing that a later era would settle on the other form. However, it is unlikely that the willful Jonson would have cared to know what future generations might decide.

Syntactic changes. The manner of combining words into phrases and sentences is the matter of syntax. Sentences are formed in all languages, and the manner of forming them is arbitrary. It is arbitrary that in French adjectives follow the noun they modify, whereas in English they precede. Either system works perfectly well, of course. And like all aspects of language, syntax is not permanently fixed but is subject to capricious changes in the course of time. In older English there was more variation in some aspects of sentence construction than is true now. Verbs could precede subjects or follow objects, an order that is now rare in declarative sentences. The loss of objective case forms in noun paradigms in ME resulted in a greater dependence on word order to assure clarity. The dominant word order came to be subject-verb-object (SVO). Chaucer's phrase "It am I" is unambiguous, for the first person verb form makes it clear that the subject is *I*. But the SVO order was so common that speakers shifted the verb to the third person form, since *It* had to be the subject and *I* the complement, and thus the sentence took the order "It is I." The shift to "It is me," long opposed by grammatical purists, is a further natural consequence of the SVO order. Speakers are little inclined to observe a distinction between the nominative complement of *to be* and the object of another verb, in this matter agreeing with French speakers who say "C'est moi," not "C'est je."

The sixteenth and seventeenth centuries were an era of

shifts in syntactic arrangement, as well as in vocabulary, spelling, and morphology. All ages are times of linguistic change, but the degree of change varies with circumstances. The long era from 1300 to 1700 was a time of great change in the English language. Since 1700 the rate of change has been a good deal slower, presumably owing to the increase in the number of the literate and the ever greater availability of printed matter. The written word took on an almost sacred character among the literate, who included nearly all whose opinion conveyed authority. Neologisms and phrasing that did not have the sanction of tradition came to be frowned on, and the freedom to experiment with words and phrases that had been exercised by Shakespeare and his contemporaries grew sharply restricted. English, like all living, spoken languages, will continue to change; the introduction of new words and the decline in use of some old ones is observable in anyone's lifetime, and phonology can never be stable, but changes in morphology and syntax can be expected to be slow as long as the conserving influence of writing continues.

Syntax is the large, complex area of English grammar. Morphology is simpler, having few irregular forms, like the noun plurals *children* and *sheep*, the sixty or so strong verbs, and a few invariable verbs, like *put*, *cast*, *set* that have uninflected preterits. Syntax, however, is so intricate and complex that a complete survey of its variations has not yet been made. Extensive studies of English syntax have been published by Jespersen, Kruisinga, Poutsma, and Curme, among others, but the full extent of the field has not been measured. All the detail of syntactic change in Renaissance English cannot be considered here, but some interesting shifts will be discussed.

An oddity not uncommon in Renaissance English was the use of *his* in the genitive case construction of a noun, as in "Mars his arms" for "Mars's arms." It came to be generally supposed that the genitive *s* was a contraction of *his*. So Addison put it in 1711 (*Spectator* No. 135): *s* "does the Office of a whole Word, and represents the *His* and *Her* of our Forefathers." How *s* could be a contraction of *her* Addison did not explain, nor was he aware that the OE genitive inflection was *es*, not *his*. Some uneasiness over the *his* construction was occasionally felt. Jonson, in *The English Grammar*, called "the prince his house" "monstrous syntax," although examples of the construction occur in his writing, as in the titles of his tragedies, *Sejanus his Fall* and *Catiline his Conspiracy*; in *The Poetaster* Jonson wrote "Horace his study" and "Mecænas his house," among other examples. *His* was not uncommonly used after sibilants, as though the combination /ɪshɪz/ sounded better than /ɪsɫz/. That the *s* in "women's beauty" and "Elizabeth's reign" was not a contraction of *her* was eventually understood, and the *his* construction faded out in the course of the eighteenth century. The idea of contraction left its mark, however, in the use of the possessive apostrophe, which aids the reader's eye in instantly distinguishing "king's reign" from "kings reign," but since the apostrophe is silent its proper use is a literacy test which half the world, at least, regularly fails.

Double comparatives and superlatives, like Shakespeare's familiar "This was the most unkindest cut of all" (*Julius Caesar*: 3.2.187), condemned as redundant and therefore illogical in the eighteenth century and "corrected" by Shakespeare's eighteenth-century editors, were not thought of as foolish in the Renaissance. Ben Jonson seems to approve of the construction in *The English Grammar*. He cites two examples from Sir Thomas More, "more readier" and "most basest," and goes on to comment: "And this is a certain kind of English Atticism, or eloquent phrase of speech, imitating the manner of the most ancientest and finest Grecians, who, for more *emphasis* and vehemencies sake, used so to speak." Jonson presumably wrote "most ancientest" deliberately. A. C. Partridge in *The Accidence of Ben Jonson's Plays, Masques and Entertainments* cites three other examples in Jonson's work: "more stricter," "most best," "most affablest." The construction was not uncommon in Shakespeare: in *King Lear* "more worthier," "most best," "most dearest" occur close together (1.1), and in act 2, scene 3 Edgar speaks of his "most poorest shape." The loss of the construction from standard English can perhaps be regretted. The nonstandard speaker who can say, "Annie was the bestest wife and the onliest woman I ever loved" has a means of being emphatic that is denied speakers of "good" English.

A curious development in early modern English, one that has been much discussed and puzzled over by grammarians, was the growing use of periphrastic *do* as an empty auxiliary. In earlier English *do* had a causative sense that was later disused: "The King did them hang" meant the King caused them to be hanged. In modern English stressed auxiliary *do* has the function of giving emphasis in affirmative declarations: "But I *do* mean it"; "I *did* lock the door"; and in polite exhortation: "*Do* have some more cake"; "*Do* come again." Now, in questions and negative constructions the empty auxiliary is required; its absence is a mark of the obsolete, as in the opening scene of *Hamlet*, where we read: "Looks it not like the King?" Current English requires "Does it not look" (or "Doesn't it look," with a less emphatic negative element). The use of *do* in questions permits the subject to precede the meaningful verb "look," and thus the prevailing SVO word order is attained, which could be argued to be a sound reason for the use of the auxiliary. Interrogative sentences without *do* were common in Renaissance English. In the second scene of *Hamlet* we find: "Hold you the watch tonight?" "Then saw you not his face?" "What, looked he frowningly?"

The omission of *do* in negative sentences is an archaism to the modern ear. Samuel Daniel wrote: "The Druids . . . committed not their mysteries to writing"; Hamlet's mother urged him, ". . . go not to Wittenberg," which now would have to be "Do not go" (or "Don't go," with a deemphasized negative). Finding a reasonable cause for preferring the periphrasis is difficult. The *do*-construction permits the negative particle to precede the meaningful verb rather than follow it and is thus perhaps less emphatic, though still clear, but the advantage of this shift in position is debatable. As usual, the Renaissance tolerated the old and the new side by side, as in the passage from the King James Bible: "Consider the lilies of the field . . . they toil not, neither do they spin."

The empty auxiliary in affirmative declarations without

emphatic function occurred not uncommonly in Renaissance English, as in Hamlet's remark: "The funeral baked meats / Did coldly furnish forth the marriage tables." Here, the periphrastic *do* is a convenience to meter, but has no other use. This construction persisted through the seventeenth century, being familiar as an occasional "quaintness" in Pepys's *Diary* of the 1660s, for example, but it eventually disappeared.

Another syntactic development in Renaissance English was a growing preference for the "expanded form" of the verb to express action that is extended in time rather than momentary. In this construction a finite part of the verb *to be* is combined with a present participle, as in "It is raining." Raining is commonly an action of some duration, and the "durative aspect" of the action is neatly conveyed by the expanded form. This means is not available in French or German, in which one can only say "It rains" (*Il pleut*, *Es regnet*), although, of course, the idea of duration is easily enough supplied by adding an adverbial element. In English, habitual action is expressed by the simple verb: "It rains every day in Pago Pago." Completed past action may be expressed simply: "It rained yesterday," but the expanded form provides a "frame" for another action: "Was it raining when you left the office?" This convenient means of expressing duration existed in OE, when an occasional example turns up, as in "Hīe wǣron feohtende" (They were fighting), but its use did not become common until well into the ModE era. In Renaissance English examples of the simple verb when the expanded form would now be natural occur frequently, as in *Hamlet*: "The wind sits in the shoulder of your sail" (is sitting); "Look, my lord, it comes!" (is coming). When Gertrude asks Polonius to be less prolix ("More matter, with less art,") he replies: "Madam, I swear I use no art at all," rather than the later modern "am using," since habitual action is not the idea in context. So, too, in "What do you read, my lord?" (are you reading); "You go to seek the Lord Hamlet" (are going); "How chances it they travel?" (are traveling). The expanded form occurs, as when Ophelia says, ". . . as I was sewing in my closet . . . he comes before me," or when Antony tells Cleopatra, "I am dying, Egypt, dying," but it is often avoided, its attraction becoming more obvious after Shakespeare's generation.

Prepositional use in English is a matter of arbitrary idiom that native speakers of the language acquire gradually and without remembered pain, but it is a frustrating difficulty for those learning English as a second language, since prepositions are grammatical function words that are often empty of meaning. It is arbitrary that we talk *about* something, but speak *of* it, talk *to* people, but confer *with* them *in* the morning or *at* night. In "make *up for* lost time" and "put *up with* inconvenience" the prepositions have lost their adverbial meaning. The arbitrariness of prepositional use is indicated by current regional variations: Americans get *on* a train, but the British get *in* it; people variously live *in* or *on* Elm Street and tell time as a quarter *of*, *to*, or *till* eight. In Southern American "wait *on*" can mean "be in expectation of" or "anticipate" ("I am waiting *on* the mailman"), a sense that requires "wait *for*" in other dialects.

Prepositional idioms have shifted a great deal since Early Modern English, Shakespeare's practice being copiously discussed and illustrated in the grammars by Abbott and Franz, the latter devoting sixty-seven pages to the subject. A few examples of Shakespeare's prepositions that differ from the current idiom will illustrate: "Let us *on* heaps go offer up our lives" (*in* heaps); "Our fears *in* Banquo stick deep" (fear *of*); "*In* such a night as this" (*on* such a night); "And the offender's life lies *in* the mercy / Of the duke only" (*at* the mercy); I am provided *of* a torch-bearer" (provided *with*); "I wonder *of* their being here together" (wonder *at*); "He came *of* an errand" (came *on*).

A little more than a century after Shakespeare wrote, his editors were changing some of his prepositions to accord with shifting idioms. It is difficult to generalize as to possible advantages derived from change in this matter. Franz (*Shakespeare-Grammatik*, pp. 360–61) offered the opinion that prepositional use has become "clearer and more precise, but also more narrow-minded and intolerant." Uncertainty persists as to whether *averse to* or *from* is "correct," *compared to* or *with*, *different from* or *than*. Concern over the propriety of such uses became the business of the linguistically precise in the eighteenth century and since, but such concern seems not to have troubled the contemporaries of Shakespeare.

NOTES AND BIBLIOGRAPHY

Herford, C. H., et al., eds. *The Works of Ben Jonson*. 11 vols. Oxford: At the University Press, 1925–52. Ben Jonson's *The English Grammar* is accessible in vol. 8 of this edition of Jonson's works. Jonson's grammar, like others composed in the seventeenth century, was designed "For the benefit of all Strangers," to aid foreigners resident in England to learn to speak the language. The work is brief, but in it Jonson made several informative observations about the English of his time.

Partridge, A. C. *The Accidence of Ben Jonson's Plays, Masques, and Entertainments*. Cambridge: At the University Press, 1953. Partridge includes material on morphological change since Old English.

Franz, Wilhelm. *Shakespeare-Grammatik*. 4th ed. Halle/Saale: Max Niemayer Verlag, 1939. An admirable piece of scholarship, intelligent and thorough.

Abbott, Edwin A. *A Shakespearian Grammar*. London: Macmillan and Co., 1929. A useful book for those who do not read German.

Kökeritz, Helge. *Shakespeare's Pronunciation*. New Haven: Yale University Press, 1953.

Onions, Charles T. *A Shakespeare Glossary*. Oxford: At the University Press, 1911. This glossary contains nearly 10,000 entries, an indication of the size and difficulty of Shakespeare's vocabulary.

Jones, Richard F. *The Triumph of the English Language*. Stanford, Calif.: Stanford University Press, 1953. Surveys opinions on English in the sixteenth and seventeenth centuries.

Starnes, De Witt T. and Noyes, Gertrude E. *The English Dictionary from Cawdrey to Johnson*. Chapel Hill: University of North Carolina Press, 1946. An interesting account of early dictionaries.

7

Later Modern English,
1700 to the Present

After 1650 a new attitude toward the mother tongue became apparent in those who spoke English. In the Renaissance the educated had been generally concerned with the poverty of the vocabulary, and some had urged plans to reform the chaotic spelling, but little concern was expressed either for variance in word-forms or for uncertainty in some of the syntactic patterns. But after 1650 grammatical tolerance gave way to a spirit of captious unease with at least some aspects of English grammar which, it was felt, needed desperately to be reformed. It was said that "English has no grammar" and that consequently the well-meaning writer was often at a loss as to how he should with decent propriety express his thoughts. The poet and critic John Dryden, who wrote English with clarity, grace, and vigor, said that at times he felt obliged to express an idea in Latin in order to know how to put it in English. It seems hardly likely that Dryden did this very often, but his remark is significant in that it indicates the preference at that time for a "regulated" language like Latin over a language like English that had no rules carefully spelled out in a grammatical guidebook. Latin was a superior language because it had rules that could be learned and confidently applied, whereas the mother tongue was unruled, and consequently its proprieties were indefinite and uncertain. Latin was referred to as a grammatical model, and English constructions that differed from the model were considered faulty, a view which accounts for the conclusion that an English sentence with a final preposition must be structurally flawed, since Latin sentences concluded with terms more meaningful than particles. In his essay *The Dramatic Poetry of the Last Age* Dryden cited an instance of a final preposition in a sentence of Ben Jonson's: "The waves and dens of beasts could not receive / The bodies that those souls were frighted from." and commented, "a common fault with him, and which I have but lately observed in my own writings." In preparing a second edition of *An Essay of Dramatic Poesy*, Dryden revised the sentences that ended in prepositions and thus corrected a "fault." That the preposition-final structure must be natural, "good" English, if he and Jonson used it, obviously did not occur to Dryden, or to anyone else for a long time.

Dryden was nettled by the captious spirit of his generation, as he made clear by his remarks in *The Dramatic Poetry of the Last Age*: ". . . I live in an age where my least faults are severely censured"; and ". . . let any man who understands English, read diligently the works of Shakespeare and Fletcher, and I dare undertake that he will find in every page either some solecism of speech, or some notorious flaw in sense; and yet these men are reverenced, when we are not forgiven." Dryden went on to say, ". . . I have no way left to extenuate my failings, but by showing as great in those whom we admire," and proceeded to cite several examples of failings in Jonson's English, including "*Ones*, in the plural number," quoting Jonson's lines, "Caesar and Crassus, if they be ill men, / Are mighty ones." Dryden didn't explain the grounds for his objection to *ones*, which is still in good idiomatic standing, but presumably *one* "logically" represented an absolute concept; one could not also be more than one. The idea that language should and must agree with logic was becoming prominent in the thinking of the time. Dryden quoted: "Contain your spirit in more stricter bounds" and exhibited forgiveness by commenting: "But that gross way of two comparatives was then ordinary; and, therefore, more pardonable in Jonson." Forgiveness is denied, however, for the line, "Though Heaven should speak with all his wrath at once," Dryden commenting, "*His* is ill syntax with *Heaven*." By Dryden's day *its* was firmly established as the neuter genitive pronoun, the variants *his* and *it* having quietly dropped out. Quoting Jonson's couplet in *Catiline*, "When we, whose virtues conquered thee, / Thus by thy vices ruin'd be," Dryden observes, "*Be* there is False English for *are*; though the rhyme hides it." Dryden was six years old when Jonson died in 1637, and the difference in their times was enough to mark noticeable changes in idiom. *Be* was still an acceptable plural present indicative verb form when Jonson wrote it, which is obvious from the fact that Jonson used it (he cites it as such in *The English Grammar*). That Dryden should have supposed that Jonson, much admired for learning and skill with language, was guilty of solecism is to be wondered at now. Dryden was aware of the inevitability of linguistic change: in his preface to *All for Love* (1678), speaking of Shakespeare, Dryden remarked, "words and phrases must of necessity receive a change in succeeding ages; but it is almost a miracle that much of his language remains so pure." By "pure" Dryden presumably meant language that agreed with the idiom current in 1678.

Dryden's concern with grammatical niceties reflects the general concern of his age. The century 1650–1750 is known as the Era of Enlightenment, the Age of Reason. It was a time of passion for amelioration. Everything should, could, and would be improved by the application of reason. It was a time of an optimism that was supported by recent discoveries in astronomy, physics, and mathematics, the contributions of men like Galileo, Copernicus, Kepler, and Newton. Through reason the world, its institutions, and its people would be brought to perfection by discerning error and imperfection and then correcting all such. In political matters it was supposed that the Glorious Revolution of 1688 had given England a perfect constitution, a political system that would endure unchanged forever. Everything else was to be similarly improved and made permanent, including the English language. Some entertained the idea of universal language, the notion that there was once one language that came into being naturally perfect, corruptions of various kinds then being induced through human error. It was necessary only to identify these corruptions and correct them in order to restore language to its pristine purity. Language thus made perfect once again would also become fixed, to change no more.

That language changed with time was obvious to all who read Shakespeare and Jonson—and Chaucer. That linguistic change could not be prevented was, however, not understood. Change was considered lamentable, because it interfered with intelligibility. As Pope put it, "Our sons their fathers' failing language see, / And such as Chaucer is, shall Dryden be." The poet Waller complained of the perishability of verse through language change:

> But who can hope his lines should long
> Last in a daily changing tongue?
> . . . .
> Poets that lasting marble seek,
> Must carve in Latin, or in Greek;
> We write in sand, our language grows,
> And like the tide, our work o'erflows.
> Chaucer his sense can only boast;
> The glory of his numbers lost!
> Years have defaced his matchless strain;

Chaucer was admired as a storyteller but not as a poet, for it was supposed that his lines did often not scan. That unstressed vowels which were silent in the seventeenth century were not so in the fourteenth was a fact not understood. The age could not read Chaucer's line, "And smalë fowlës makën melodië" for the perfect pentameter and lovely line that it is.

The hope of fixing the language in a perfected form was expressed in 1712 by the influential writer Jonathan Swift in *A Proposal for Correcting, Improving and Ascertaining the English Tongue*, an essay addressed as a letter to the Earl of Oxford, then Lord High Treasurer and Prime Minister, Swift's powerful patron and employer. The business of correcting, improving, and ascertaining would be undertaken by an academy formed on the model of the French Academy:

> The persons who are to undertake this work, will have the example of the French before them, to imitate where these have proceeded right, and to avoid their mistakes. Besides the grammar-part, wherein we are allowed to be very defective, they will observe many gross improprieties, which however authorized by practice, and grown familiar, ought to be discarded. They will find many words that deserve to be utterly thrown out of our language; many more to be corrected, and perhaps not a few, long since antiquated, which ought to be restored, on account of their energy and sound.
>
> But what I have most at heart, is, that some method should be thought on for ascertaining and fixing our language for ever, after such alterations are made in it as shall be thought requisite. For I am of opinion, that it is better a language should not be wholly perfect, than that it should be perpetually changing; and we must give over at one time or other, or at length infallibly change for the worse: As the Romans did, when they began to quit their simplicity of style for affected refinements; such as we meet in Tacitus and other authors, which ended by degrees in many barbarities, even before the Goths had invaded Italy.

Swift supposed that English in his time was being corrupted by the introduction of "barbarisms." Besides citing Latin as a language that had decayed through change, he argued that French was declining by "the affectation of some late authors, to introduce and multiply cant words, which is the most ruinous corruption in any language." Swift thought that "The period wherein the English tongue received most improvement, I take to commence with the beginning of Queen Elizabeth's reign, and to conclude with the great rebellion of forty-two." Since then, injury had followed injury, induced by the "enthusiastick jargon" of the Puritans and then by the licentiousness of the court of Charles II, which, "from infecting our religion and morals, fell to corrupt our language." Corruption could be reversed and new instances of it prevented by the exercise of authority, presumably that of an academy sponsored by the government. The aid of the government in the form of monetary support of the academy was a necessity. The long, expensive War of the Spanish Succession was still going on, and the Tory government was practicing economy, but Swift urged the Lord High Treasurer to spare some means for his project. He hinted that, as in France, government pensions might be well bestowed on worthy men whose time would, presumably, be spent in doing the projected academy's work.

In the *Proposal* Swift offered no examples of the "gross improprieties" in "the grammar-part" that he objected to. He was specific only in complaining of the loss of the unstressed vowel in the inflectional syllable -*ed*, citing "*drudg'd*, *disturb'd*, *rebuk'd*, *fledg'd*, and a thousand others." Swift's objection had an esthetic basis: ". . . by leaving out a vowel to save a syllable, we form so jarring a sound, and so difficult to utter, that I have often wondered how it could ever obtain." To Swift, English "was already overstocked with monosyllables." The loss of unstressed vowels was a process begun in the fourteenth century that was continuing in the seventeenth, especially in the inflectional -*ed* syllable. In Shakespeare's use *banishëd* could have three syllables or two, /bænɪšt/, as in his line in *Romeo and Juliet* (3.3.19): "Hence banishëd is banish'd from the world," a metrical convenience that was eventually lost. Adjectives that end in -*ed* retain the vowel: *wickëd*, *nakëd*, *raggëd*, *ruggëd*, *crookëd*. A few forms that function as both verb and adjective retain the vowel in the adjectival function, as in *agëd* man, *blessëd* event, *learnëd* person. Adjectival *learned* had lost its unstressed vowel in the later seventeenth century, as indicated in Dryden's spelling: ". . . some are unlearn'd, or (as Chaucer calls them) lewd, and some are learn'd" (*On Translating the Poets*), and adjectival *learned* is monosyllabic in Pope's poetry. In this instance, at least, Swift's desire to restore the unstressed vowel was met, but otherwise his complaint was ignored by the generality of speakers, who chattered thoughtlessly on, unaware of the disapproval of the angry man of letters.

In an earlier essay he had contributed to Steele's *Tatler* in 1710, Swift had objected to contracted forms like *cou'dn't, han't don't* (haven't done it), *he's, sha'n't,* to the clipped forms *phizz, hipps, mob, poz, rep* (for physiognomy, hypochondria, mobile, positive, reputation), and to popular slang terms: *banter, bamboozle, sham, bubble, bully,* especially when clergymen delivered them from the pulpit. Swift was a linguistic conservative, reluctant to accept neologisms, more inclined to seek a way to restore words once esteemed that had perished.

In his *Proposal* of 1712, Swift expressed gratitude for the support given his views by another influential man of letters, the admired Joseph Addison, who in *Spectator* No. 135 (1711), although he remarked that monosyllabism suited the natural taciturnity of the English, repeated Swift's objections to contractions and clippings and supported Swift's opinion. Addison agreed that questions of variable usage ". . . will never be decided till we have something like an Academy, that by the best authorities and rules drawn from the analogy of languages shall settle all controversies between grammar and idiom." By "idiom" Addison presumably meant English as it was used and by "grammar" English as it ought to be used.

The views expressed by Swift and Addison are important because they were not eccentric views, but were those generally held by the educated at that time. Swift's call for an academy was not answered by the establishment of such a body, but the idea was generally considered a good one. The idea was not new in 1712. Early in the seventeenth century Samuel Daniel had suggested the desirability of having some authority pass on the admissibility of new words. When the Royal Society was founded in the 1660s that body considered for a while undertaking a study of the English language with a view to improving it, but the idea was dropped as not suited to the proper concerns of its members. In 1698, Defoe published in *An Essay on Projects*, a collection of schemes for improving the world, a proposal for a linguistic academy made up of thirty-six gentlemen whose authority no one would dare flout. Coining words without permission would then be equivalent to counterfeiting money. Academies were functioning in other countries. In Italy the Accademia della Crusca had been working since the late sixteenth century to guard the purity of the Italian language and produce an authoritative dictionary, the first edition of which appeared in 1612, and in France the famous French Academy had been established in 1635 with the support of Cardinal Richelieu and after years of labor produced a dictionary in 1694 which was supposed to be a guide to propriety in the use of words for all right-thinking speakers of French.

The idea of an academy continued to be promoted through the eighteenth century—and is still occasionally suggested—but in the latter part of the century opposition to the idea was cogently expressed, by Samuel Johnson among others. It was pointed out that academies had not prevented Italian and French from changing (probably for the worse) and that Englishmen, unlike the French, were too liberty-loving to submit to dictation by any body of men, however constituted.

Prescriptive Grammar. Although no academy was organized in England, the desire to have the English language corrected, improved, refined, ascertained, and fixed continued to be expressed. By "ascertaining" was meant making certain, stating definite rules for proper words in proper places. Though no official body existed for doing this, it was thought that reason in collective action would somehow accomplish ascertainment. The nation needed an authoritative grammar and an authoritative dictionary. Through the seventeenth and eighteenth centuries a number of grammars appeared that were meant for school use and for assisting foreigners in learning some English for practical, commercial purposes. These grammars were concerned with pronunciation, spelling, and morphology and touched little on matters of syntax, but beginning in the 1760s grammars dealing with syntactic questions were presented to a reading public that was eager to have definite, authoritative answers. The appearance of Samuel Johnson's famous dictionary in 1755 seems to have stimulated others to attempt to do for grammar what Johnson was thought to have done for the vocabulary—to determine propriety and hopefully to fix it forever. In the introduction to his dictionary Johnson had discussed grammar in fifteen pages, but had dismissed syntax in twelve lines, which was a disappointment to those who had expected more.

In 1761, Joseph Priestley published *The Rudiments of English Grammar*. Priestley was what the century called a "virtuoso," a man interested in various kinds of learning. He was a scientist of distinction, having among other things identified the element oxygen. His grammar was notable for his recognizing that the usage of reputable writers is the reliable guide to linguistic propriety. Priestley accepted forms like *it is me* and the double comparative *lesser* because he observed their use by reputable writers like Addison. The importance of usage had been recognized before, the authority of the Roman grammarian Quintilian and of Horace to the effect that "custom is the certain mistress of language" having been frequently cited, but Priestley was alone in his age in adhering to this principle.

Immediately after the appearance of Priestley's book Robert Lowth published his *Short Introduction to English Grammar* (1762), a work so much in demand that more than twenty editions of it appeared before the end of the century. Lowth was an intelligent and able man, an Anglican clergyman who rose to be Bishop of Oxford and then of London. He wrote in a simple, readily intelligible style, a characteristic not always found in "grammarography." That and his willingness to be decisively authoritarian about problems in usage account for his popularity. Lowth set a trend that was soon followed by others. In 1763, John Ash published *The Easiest Introduction to Dr. Lowth's English Grammar*, meant for the instruction of children, to induce in the young as early as possible the principles of good English. Another popular work appeared in 1776, George Campbell's *Philosophy of Rhetoric*, and in 1795, Lindley Murray published at York a phenomenally successful book called *English Grammar*, which remained in use for decades and provided a model for other writers of school-book grammar for decades more. Murray was an American who after the Revolution moved to England and lived near York as a retired gentleman. There he was induced to compose an English grammar suitable for use in a Quaker school for girls. Murray had no pretensions to originality. He culled material from earlier grammars and, like Lowth, had a knack for clear, decisive, authoritarian exposition. There was nothing in Murray to puzzle the mind.

These writers and those who followed them in the next century had no particular qualifications for the study of grammar except for a disposition to declare what they thought was right and wrong about the English language. Some, like Lowth and Campbell, were clergymen, and as such had a knowledge of Greek, Latin, and Hebrew, which gave them an opportunity to reflect, at least, on the idea of comparative grammar. Lowth mentions having seen an Old English grammar written in Latin by George Hickes, but neither comparative nor historical linguistics had as yet been systematically undertaken, as they were to be in the nineteenth century. Some of the others who wrote on grammar had little background to work with, like Robert Baker, who in 1770 published *Reflections on the English Language*, "being a detection of many improper expressions used in conversation, and of many others to be found in authors." Baker modestly admitted that he had small Latin and no Greek, owned few books, and couldn't afford a copy of Johnson's dictionary, but nevertheless felt that he owed the world his views on what constituted propriety in English.

Lowth had no hesitancy in defining specific improprieties despite their use by reputable writers, as in "*You was* . . . is an enormous solecism: and yet authors of the first rank have inadvertently fallen into it." Lowth quotes Addison and Pope, among others, as offenders in this matter. How painstaking writers like Addison and Pope could manage inadvertency Lowth did not explain, nor did he explain the grounds for his objection. Presumably, since *you* was historically a plural form, the verb must also be plural for the sake of concord in number. That cultivated speakers in Lowth's time said "you was" is attested by the occurrence of the phrase in plays, in Sheridan's *School for Scandal* (1777), for example, where it is spoken by quite proper ladies and gentlemen. The American lexicographer Noah Webster defended *you was* in *Dissertations on the English Language* (1789): "This practice is not merely vulgar; it is general among men of erudition who do not affect to be fettered by the rules of grammarians, and some late writers have indulged it in their publications." As it happened, *you was* disappeared from reputable practice and survives as "merely vulgar." Whether the influence of Lowth and those who echoed him had an effect is impossible to know. Its survival would have been advantageous in referring to a single person, but survival depends on unpredictable whimsy.

On a few occasions Lowth expressed a becomingly modest "I think," but he was usually quite certain. One "I think" occurs in "*Whose* is by some authors made the possessive case of *which*, and applied to things as well as persons; I think, improperly." Lowth quotes Dryden: "The question, whose solution I require," and Addison: "Is there any other doctrine, whose followers are punished?" The problem here was that *which* had an incomplete paradigm. In early English *who* and *which* had been interrogative pronouns, their use as relatives developing in late ME and early ModE. Only gradually did it come about that *who* referred to persons and *which* to things. The King James Bible put it: "Our Father, which art in heaven . . ." A minor grammarian named John Clarke commented: "How ridiculous must it appear in many clergymen, undoubtedly men of education, who continually use false English when they repeat the Lord's Prayer, 'Our Father, which art . . .'" Unfortunately Clarke was born too late to prevent the effects of ignorance in the translators of 1611.

From the beginning *who* had a complete paradigm, but *which* did not:

N.	who	which
G.	whose	*whiches (or *which's)
D.	whom	*whichem

Consequently, the possessive function of *which* required syntactic means, *of which*. According to Lowth, Dryden should have written: "The question, the solution of which I require . . ." In this matter, standard usage has ignored Lowth. The nicest people still use *whose* in impersonal reference. George O. Curme in *Syntax* cites such a use of *whose* in the impeccable novelist Galsworthy: ". . . a little white building *whose* small windows were overgrown with creepers."

Another problem in the use of relative pronouns was the alternative use of *that* for *who* and *which*: "The man *who* called"; "The man *that* called"; "A book *which* I read"; "A book *that* I read." Sir Richard Steele discussed the problem in a humorous way in *Spectator* No. 78 (1711), in the form of a mock letter called "The humble petition of *Who* and *Which*." The pronouns complain that they are sometimes supplanted by "the jacksprat *That*" and appeal to Mr. Spectator to use his influence to defend their rights. Two papers later, in *Spectator* No. 80, Steele allows *That* a rebuttal, entitled "The just remonstrance of affronted *That*." Steele's touch is so light that it seems improbable that he regarded this problem of variation as a serious one. Grammatical comment in the latter part of the century prefers *who* and *which*, but does not proscribe *that* absolutely. That this variation was considered a problem stemmed from a yearning for the absolute. Where variation existed, one variant ought to be prescribed in every instance, the other variant being consequently proscribed. The usage of the polite still permits the nonproscribed alternation of *that* with *who* or *which*. Several other pronoun practices were a source of perturbation. Lowth declared: "Some writers have used *ye* as the objective case plural of the pronoun of the second person; very improperly and ungrammatically." Lowth cites Prior and Milton as ill-doers in this detail and doesn't seem to be aware that by his generation *ye* was being used only as a conscious archaism.

Lowth lays down the rule that "The verb *to be* has always a nominative case after it; as, 'it was *I*, and not *He*, that did it.'" This rule as Lowth phrased it became a shibboleth that induced anxiety in some who were not ordinarily perturbed by the other rules of grammar. Winston Churchill set off a small furor among purists in 1946 by saying, "This is me, Winston Churchill," but he has plenty of good company. Shakespeare's object pronoun is familiar in *Macbeth*: "Lay on, Macduff, / And damned *be him* that first cries 'Hold, enough!'" Shelley in his *Ode to the West Wind* wrote, "Be thou, Spirit fierce, / My spirit! *Be* thou *me*, impetuous one!" Correcting Shelley's pronoun to *I* to fit Lowth's rule could seem worse than inappropriate. What the Germans call *Sprachgefühl*, a feeling for language, a sense of the appropriate, could apply here to support Shelley. Grammar and idiom sometimes collide, and the eighteenth-century reformers' search for the absolute could not help but fail.

Lowth supplied the theory of the ellipsis of a verb understood after *than* or *as*: "When the qualities of different things are compared, the latter noun is governed, not by the conjunction *than*, or *as*; (for a conjunction has no government of cases,) but by the verb or the preposition, expressed or understood. As . . . 'You are not so tall as I [am]'" Lowth cites examples of erroneous use from Swift: "than me," Hobbes: "as them," and Prior: "as thee." In Shakespeare's *Antony and Cleopatra*, when Cleopatra receives the bad news of Antony's marriage to Octavia, she asks the messenger, "Is she as tall as me?" (3.3.14). In one of his "Cloe" poems Prior wrote, "For thou art a girl as much brighter than her, / As he was a poet sublimer than me." It would seem from these examples that English speakers were not inclined to keep in mind a distinction between conjunctions and prepositions. It may be that the dominating SVO word order unconsciously dictated the objective pronouns, although what writers were "thinking" when they composed sentences cannot be successfully guessed. Lowth's ellipsis theory won acceptance and survives today as the school grammar solution to the problem of case form after *than* or *as*.

Lowth was troubled by the objective case form of the third person reflexive pronouns: "*Himself, themselves*, seem to be used in the nominative case by corruption instead of *his self, their selves*: as, 'he came *himself*'; 'they did it *themselves*'; where *himself, themselves*, cannot be in the objective case. If this be so, *self* must be in these instances not a pronoun, but a noun." Analogy was an important guiding principle in the thinking of the grammatical reformers. In the first and second person reflexive forms the pronouns are in the genitive case: *myself, ourselves, yourself, yourselves*. That the third person forms are in the dative case is a breakdown in analogy. Curiously, speakers of nonstandard English apply analogy in *hisself* and *theirselves*, but this suggestion of Lowth's was not repeated by the grammarians who came after him and has not appeared in standard English use.

Lowth cited another problem in analogy: "Adjectives are sometimes employed as adverbs, improperly, and not agreeably to the genius of the English language." He gave as examples "extreme elaborate" from Dryden and "extreme unwilling" from Swift, mentioning other instances in the writing of Addison and Pope. In an ideal language the parts of speech would be distinguished by their form: all adverbs should end in *-ly*, but no adjective should. But English is not ideal; some adjectives have an *-ly* affix, like *godly, lowly, friendly, ghastly, kingly, early*. Some grammarians advocated adding *-ly* to all adverbs, producing forms like *soonly, lowlily, friendlily*. This artifice has been sometimes seen in print—"smiled friendlily," "behaved sillily"—but is not in general practice.

The problem of concord in number was troublesome. Lowth thought the pattern, *this means, that means* illogical: "Ought it not to be, by *these means*, by *those means*? or by *this mean*, by *that mean*, in the singular number?" Despite Lowth, *means* has remained a singular and the ideal of consistency in logic and analogy is still unattained. Some plural noun forms like *means, measles, mathematics* agree with singular verbs.

Politics is plural in the British dialect, but singular in the American, as in "Politics are/is a strange business." Lowth also pointed out inconsistency in "this forty years" and "these kind," patterns that still persist in the practice of the less meticulous. The number discord in the pattern "Many a man is . . ." was noted by Campbell and Murray and considered somehow acceptable. The idiom is ancient, appearing in the earliest English, and has escaped attack. The scholarly eighteenth-century poet Thomas Gray could write, "Full many a rose is born to blush unseen" without fear of being accused of a barbarism.

The illogic of the double comparatives *lesser* and *worser* was noted. Lowth commented: "*Worser* sounds much more barbarous, only because it has not been so frequently used," suggesting that Lowth might tolerate *lesser* because he heard it more often. In time, *worser* dropped out of standard use, but *lesser* survives in phrases like "lesser evil," "lesser depth."

The reformers made a good suggestion, that came to nothing, in preferring distinct forms for the principal parts of all strong verbs, like *sing, sang, sung* and *write, wrote, written.* Lowth suggested the paradigms *sit, sat, sitten* and *spit, spat, spitten.* Of *sit* he remarked, "Frequent mistakes are made in the formation of this verb. The analogy plainly requires *sitten*; which was formerly in use." The *OED* cites examples of *sitten* as late as the early nineteenth century, but the conveniently distinctive participle perished thereafter. And *spit* has become an invariable verb in the practice of some reputable writers. Distinctive preterits like *clang, slank, wrang* may be theoretically convenient, but they are not standard.

The grammarians proscribed the double negative on the grounds that logically two negatives canceled out to produce an affirmative, as in algebra. Multiple negation was commonplace in early English. In the General Prologue to *The Canterbury Tales*, Chaucer said of the Knight, "He nevere yet no vileynye ne sayde / In al his lyf unto no maner wight," which could be modernized as, "He didn't never say nothing bad to nobody in his whole life." By the sixteenth century multiple negation had become rare, for reasons unknown.

There are few examples of it in Shakespeare. It flourishes still in nonstandard speech: "I didn't do nothing" is said by millions and is mistaken by no one as an affirmative. The loss of rhetorical emphasis by denying the repetition of negation in standard English is regrettable. Change is not necessarily progress.

Besides logic, reason, and analogy, etymology was considered a criterion in determining grammatical propriety. After objecting to some of the prepositions used by Swift, Dryden, and Addison, Lowth remarks, "So the noun *aversion*, (that is, a turning away,) requires the preposition *from* after it; and does not properly admit of *to*, *for*, or *towards*, which are often used with it." *Aversion* did indeed mean "turning away" in the Latin that was the source of the word, but Lowth's contemporaries did not always have etymology in mind when they used the word in an English sentence.

Shall-will.   A curious and troublesome consequence of the effort to correct and improve the English language was the attempt to make sharp distinctions between *shall* and *will* in expressing future time. *Shall* in some situations may convey the sense of obligation, compulsion, necessity, or a threat, but in the first person is supposed to convey a simple, nonmodal prediction. But the meaning of *shall* is sometimes clouded. Early in World War II, when General MacArthur was compelled to leave his command in the Philippines, he declared, "I shall return," but whether he meant a calm prediction of future certainty or meant to imply an obligation to return was not clear. As an American English speaker, the General may have meant to convey both senses.

English has no future tense in its morphological system, Germanic speakers having lost that part of their inherited linguistic machinery in prehistoric time. Future time has ever since been expressed by the present tense: "We leave in the morning"; "He is returning next week," or by auxiliary verbs plus the infinitive: "I can, could, may, might, must, shall, will, should, would return." In OE *shall* and *will* had infinitive forms, *sculan*, *willan*, and inflection for person and number, which survived into early ModE in the second-person singular forms, *thou shalt*, *thou wilt*. *Should* and *would* were the preterits of *shall* and *will*. Semantically, *sculan* in OE had the sense of necessity, compulsion, obligation, or duty, and *willan* meant volition or desire. By late ME and early ModE *shall* and *will* had lost their full-verb status, had become auxiliary verbs, and did not always convey the modal senses of compulsion or volition. In the seventeenth century the auxiliaries were used interchangeably, without clear and consistent distinction in their uses. In *The English Grammar*, Ben Jonson indicated no distinction between *shall* and *will*: "The futures are declared by the infinite, and the verb, *shall*, or, *will*: as *Amabo*: I *shall*, or, *will* love. *Amavero* addeth thereunto *have* . . . I *shall* have loved: or, I *will* have loved. . . . In *Amabor*, it is governed of *shall*, or *will*: as, I *shall*, or, *will* be loved." No consistent distinction between the functions of *shall* and *will* can be discerned in the practice of Shakespeare or Daniel or any other seventeenth-century writer whose usage has been studied. The obligatory sense of *shall* is conveyed in the biblical "Thou shalt not," but in many other situations *shall* appears to be a function word empty of meaning, a mere sign of futurity.

In 1653, in an English grammar written in Latin for the use of foreigners, *Grammatica Linguae Anglicanae*, John Wallis stated that simple futurity was expressed by *shall* in the first person and by *will* in the second and third persons. He did not say whether he drew this conclusion from his observation of usage or decided to create a distinction between the auxiliaries that had not existed. The idea of distinction was attractive and became one of the rules of eighteenth-century grammar. The anonymous *A Pocket Dictionary*, published in 1753, stated, "As some are apt to mistake the use of *shall* and *will*, the signs of the future tense, it must be observed that when we only simply foretell, we use *shall* in the first person, and *will* in the rest; but when we promise, threaten or engage, we use *will* in the first person, and *shall* in the others."

In 1762, Lowth had a brief statement: "*Would* expresses the intention of the doer; *should* simply the event. *Will* in the first person promises or threatens; in the second and third persons only foretells: *shall* on the contrary, in the first person simply foretells; in the second and third persons commands or threatens."

The system of *shall* and *will* was worked out as in the paradigms:

Nonmodal	Modal
I, we shall	I, we will
you will	you shall
he, they will	he, they shall

In the first person *shall* was no longer to convey the original sense of obligation or compulsion; in the second and third persons *will* did not mean volition or determination. The system was gradually elaborated: In putting questions the proper auxiliary was the one expected in the answer. Nonmodal: "Shall you be there?" "Yes, I shall." Modal: "Will you help me?" "Yes, I will." The first speaker must think through the answer before he puts the question.

The rule for *shall* and *will* determined the choice between *should* and *would*. *Should* in the first person is nonmodal: "I should think so" does not mean "I ought to think so." In dependent clauses the choice is determined by the auxiliary that would be used in the corresponding independent statement. Thus, *should* is required in, "He said that he should be there" because the underlying statement is, "I shall be there."

This system is complicated, really too complicated to be workable. The brothers Fowler, H. W. and F. G., who were arbiters of grammatical propriety in the early twentieth century, devoted more than twenty pages in *The King's English* to a careful explanation of the use of *shall* and *will*. They prefaced the discussion with a remarkable statement:

It is unfortunate that the idiomatic use, while it comes by nature to southern Englishmen (who will find most of this section superfluous), is so complicated that those who are not to the manner born can hardly acquire it;

and for them the section is in danger of being useless. In apology for the length of these remarks it must be said that the short and simple directions often given are worse than useless. The observant reader soon loses faith in them from their constant failure to take him right; and the unobservant is the victim of false security.

The Fowlers were intelligent men, and it is significant that they saw nothing humorous in their solemn prologue. They provided examples of correct and incorrect usage of *shall*, *will*, *should*, *would*, and among those who got the matter wrong were Wilde, Yeats, Stevenson, the London *Times*, the eminent politician Gladstone, and the highly reputable grammarian Henry Sweet.

This complex system of *shall* and *will* is a dialect matter, regional and social. It was accepted as law in southern England, in London and its environs, by those who made up the "Establishment," and became a mark of social distinction in that circle. Elsewhere, in Scotland, Ireland, and the United States, the system has not been generally observed. Among the ill-doers whom the Fowlers noted, Wilde and Yeats were, after all, Irish, and Stevenson was a Scot. There have been many attempts to provide rational explanations for the system, one being that the English say "I shall" because they are too polite to suggest imposing their will on others. The Scots say "I will" because they are not polite. This idea led the Danish grammarian Otto Jespersen to wonder, "But are English people really more polite than other nations?" The rationale for the system is elusive, but is presumably to be found in the prescriptive drive of the Age of Reason, the desire to improve the English language. It was sensed as intolerable that *shall* and *will* should be aimlessly interchangeable. If no distinction existed, one must be created.

It has been pointed out that in English three ideas—obligation, volition, and nonmodal futurity—must be expressed with only two auxiliaries, *shall* and *will*, which is difficult, or perhaps impossible. German has three auxiliaries, *sollen*, *wollen*, and *werden*. *Shall* and *will* are cognate with *sollen* and *wollen*, respectively; OE had a cognate with *werden—weorðan*—but speakers fumbled it away in the Middle English era. Of course, all is not lost. Obligation is clearly expressed with *must* and *ought to*, and volition with *want to* and *wish to*.

In American English *shall* is in rare use. It occurs in invitational questions: "Shall we dance?" but not often in other situations. In American military correspondence *will* is used in commands: "You will proceed by the most convenient transportation," which could be rationalized as meaning that noncompliance is out of the question, so that *shall* is unnecessary. The more frequent use of *shall* is a characteristic of British English and may still be observed in the usage of recent novelists, like Aldous Huxley and Evelyn Waugh, and of writers who may be irreverent in other matters, but are obedient to the law of *shall* and *will*.

The successful establishment of the artificial system of *shall* and *will* among the southern English is a remarkable instance of prescriptivism actually working, if only in one dialect of several, but for the most part prescriptions were ignored in the flow of living usage. Some usages were proscribed out of a merely personal dislike, similar to Swift's dislike of monosyllables like *drudg'd*, clipped forms like *mob*, and new slang like *banter*. Against these forms Swift raged in vain, for all survive in good practice today. Samuel Johnson disliked the form *noways*, which he said was used only by "ignorant barbarians." George Campbell in *The Philosophy of Rhetoric* (1776) took issue with "our learned and ingenious lexicographer," pointing out that "These ignorant barbarians . . . are only Pope, and Swift, and Addison, and Locke, and several others of our most celebrated writers." Here Campbell sides with Priestley in citing reputable usage as the guide to propriety. On another occasion Campbell remarks, ". . . it is to no purpose to Johnson to pronounce the word *news* a plural, (whatever it might have been in the days of Sidney and Raleigh,) since custom hath evidently determined otherwise." Campbell disagreed with Lowth, whom he referred to as "This ingenious gentleman," on a number of points, including

Lowth's insistence on *aversion from*. Campbell remarks that:

> . . . the words *averse* and *aversion* are more properly construed with *to* than with *from*. The examples in favour of the latter preposition are beyond comparison outnumbered by those in favour of the former. The argument from etymology is here of no value, being taken from the use of another language. If by the same rule we were to regulate all nouns and verbs of Latin original, our present syntax would be overturned. It is more conformable to English analogy with *to*; the words *dislike* and *hatred*, nearly synonymous, are thus construed.

The grammarians disagreed among themselves over various matters of usage, such as whether *had rather* was good English, and a game developed in finding examples of bad English not only in Addison and Swift but also in the writing of other grammarians. Noah Webster (*Letter to Dr. Ramsay*) put it that "I have no hesitation in affirming, that the grammars now taught in our schools introduce more errors than they correct."

Campbell was not consistent in supporting usage, but had his crotchets, too:

> There are a few phrases . . . which, though favoured by custom, being quite unnecessary, deserve to be exploded. Such, amongst others, are the following: the *workmanship* of God for the work of God; a *man of war*, for a *ship of war*; and a *merchantman* for a trading vessel. The absurdity in the last two instances is commonly augmented by the words connected in the sequel, in which, by the application of the pronouns *she* and *her*, we are made to understand that the man spoken of is a female. I think this gibberish ought to be left entirely to mariners; amongst whom, I suppose, it hath originated.

Ben Jonson in *The English Grammar* had noted the gender anomaly in referring to ships, but seems to have thought it merely amusing. Of the neuter gender he wrote, ". . . under which are compriz'd all inanimate things; a ship excepted: of whom we say she sails well, though the name be Hercules, or Henry, or the Prince." Incidentally, Campbell used as a heading for his second chapter the phrase, "Good use not always uniform in her decisions," and was apparently not disturbed by assigning a feminine pronoun to the neuter *use*.

Campbell supplied a definition of good English that has not yet been improved on: that English which is "reputable, national, and present." National use he defined as being neither provincial nor foreign. As provincial use he supplied examples of Scots pronunciation of *good*: ". . . in the south of Scotland they said *gude*, and in the north *gueed*" (/gud/ and /gid/?). Analogous constructions drawn from Latin and French, sometimes cited by grammarians, Campbell rejected as not pertinent to English and thus not national. Present use he defined as not that of the moment, for today's speakers and writers sometimes use words and turns of expression that will prove fugitive, but the usage of the recent past, use that has already been tested and found viable. Reputable use is difficult to define: Campbell defined it as ". . . whatever modes of speech are authorized as good by the writings of a great number, if not the majority, of celebrated authors." This definition is not ideally precise, but it is still the prevailing one, sometimes stated as "the best use of the best speakers and writers," to the best of one's ability to determine what the best use is.

The effect of the prescriptive movement, the attempt to make English better by applying logic, analogy, "right reason and the law of Nature" to English, is difficult to determine. Prescriptivism continued to be supported through the nineteenth and twentieth centuries. In the nineteenth a new rule was "discovered," proscribing the split infinitive. It was declared an appalling solecism to permit an adverb to intervene between the sign of the infinitive, *to*, and the verb, as in "to greatly dare." In OE *to* had semantic content, meaning "towards," "in the direction of," or "for the purpose of." In time the particle lost its meaning and survived only as a function word, an empty sign of the infinitive function of the verb. Its appearance or nonappearance is a matter of idiom. *To* appears in "He needed someone to *compel* him *to act*," but it does not appear in "He needed someone to *make* him *act*." An intervening word between *to* and the verb is rarely ambiguous and is sometimes unavoidable. In "He was so reluctant to go that he managed *to just miss* the train," the split position is the only possible one, and the split is probably best in "Some confirmed bachelors are unwilling *to even think* of marrying." In "Our team was expected *to again finish* last," the split can be avoided by making *again* final in the sentence, but the split position provides the adverb with an attractive emphasis, and there is certainly no need to bother to avoid the split. No objection was raised to the separation of similar verb-phrase elements in examples like, "I *will gladly do* it." Split infinitives were not common in earlier English, in Shakespeare, for example, but did occur on occasion in later use. Prohibiting them had no rational basis; it was purely arbitrary, but curiously became a shibboleth that generations of writers were made to fear.

Prescriptivism has been defended as a force that warned speakers and writers to be attentive to the correctness of their language, but it has also been attacked as the cause of prose style that is "correct" but lifeless, inducing so much fear of being incorrect that the writer is afraid to give free flow to the expression of his ideas. Emerson's remark could be paraphrased here: "A foolish correctness is the hobgoblin of little minds." Prescriptive grammar induced a state of paralyzing anxiety in American society. School "grammar" is still thought of by many good citizens as something arcane, a mystery too deep to be penetrated by any but witches, strange gurus, and "English teachers."

There is, of course, a standard English, a standard that is not only national, but international, with a small number of inconsequential variations in pronunciation, spelling, vocabulary, and grammar. This standard is the usage of the reputable speakers and writers of the English-speaking world. There are many varieties of nonstandard English, too. In the eighteenth century, English usage was divided into that of the "polite" and that of the "vulgar;" the polite being persons of education, refinement, and culture, and the vulgar being the poor—like Shaw's Eliza Doolittle in *Pygmalion*—who were denied the advantages of extended education, access to books, and conversation with polite persons. A certain number of years of formal schooling is no guarantee of the acquisition of standard English, just as the lack of much schooling does not necessarily deny one the use of good English. Shakespeare, Pope, and Burns had limited formal education, but wrote like angels anyway, and Shelley and Poe were expelled from college without detriment to their mastery of the mother tongue. It may be unfortunate in a democratic society, but it is nevertheless true that some people speak and write English better than others. Precisely why this is so is difficult to say. For one thing, language is enormously complex, and some individuals are gifted with the ability to master its niceties and nuances. Mastery is acquired by observation, mainly through reading, begun early and continued long. Some individuals appear to be unwilling or unable to observe all the varieties of ways of expressing ideas in the mother tongue, and drilling all comers in these ways in school has failed to graduate English users of a uniformly high degree of skill. The linguistic hewers of wood and drawers of water will always be with us. Standard English has its prescriptions: it prohibits the double negative and certain verb forms. "Gabriel done blowed his horn for Grampaw" may be picturesque, but it isn't standard English, nor is "Where was you borned at?" nor "He taken it hisself," nor "Hit don't make me no never mind." Good English is socially of considerable consequence. In one of Joyce's *Dubliners* stories, "The Boarding House," a fairly genteel man in his thirties, Mr. Doran, is maneuvered into marriage with nineteen-year-old Polly. He reflects, "She *was* a little vulgar; some times she said 'I seen' and 'If I had've known.' But what would grammar matter if he really loved her?" Polly's grammar did, of course, matter.

A problem in determining reputable usage is that reputability is not a rigid absolute. Variations in the grammatical practice of reputable speakers and writers sometimes occur that shock the sensibilities of other reputable speakers and writers, and whether it is socially better to quietly tolerate (note split infinitive) or vigorously protest offences against linguistic decorum is difficult to decide. Around 1960 the philosopher Jacques Barzun published vehement protests against the frequent use of *disinterested* in the sense of "uninterested" rather than "unbiased." A useful word was being destroyed by heedless malpractice. Another example of misuse that annoys the precise is the form *predominate* used as an adjective, as in "a predominate idea." The suffix *-ate* marks a verb, not an adjective, which is marked by *-ant*, and thus the conventional form is *predominant*. The conservative desire to defend the purity of the mother tongue has much to be said for it, but conservation is a losing battle. It is easier, and finally better, to tolerate the linguistic failings of others than to make a useless outcry against them. Reputable speakers cannot be equally reputable at all times in an absolute sense. Churchill had enough confidence in his reputability to say, "This is me, Winston Churchill." If the purist anger that his remark aroused was brought to his attention it must have merely amused him.

The prevalence of pronoun misuse in examples like "between you and I" presents an interesting problem to the speaker who would use the correct *me*; he may know that perhaps the majority of his listeners will think him wrong. "Between you and I" is an ancient pattern, occurring in Shakespeare: ". . . all debts are cleared between you and I" (*Merchant of Venice*, 3.3.322). Renaissance writers and their publishers did not give themselves the concern over matters of grammar that became important later. In today's English, the frequency with which subject case forms of pronouns in the object function occur in speech and in casually edited print has been attributed to "hypercorrectness," a feeling that "he and I" is bound to be better English than "him and me"—"Prizes were awarded to both he and I." Hypercorrectness may also account for the prevalent *whom* before a parenthetic phrase: "He was not the man *whom* I thought he was."

The prescriptivists went astray by refusing to acknowledge that reputable usage is the only reasonable criterion of good English and by supposing that "grammar" was different from, and superior to, usage. As Lowth put it in the preface to his *Short Introduction*: ". . . our best authors for want of some rudiments of this kind have sometimes fallen into mistakes, and been guilty of palpable errors in point of grammar." Grammatical purism has been under persistent attack by students of language behavior (linguists) through the twentieth century, but has as yet lost little of its vitality. The idea that the grammarian's job is simply to observe and record usage without condemning any of it has as yet not won the consent of the majority. The grammarian may point out that a distinction between *may* and *might* is not always understood, as when someone writes: "Germany *may* have won the war if she had not attacked Russia in 1941," but if the grammarian regrets the failure to grasp nuance, he does not say so. He merely records fact as he finds it.

Johnson's Dictionary.   A notable event in the history of the English language occurred in 1755 with the publication of Samuel Johnson's *Dictionary*. English dictionaries had been steadily improving since the early versions, and definitions like "Dog. An animal well known," no longer appeared. Nathaniel Bailey produced a successful dictionary in 1721 and prepared a revised edition in 1731 which was much used through the next generation. Bailey defined more words than his predecessors had done and supplied some etymologies, which were appreciated. However, there was some dissatisfaction with Bailey's inadequacies, and thus the ground was prepared for Johnson's great effort. Johnson began work on his dictionary in 1747. He was then thirty-eight years old. The son of a bookseller in Lichfield, he had attended Oxford but had been obliged through poverty to leave without his degree. He opened a school for boys near Lichfield that attracted three pupils, one of whom by happy chance was David Garrick, who became the most celebrated actor of the age. In 1737 Johnson and Garrick moved to London where Garrick was to continue his schooling and then study law, a notion he soon thought better of. Johnson, meanwhile, made a precarious living as a translator from French and Italian and by writing on whatever topics the booksellers were willing to print. By 1747 Johnson had a reputation as a learned and able man, well suited to undertake the compilation of the authoritative dictionary that had been so long called for. Johnson was willing to assume authority. In his Preface he stated that "... every language has ... its improprieties and absurdities which it is the duty of the lexicographer to correct or proscribe." He would settle for all time the meanings of words, their spelling and pronunciation, and would illustrate the use of words by quotations drawn from celebrated authors, ranging as far back as Sir Philip Sidney.

Johnson contracted with a group of booksellers to undertake this arduous task, the booksellers agreeing to pay him fifteen hundred and seventy-five pounds for his expenses. They gambled that Johnson would finish the work, but he did, and the profit was theirs. Boswell in his *Life of Johnson* remarked:

> He had spent during the progress of the work the money for which he had contracted to write his *Dictionary*. We have seen that the reward of his labour was only fifteen hundred and seventy-five pounds; and when the expenses of amanuenses and paper and other articles are deducted, his clear profit was very inconsiderable. I once said to him: 'I am sorry, sir, you did not get more for your *Dictionary*.' His answer was: 'I am sorry too. But it was very well. The booksellers are generous, liberal-minded men.' He, upon all occasions, did ample justice to their character in this respect. He considered them as the patrons of literature; and, indeed, although they have eventually been considerable gainers by his *Dictionary*, it is to them that we owe its having been undertaken and carried through at the risk of great expense, for they were not absolutely sure of being indemnified.

Johnson supposed the work would be finished in three years; it took him seven. Johnson had the help of six copyists, five of whom, Boswell was pleased to say, were Scots, but the labor of definition was Johnson's own. He used the work of his predecessors, as all lexicographers since Cawdrey have done, but much of his work was original. He labored on under difficulties, and his bookseller patrons grew impatient with delay, but eventually the job was done. Johnson had in the beginning been encouraged by the Earl of Chesterfield with a promise of patronage, but the Earl thereafter forgot Johnson until it was announced that the *Dictionary* would soon appear, whereupon Chesterfield praised Johnson, apparently hoping that the work would be dedicated to him. This situation gave occasion to Johnson's composing a response to the Earl that became famous. Johnson wrote, in part:

> Seven years, my Lord, have now passed since I waited in your outward rooms, or was repulsed from your door; during which time I have been pushing on my work through difficulties, of which it is useless to complain, and have brought it, at last, to the verge of publication, without one act of assistance, one word of encouragement, or one smile of favour. Such treatment I did not expect, for I never had a Patron before. . . . Is not a Patron, my Lord, one who looks with unconcern on a man struggling for life in the water, and, when he has reached ground, encumbers him with help?

Johnson's rewards for his labor were, in the end, considerable. "Dictionary" Johnson, "the Great Lexicographer," was praised as a benefactor to his country. At a time when rivalry with France ran high, it was remarked that a single Englishman had matched the achievement of the French Academy. As Garrick put it, "Johnson, well armed like a hero of yore, / Has beat forty French, and will beat forty more." According to Boswell, Johnson was complacent over a report that the Accademia della Crusca found it difficult to believe that his dictionary was the work of only one man. Johnson gained international fame and, in 1762, was granted a government pension of three hundred pounds a year.

His dictionary, as Johnson was well aware, was imperfect and was soon attacked for its defects. His definition of *network* as "Any thing reticulated or decussated, at equal distances, with interstices between the intersections" was considered hilarious by some of the London wits. Johnson anticipated objections in his Preface by pointing out the difficulty of defining:

> To explain, requires the use of terms less abstruse than that which is to be explained, and such terms cannot always be found. For as nothing can be proved but by supposing something intuitively known, and evident without proof, so nothing can be defined but by the use of words too plain to admit of definition. Sometimes easier words are changed into harder; as, *burial*, into *sepulture* or *interment*; *dry*, into *desiccative*; *dryness*, into *siccity* or *aridity*; *fit*, into *paroxysm*; for, the *easiest* word, whatever it be, can never be translated into one more easy.

For the most part Johnson's definitions were models of clarity, precision, and thoroughness. He defined *carry* in thirty-five senses and *do* in twenty-seven, *bar* as a noun in fourteen senses and in ten as a verb. There were a few slips, such as defining *windward* and *leeward* in identical terms. Boswell has an anecdote on another error: "A lady once asked him how he came to define *Pastern* the *knee* of a horse: instead of making an elaborate defence, as she expected, he at once answered: 'Ignorance, madam, pure ignorance.'" In a few of his definitions he exercised his jocularity or prejudice. A *lexicographer* was "a harmless drudge," although Johnson himself was certainly not harmless. *Oats* he defined as "a grain, which in England is generally given to horses, but in Scotland supports the people." An inveterate Tory, he despised the opposite party and defined Whig as "the name of a faction." He had long been annoyed by the granting of pensions to men he thought unworthy and defined *pension* as "An allowance made to any one without an equivalent. In England it is generally understood to mean pay given to a state hireling for treason to his country." When Johnson was added to the pension list it was thought amusing that he would have to live with his definition, but he cheerfully admitted being happy to do so for three hundred pounds a year. He let the definition stand through the seventh edition, which appeared in 1785.

Johnson's dictionary was a bookish one and lacked the

thousands of words used by the various trades and occupations. He conceded that he had been unable to go down into mines or on board ships to learn the terms of navigation. He drew his words from literature and included a number of words that had been tried experimentally during the "enrichment" phase of the Renaissance, but had failed to survive and were not a part of the living vocabulary. Noah Webster disapproved of Johnson's including such oddities as *ariolation*, *clancular*, *exolution*, *exenterate* and, Webster said, "thousands of such terms."

As to etymology, Johnson was well equipped to trace the origin of words drawn from Latin, Greek, French, and Italian. When he didn't know the etymology he made the mistake of guessing. Of *peacock* he surmised that the bird got its name from the peak on its head, although he correctly etymologized *peahen*, as "*pea* and *hen*; *pava*, Latin."

Johnson was willing to provide an authoritative opinion as to the propriety of words by giving them labels, such as "proper," "improper," "corrupt," "cant," "barbarous," "vulgar." Like Swift, Johnson was conservative and provided pejorative labels for new, slangy words: *banter* he declared "a barbarous word, without etymology"; *fib* was "A cant word among children," although its use by Pope was cited; *bamboozle* was "a cant word not used in pure or in grave writings"; of *nowadays* Johnson wrote, "This word, though common and used by the best writers, is perhaps barbarous"; and of *phiz*, "This word is formed by a ridiculous contraction from *physiognomy*, and should therefore, if it be written at all, be written *phyz*." He approved of *sherbet* because it came from Arabic, but *punch* was a bad word because it had no known etymology. Users of the dictionary expected such guidance, so that they might know whether a given word was vested with due decorum or not. Dictionary makers who followed Johnson continued his practice of providing labels, sometimes quite whimsically, until the appearance in 1966 of *Webster's Third New International Dictionary* aroused a storm of protest in the United States because of the editors' sparing use of labels like "substandard" and "nonstandard." Some professed to see ruin at the door by the abdication of authority that the compilers of dictionaries were supposed to assume.

An important use of Johnson's dictionary was as a guide to that troublesome matter, proper spelling. Johnson had an opportunity to introduce some useful improvements in spelling, but, if he had such an idea in mind, he was not consistent in carrying it out. He sensibly omitted the unnecessary medial *e* in *immovable*, but not in *moveable*; he reduced the double *l* in *downhil*, but not in *uphill*; omitted the *u* in *exterior*, but not in *interiour*. Johnson could have used the authority willingly conferred on him by his contemporaries to reduce spelling to a better system, but he did not make the effort to do so.

Johnson was expected also to settle matters of variable pronunciation, but he did not do this, professing diffidence; he pointed out that the best speaker of the House of Lords (Chesterfield) and the best speaker of the House of Commons differed in the pronunciation of the word *great*. Johnson felt he could not arbitrate between equally reputable speakers of the mother tongue. He did indicate a preference for syllable stress in words that were unsettled: *academy* and *balcony* were variably stressed on the first or second syllable and *European* on the second or third. Curiously, Johnson's authority was not successful in establishing *ácademy* and *balcóny*.

Johnson's dictionary was eventually displaced by works that improved on his model, but the use of his book continued beyond his death in 1784. In Thackeray's novel, *Vanity Fair*, the headmistress of a school for women makes a gift of Johnson's *Dictionary* to the graduates of her school. Becky Sharp ungratefully throws her copy out the carriage window, but as late as 1812 some thought young ladies well advised to rely on Johnson as a safe guide to proper English. Dependence on the assumed authority of some dictionary persists today, although it should be evident that any lexicographer may, like Johnson, be learned, but is human and fallible.

The orthoepists. Although Johnson was reluctant to legislate in matters of the variant pronunciation of some words, others were not, and a number of books on this troublesome matter appeared in the later eighteenth century. The authors gave their art the name "orthoepy," a coined compound meaning "correct pronunciation."

Johnson had remarked that, "For pronunciation the best general rule is, to consider those the most elegant speakers who deviate least from the written words." This ideal condition was generally supported by the orthoepists, although there were obvious limits to its application. No one advocated pronouncing all the symbols written in *Wednesday*, but the idea of "spelling pronunciation" restored the /l/ in *fault* and *vault*—which rhymed in eighteenth century poetry with *ought*—and in *soldier*, which the semi-literate spelled "soger," indicating a loss of the liquid phoneme. Spelling presumably restored the /w/ in *Edward* and *awkward*—the orthoepists indicated they were pronounced /ɛdəd/ and /ɔkəd/ by Londoners—and /k/ was restored in *verdict* and *perfect*. The reformers urged the restoring of medial /d/ in *London* and final /d/ in *island*, which were not being heard, and of the medial vowel in *venison* and *medicine*, which, however, remained unrestored in British speech, although Americans obediently sound it. The gap between the spelling of *iron* and the pronunciation "i'urn" was pointed out, but in this instance the gap has remained. On the whole, pronunciation has moved very little in the direction of agreeing with spelling, although the matter is still sometimes argued; some are distressed by the pronunciation "stummick" for *stomach*, since the spelling does not give sanction to /ɪ/ in the unstressed syllable.

Analogy was another principle looked to for guidance in improving current pronunciation. Boswell reported that Johnson pronounced *heard* /hɪəd/ by analogy with *ear* and *hear*. That *hear* was not analogously pronounced with *bear* and *wear* Johnson did not remark on. *Beard* was variously pronounced, and it was recommended that the pronunciation be determined by adding *d* to *bear*, which allowed the application of spelling analogy.

The strength of the spirit of reform in the later eighteenth century accounts for the proliferation of books on orthoepy and for the popularity of such books, some of them going through several editions into the nineteenth century. A curious feature of this movement was the early prominence of Scots, among them James Buchanan and James Elphinston, to whom a genteel pronunciation was important, since when they migrated to London to win fame and fortune they found their dialect ridiculed by the natives. When Boswell arrived in the metropolis he took speech lessons from Thomas Sheridan, the father of the playwright, Richard Brinsley Sheridan. Thomas Sheridan was a prominent lecturer, teacher, and writer on the topic of good speech and "elocution." Sheridan argued that serious attention paid to elocution would not only improve the English language but would raise the general tone of English society, just as Rome owed its greatness to the attention paid to oratory. Johnson did not think much of Sheridan's pretensions; "What does he pretend to teach?" asked the sage. Sheridan had the disadvantage of being Irish, and an anonymous critic warned readers against him, for "to the last period of his life his origin was obvious in his pronunciation." A Londoner named William Kenrick, who published a pronouncing dictionary in 1773, put it that "There seems indeed a most ridiculous absurdity in the pretensions of a native of Aberdeen or Tipperary, to teach the natives of London to speak and to read."

The most popular work on orthoepy was John Walker's *Pronouncing Dictionary*, published in 1791, which was regarded as a reliable reference book for decades. Like Sheridan, Walker had been an actor and in this way had developed an early interest in pronunciation. Walker agreed that usage should determine propriety in pronunciation but, since usage varied, it was admittedly a troublesome criterion. Walker recognized the usage of the multitude, the academic and professional, and the courtly, suggesting that the practice of two out of three should decide in matters of divided usage. Decisions were sometimes hard to make: Walker and Sheridan preferred that *celery* should be pronounced as spelled, but "sallery" was just as often heard; Walker declared "chaw" for *chew* vulgar, but other orthoepists accepted either pronunciation. Johnson said "chaw" was "frequent and perhaps proper."

Many good speakers fronted the nasal /ŋ/ to /n/ in "readin,"
"writin," "singin," and whether this was proper remained uncertain. *Dictionary* apparently came to be pronounced as
spelled, for Walker remarks:

> A few years ago this word was universally pronounced as
> if written *Dixnary*, and a person would have been thought
> a pedant if he had pronounced it according to its orthog-
> raphy; but such has been the taste for improvement in
> speaking, that now a person would risk the imputation of
> vulgarity should he pronounce it otherwise than it is
> written.

Spelling also affected the pronunciation of *merchant* and *service*. According to Walker, "Thirty years ago, everyone pronounced the first syllable of *merchant* like the monosyllable
march.... Service and *servant* were still heard among the
lower order of speakers as if written *sarvice*, *sarvant*." *Clerk*,
sergeant, *Derby*, and *Berkeley*, however, continued to resist the
attraction of spelling and analogy in British speech.

There was uncertainty over *imbecile*, some orthoepists preferring a second syllable stress /ɪmbésɪl/ and others the third
syllable /ɪmbəsíl/. A century later this question was still unre-
solved, according to James Russel Lowell (Introduction to
The Biglow Papers, Second Series):

> I had been so used to hearing *imbecile* pronounced with
> the accent on the first syllable, which is in accordance
> with the general tendency in such matters, that I was
> surprised to find *imbécile* in a verse of Wordsworth. The
> dictionaries all give it so. I asked a highly cultivated
> Englishman, and he declared for *imbecéel*. In general it
> may be assumed that accent will finally settle on the syl-
> lable dictated by greater ease and therefore quickness of
> utterance.

An intrusive /j/ was heard after /g/ and /k/ often enough to
be considered allowable in words like "gyarden" and "cyard."

Like the grammarians of the age, the pronunciation reformers did not always agree with one another as to which variant

was to be preferred. Anselm Bayley considered /æ/ better in *man*, *hand*, *bath*, but William Kenrick was sure that /a/ was the proper vowel. Bayley thought *speak* should rhyme with *break* (/spek/), but Kenrick argued that /spek/ was Irish. The Irish continued to pronounce *tea* /te/ after the English had shifted to /ti/. /te/ had been general earlier, as in Pope's rhyme in *The Rape of the Lock* (1711): "Here thou, great Anna, whom three realms obey, / Dost sometimes counsel take, and sometimes tea."

The diphthong /aɪ/ in words spelled *oi* caused some perturbation because of the disharmony of pronunciation and spelling. *Join* regularly rhymed with *line* in Pope and other poets. Kenrick declared it a "vicious custom" to pronounce *oil* and *toil* "exactly like *isle*, *tile*," but he admitted that "it would now appear affectation to pronounce other than *bile*, *jine*" for *boil* and *join*. Eventually speakers shifted to /ɔɪ/ or /oɪ/, presumably to agree with the spelling.

Nature shifted gradually from /netɚ/ to /netjuɚ/ to /netʃɚ/. Some American dictionaries cited /netjuɚ/ as the "correct" pronunciation as late as the mid-twentieth century.

The pronunciations that came to be disused in standard speech were brought to America by migrants, and forms like "jine," "rile," "varmint" (vermin), "nater," "soger" are familiar to readers of American fiction, like Lowell's *Biglow Papers*, that made literary use of "rustic" speech.

The ideal the orthoepists hoped to reach, to bring about a single, universal pronunciation system in harmony with spelling and analogy, failed, as did the grammarians' hopes of making syntax consistent with analogy and logic. Pronunciation varies according to regional and social dialect. Whether *advertisement* is stressed on the second or third syllable is a regional distinction, as are the variants /iðɚ/ and /aɪðə/. Australians sound *race* as a homophone with *rice*; this pronunciation is regional, not "wrong." A living language is under the government of all the people who speak it, most of whom are out of the reach of academic rules.

Semantic change.   The Greek philosophical dictum, *panta* *rhei*, all things change, applies to all aspects of language, including the meaning of words. Speakers sometimes give a new meaning to a word, and one or more of the older senses of a word may come in time to be disused and to be glossary items in editions of older literature. Readers of Chaucer must keep in mind that *lust* as Chaucer used it meant "pleasure" or "desire" of a harmless sort. The pejorative sense was acquired later and drove the original meaning out of use. Curiously, *lusty* is still innocent but *lustful* is not. So, too, *lewd* in ME meant "ignorant"; "the learned and the lewd" was a contrasting pairing in Chaucer's time, and again the pejorative sense prevailed over the innocent one. Words may broaden their area of meaning: *go* in one sense meant "walk," as in Chaucer's phrase "whether he go or ride," but when the word came to mean movement of any sort, the narrower sense was lost. Words may also contract their area of meaning: *meat* in older English meant food of any kind, but came to refer to food of the flesh sort only. The general sense was meant in the proverb, "One man's meat is another man's poison," and the obsolete compound *sweetmeat* did not refer to flesh. *Corn* meant grain of any kind, but in American use was restricted to mean the Western Hemisphere plant "Indian corn" or "maize." In OE *starve* meant "die" by any means, but came to refer to death by a specific means. *Slay* meant "strike" in general, but narrowed to refer to the action with a particular consequence. The German cognates of *starve* and *slay*, *sterben* and *schlagen*, conservatively retain the original broader sense. So, too, in German *lust* still has its innocent sense; a *Lustgarten* in Germany is not the sort of place an English speaker might suppose it to be.

The etymological meaning of words, whether native or borrowed, is not necessarily a clue to the current sense. Robert Lowth argued that "aversion to" had to be incorrect because in Latin an aversion was a turning away, and thus a semantic contradiction was involved in using *to* rather than *from*. But English speakers did not choose to be etymologically precise. A *carol* in Old French was a dance, not a Christmas song; *arrive* in Latin meant specifically to reach the bank of a river;

delapidated has as its base word the Latin *lapis*, meaning "stone," but in English wooden structures may be referred to. *Holiday* has moved from its original sense of "holy day" (the Fourth of July is not a religious occasion), and in British use the term may extend more than a day, as in "a week's holiday in France."

Older meanings sometimes survive as metaphors. "Sail" had been used so long as a term for sea navigation that it survived after steamships were moving without canvas sheets to catch the wind. "Pen" as a writing instrument derived its name from Latin *penna*, meaning "feather," when pens were goose quills.

Words can go through several semantic shifts. The Italic word *virtue* had as its base the Latin *vir*, meaning "man," and the original sense of *virtue* was "manliness," "valor," "fortitude"—the soldierly qualities. In medieval use the word was generalized to signify quality, excellence, or power of various kinds, as in the "virtue" of plants and precious stones. When the word was specialized in "woman's virtue" to mean feminine chastity, it had traveled far from its etymology in *vir*. *Nice* in Old French and ME meant "foolish." The word then took on a variety of meanings: the *OED* records, among others, "lascivious," "extravagant," "elegant," "strange," "indolent," "effeminate," "delicate," "shy," "fastidious," "precise," "refined," "discriminating." The *OED* remarks, "In many examples from the sixteenth and seventeenth centuries it is difficult to say in what particular sense the writer intended it to be taken." The word survives in the sense of "mildly agreeable," as in "nice day," "nice party," "nice person" and has traveled far from the sense of "foolish." *Silly* went through a similar number of changes. In OE *sælig* meant "blessed" or "happy." In late ME and early ModE the word took on the sense of "pitiable" or "helpless" or "harmless," as in "silly sheep." Then the word came to mean "simple," "ignorant," "foolish." Coleridge's use of the term in *The Rime of the Ancient Mariner*, "The silly buckets on the deck," is puzzling, but presumably he meant "simple" or "homely," since "foolish" is not applicable.

Meaning can be weakened through hyperbole, as in "My feet are killing me," or the "killing looks" of a coquette. In OE *cwellan* (quell) meant "kill"; *cwealm* (qualm) meant "death"; and *sweltan* (swelter) meant "die." Now insurrections are quelled, a qualm is a minor discomfort, and swelter has narrowed its sense to unpleasant warmth.

The frequency with which the pejorative change occurs has led some to wonder if this aspect of language reveals a dark side of the human mind. Certainly linguistic changes sometimes have a psychological origin, as in the operation of analogy. Even a little observation of human behavior informs us that man is a fault-finding animal, quick to disapprove of others. This disposition accounts for a number of pejorative semantic changes. In early English *knave* meant "boy," as the German cognate, *Knabe*, still does. As late as the Renaissance, a new-born infant was identified as either a knave-child or a lass, but today a new-born male has not had time to become a knave. In ME a *villain* was a laborer on a *ville*, an estate; the pejorative change in meaning reflects the landowners' opinion of the working stiffs who tilled the soil. This attitude accounts also for the decline in the moral sense of *boor*, which originally meant dweller on the land, or farmer, as do the German and Dutch cognates, *Bauer* and *Boer*. *Hussy* is the reduced form of the harmless compound, *housewife*. Earlier, *debonair* (with a good air) meant "modest," but now conveys the sense of affected coyness. *Genteel*, a variant of *gentle*, referred in the seventeenth century to the good manners of the well bred, but came to mean the vulgar affectation of such manners, a mark of the "pushiness" of the ambitious middle class. *Sanctimonious* was originally complimentary but now suggests hypocrisy, as in "sanctimonious old fraud." *Propaganda* meant the diffusion of doctrine that was not designedly false, but now has a pejorative sense. *Suggestive* is etymologically colorless, but "suggestive remarks" are not blameless; and although an "informer," one who informs, is exclusively pejorative, an "informant" is harmless. *Harbor* as a verb means "to shelter," but only criminals are harbored, never visiting aunts from Baltimore. The pejorative drift is a constant factor in the use of living language and needs to be promptly perceived when it occurs to avoid giving offence inadvertently.

The elevation of the meaning of words to a higher level of esteem also occurs. *Knight*, which meant simply "young man," was elevated to an aristocratic title in the later Middle Ages. *Chivalry* was derived from the French word for horse (cheval), but was applied to the ideal manners of horse-owning aristocrats. The military importance of cavalry accounts for the elevation of *marshal* and *constable* as titles of consequence, both terms originally meaning "stable attendant." *Steward* meant "sty keeper," but in a courtly household it came to be the title of a person who was responsible for the food supply. The political terms "Tory" and "Whig" were applied derisively in the seventeenth century, but through familiarity they achieved a respectable level, as did sectarian terms like "Puritan," "Quaker," and "Methodist."

New words.   Since 1800 the English language hasn't changed much except for large additions to the vocabulary. Phonology is, of course, always somewhat wavering, but no change as gross as the Great Vowel Shift has occurred in the last two hundred years. Morphology and syntax have remained reasonably stable; there is little in the language of Wordsworth that seems unidiomatic to the reader at the end of the twentieth century. But the current language has thousands of vocabulary items that would baffle Wordsworth, were he aware of them. The expansion of the British Empire in South Africa, Australia, and India led to the literary borrowing of exotic words, like the Boer words *spoor*, *veldt*, and *trek*, the aboriginal Australian words *kangaroo*, *wombat*, *koala*, *boomerang*, and a number of East Indian words like *Brahmin* (used metaphorically in the sense of "aristocrat," as in "Boston Brahmin"), *nirvana*, *pundit*, *juggernaut*, *coolie*, *bungalow*, *thug*.

The two world wars were strong collective experiences and produced a number of borrowings from French and German; among them, from French, were *camouflage*, *barrage*, *liaison*, *ace*, and *cootie* (for that common trench companion, the louse). From German, in World War I, came *strafe*, meaning "punish," and *flak*, meaning "anti-aircraft fire," an acronym of the compound *Fliegerabwehrkanone* (flyer defense cannon); in World War II *panzer*, *ersatz*, *stuka*, *blitzkrieg*, and *luftwaffe* were quite familiar, though they are less so now.

Russian words have so far not been readily assimilated into English. Readers of translations of Russian novels know that a *samovar* is what Russians make tea in and that a *droshky* is a carriage or sled; at the time of the Russian Revolution *Bolshevik* and *tovarish* (comrade) had some English currency; in the 1950s *sputnik,*, meaning "space satellite," had a brief run, but has faded from use. It may be that the Slavonic languages are as yet too strange and distant for easy assimilation in English.

French has contributed recently in the areas of cookery and dress: *chef*, *cuisine*, *gourmet*, *rotisserie*; *chemise*, *brassiere*, *lingerie*, *modiste*, *chapeau*, *chartreuse*. Some other fashionable French terms are *rapport*, *impasse*, *apropos*, *beaux arts*, *détente*, *belles-lettres*, *littérateur*, *rendezvous*.

Remarkable advances in the various sciences and a general interest in the results account for the proliferation of Latin and Greek compounds that are familiar to the literate: *stratosphere*, *peritonitis*, *cardiac*, *orthodontist*, and *antibiotics*, for example. Learned terms in psychology and sociology also have general currency, like *behaviorism*, *infrastructure*, *introvert*, *claustrophobia*, *agoraphobia*, *neurosis*, *egocentric*, and *Angst*.

The various technical vocabularies, in physics, chemistry, botany, medicine, and so forth, are the province of specialists, but the general vocabulary has increased so broadly that the literate who read on several topics are more dependent on dictionaries than was true in the past.

Slang. A special branch of the vocabulary is slang, a term that is difficult to define. Slang is generally recognized as a nonstandard variety of language, but the disapproval of it that was vigorously expressed in the eighteenth and nineteenth centuries has given way to some tolerance and recognition of it as interesting. Slang at its best has a metaphoric picturesqueness and vigor that is attractive. When it expresses irreverence or defiance of authority it pleases some who hear it and annoys others.

There is a good deal of slang in current American use, but slang is neither new nor peculiar to Americans. To illustrate its antiquity, the French term for "head," *tête*, has been in respectable use for centuries, but its late Latin form, *testa*, meant "cooking pot," an instance of the tendency to find the human head an object of humor, as English terms like *bean*, *nut* ("He's off his nut"), *belfrey*, *noddle*, and *noodle* ("That's using the old noodle") testify. Slang is presumably universal; it is certainly copious in French, some of whose speakers call a policeman a *flic* and a young woman a *poule* (literally, "hen").

Sixteenth- and seventeenth-century literature made frequent use of some slang, like *doxy* and *drab* for "woman," and the epithets *zounds* and *gadzooks*. In the civil war of the 1640s commonwealth men were called *Roundheads* from the shape of their haircuts. The late seventeenth-century political terms *Whig* and *Tory* were originally slang, derived from Gaelic and used in derision, but custom soon gave the terms respectability. Also slangy and derisive was the term *Quaker*, applied to a new religious sect. Custom elevated some eighteenth-century slang to respectability, at least on the informal level—words like *mob*, *sham*, *banter*, *bully*—that survived the severe disapproval of Swift and Johnson. Other contemporary terms like *smoke* (to discover or reveal) and *bubble* (to deceive) did not survive. *Bamboozle* survived, but remains slangy. *Booze* has been slang for centuries and still is. Slang is, however, often ephemeral. In the 1920s, a young woman was a *chicken*, clipped in the 1970s to *chick*, while the meaning of *chicken* shifted to refer to timidity. Slang phrases fashionable in the 1920s—"That's not so hot," "So's your old man," "Tell it to the marines"—are no longer intelligible. Fiction writers who use the slang of their day—O. Henry, Ring Lardner, P. G. Wodehouse—need glossing for the next generation of readers.

The etymology of slang is obvious when it is metaphor drawn from the general vocabulary, like *egghead* for an intellectual, or *chatterbox* and *windbag* for an excessive talker, or *dreadnought* and *battle-ax* for a domineering older woman. But many slang terms have no known etymology, leading to unanswerable questions like "Where does *boondocks* come from?" or *cop* (policeman), or *malarkey*, or *spiffy*. Such words have a spontaneous origin in the spoken language, and when they acquire wide currency and eventually appear in print the source cannot be traced. The origin of *O. K.* has attracted a number of unlikely explanations, one being that President Andrew Jackson was a poor speller who indicated his approval by writing "Oll Korrect," which was then shortened to O. K. It has been suggested that *cop*, clipped from *copper*, was derived from the copper buttons on police uniforms or from Latin *capio*, "I seize," but this is only speculation.

Some objects and conditions attract a number of slang synonyms, like those for "woman," among them *fluff*, *twist*, *skirt*, *broad*, *dame*, *tomato*, *dog* (*tomato*, unlike *dog*, being complimentary), and there are many slang terms for "drunk": *boiled*, *fried*, *spiffed*, *loaded*, *pickled*, *sozzled*, *pie-eyed*, and others. There are some odd terms for "money," including *spondulix*, *ready rhino*, and *mazuma*.

Sport supplies some slangy metaphors. Organizations begin a new year by having a "kickoff" breakfast, for example, and although in prize-fighting "on the ropes," "throw in the towel," "down and out," and "take the count" have a literal meaning, these terms become slang when applied elsewhere.

Clever coinages like H. L. Mencken's *booboisie* and blends like *guesstimate*, *anecdotage*, *infanticipate* do not qualify as slang because they have limited use and perish early. Another area of vocabulary that is not properly slang because its use is limited to a subculture is criminal cant or argot, to which Gypsy lingo seems also to belong. Gangster movies in the 1930s made *gat* for "gun" and *moll* for "woman" generally familiar, but criminal terms like *whiz mob* for pickpockets, *cannon* for a skilled pickpocket, and *mark* for his victim are buried in the subculture. Strange Gypsy terms are occasionally recorded in serious literature, as in the "Proteus" section of Joyce's *Ulysses*: *darkmans* for "night," *strolling mort* and *wapping dell* for "woman," among others.

The examples given here could be multiplied many times. In every decade adolescents adopt new slang that baffles their parents: in the 1970s terms like *square* and *hip*; and *make out* and *put out* in sexual senses. Special activities have their own slang: in baseball a left-handed player is a *south-paw* or "wrong-armed guy"; a flashy player is a *hot dog*. In the drug culture a *reefer* is a marijuana cigarette, and *snow* is cocaine. The vocabulary of slang seems to pervade nearly every area of experience.

NOTES AND BIBLIOGRAPHY

Leonard, Sterling A. *The Doctrine of Correctness in English Usage, 1700–1800.* University of Wisconsin Studies in Language and Literature, no. 25. Madison: University of Wisconsin Press, 1929. A valuable study of the idea of grammatical reform.

Jespersen, Otto. *A Modern English Grammar.* part 4. Heidelberg, 1931. The question of *shall* and *will* is brilliantly treated in more than one hundred pages.

Wyld, Henry C. *A History of Modern Colloquial English.* London: T. Fisher Unwin, 1920. The matter of pronunciation is presented in detail.

Campbell, George. *The Philosophy of Rhetoric.* Edited by Lloyd F. Bitzer. Carbondale: Southern Illinois University Press, 1963.

Curme, George O. *Syntax.* Boston: D. C. Heath, 1931. Contains much that is valuable on historical grammar.

Partridge, Eric. *Slang Today and Yesterday*, 3d ed., New York: Macmillan Co, 1950. A number of studies of slang in various languages have been published in the past century, meaning that students of language consider slang to be more than vulgar and trivial. Partridge provides a lively treatment of the topic. His lists of slang that was current before 1930 in the English, American, and Australian dialects make clear the short life of most slang.

8

American English

The English language is now at the peak of its use as a means of international communication, and what chiefly sustains its position is no longer the power of the British Empire but the power of the United States. It was, of course, the development of the British Empire during the eighteenth and nineteenth centuries that first made English an international language, and the colonies that became the United States were part of that empire from 1607 to 1776. There are citizens of various parts of the world who are aware that Britain and America are separated by the vast Atlantic Ocean, but they are not aware of western history and often wonder that Americans speak English so well, attributing American skill to excellent schooling in a foreign language.

In fact, of course, English was brought to America by migrants, just as it had been brought to Britain from the European mainland in the fifth and sixth centuries. English was first established in the Western Hemisphere in the Jamestown colony in 1607, followed by the Massachusetts colonies planted in 1620 and 1630. Ultimately, thirteen British colonies were founded along the Atlantic seaboard that were administered as part of the British Empire until the Revolutionary War. Throughout the seventeenth and eighteenth centuries migrants from the British Isles continued to settle in the colo-

nies in considerable numbers, assuring that the dominant
language of the colonies would be English. Other languages
were absorbed by English when the descendants of the original non-English settlers mingled freely with the English-
speaking majority; Dutch, for example, was no longer dominant after New Amsterdam became New York during the
Anglo-Dutch wars of the 1660s. The Dutch left names—like
Rip Van Winkle, Schuyler, Stuyvesant, Spuyten Duyvil, Har-
lem, and Catskills, and words like *cookie, cruller, stoop,* and
spook—but not their language. Only those foreign-language
communities that could maintain isolation from the English,
like the Pennsylvania Dutch, were able to resist linguistic
assimilation.

Until the Revolutionary War the English spoken by the
colonists was not commonly thought of as a peculiar dialect.
Place names of Indian origin, like Connecticut and Potomac, were strange, of course, and some terms applied to the
terrain, like *bluff* and *foothills,* also struck English visitors
as odd; so did terms like *feed store* and *spider* (frying pan).
But between 1607 and 1776 not enough time had elapsed for
pronunciation changes to occur that would mark American
English as a distinct dialect. The periodic arrival of fresh migrants from Britain probably helped keep American phonology tied to that of the mother country. Another contributing
factor was a mobility that kept American communities from
the isolation that leads to dialectal drift. When young Ben
Franklin moved from Boston to Philadelphia, any peculiarity
in his speech, if it was noticed by his new neighbors at all,
must have quickly vanished. Colonial English was noted for
a remarkable uniformity that existed despite the distance
that separated New Hampshire from Georgia. There were, of
course, some dialectal variations. Ben Franklin in *Poor Richard* (1739) remarked in a jocular paragraph on eclipses that:

> Mercury will have his share in these Affairs, and so con-
> found the Speech of People, that when a Pensilvanian
> would say PANTHER, he shall say PAINTER. When a
> New-Yorker thinks to say (THIS) he shall say (DISS) and

the People in New-England and Cape-May will not be able to say (COW) for their lives, but will be forc'd to say (KEOW) by a certain involuntary Twist in the Root of their Tongues. . . . and there will be above seven and twenty irregular Verbs made this Year, if Grammar don't interpose. Who can help these Misfortunes!

Fifty years later Noah Webster observed in *Dissertations on the English Language*: "There is a vulgar singularity in the pronunciation of the eastern people which is very incorrect, and disagreeable to strangers; that of prefixing the sound of *i* short or *e*, before the diphthong *ow*; as *kiow*, *piower* or *peower*"; "Some of the southern people, particularly in Virginia, almost omit the sound of *r* as in *ware*, *there*"; "The pronunciation of *w* for *v* is a prevailing practice in England and America: It is particularly prevalent in Boston and Philadelphia. Many people say *weal*, *wessel*, for *veal*, *vessel*."

The Revolutionary War, an affliction suffered by both sides for seven years, left a bitter and abiding ill-will that came to be expressed, among other ways, in disdain for the other side's kind of English. Cause for ill-will was renewed by the War of 1812. The British burning of Washington was not an event of much consequence, but the fact was remembered by Americans beyond its deserving.

After the Revolution and the formation of the United States, speculative commentators on both sides of the Atlantic supposed that American and British English would drift apart: though obviously related, they would become mutually unintelligible, on the model of Dutch and German, or Danish and Norwegian. Some patriotic Americans peered longingly into the foggy future, anticipating the day when Americans would have their own language as they had their own country. Noah Webster expressed this view in 1789, in his *Dissertations on the English Language*: "As an independent nation, our honor requires us to have a system of our own, in language as well as government."

However, dialectal drift to the point of incomprehension did not occur. Such a point could be reached only with the breaking off of communication across the Atlantic, but mutually beneficial commercial and cultural communication has been steadily maintained. Through the nineteenth century most of the prestigious reading matter in English was still being published in London and read in America. The question Sydney Smith put in 1820, "Who reads an American book?" remained true enough for a while. In the twentieth century, however, communication has been accelerated and flows both ways. Plays written on either side of the Atlantic find simultaneous audiences in London and New York. Waugh is read in Michigan and Faulkner in Lancashire. Films and television provide means of mass intercommunication, so that even ephemeral slang is sometimes exchanged: many speakers of the common language are aware that a young woman is a "chick" in America but a "bird" in Britain.

Phonological differentiation.   In the course of the nineteenth and twentieth centuries a number of changes occurred in the English spoken on opposite sides of the Atlantic, leading to a readily noticeable dialectal divergence. Pronunciation features changed sufficiently to mark British and American as different dialects, though not to such a degree that intelligibility was seriously interfered with. British speech replaced the "flat a" with the "broad a," that is, retracted the tongue slightly from the position of /æ/ to that of /ɑ/, with the result that "last chance" came to be pronounced /lɑst čɑns/. American speakers did not make this shift and pronounce /læst čæns/ as Alexander Pope did. Physiologically the difference, though slight, is sufficient to place the vowels in phonemic contrast, as in the words *bond* and *band* (/bɑnd/, /bænd/), for example. Man as a conforming animal tends to react with annoyance when he hears an unfamiliar vowel in a certain environment. During World War II, when numberless copies of G. I. Joe had social encounters with British civilians, there were petty flare-ups over whether /dæns/ or /dɑns/ was "proper English." These variant vowels occur in many words that are frequently spoken in ordinary discourse and are consequently readily noticed in conversation. British speakers use

/ɑ/ in words ending in /ns/, as in *chance* and *dance*, although they have /æ/ in words ending in /nz/, like *pans* and *hands*. British /ɑ/ occurs before /nt/ in *can't* and *advantage*, before /nd/ in *command*, *demand*, when /s/ is final, as in *pass* and *glass*, and when /s/ is followed by /p/, /t/, or /k/, as in *grasp*, *last*, *ask*. It occurs in words like *path* and *bath*, that have /ə/ final, as well as in words with /f/ following, like *half* and *laugh*.

Another vowel difference that is readily sensed occurs in what is known as "short *o*," *o* before the voiceless stops /p/, /t/, /k/. Standard British retains the low, back, slightly rounded vowel /ɒ/ in words like *stop*, *hot*, and *stock*, whereas Standard American shifted to the low, mid vowel /ɑ/. By Standard British is meant the prestige dialect of Britain, the dialect of the "Establishment," of the "public schools" like Eton, of Oxford and Cambridge, and of the BBC. Geographically, this dialect has its origin in London and its environment, the "Home Counties"; socially, it is the dialect of the privileged class. The segregated poor in London have a quite different dialect, commonly known as "Cockney," and North Britons don't necessarily use the sound system of Standard British.

The treatment of the semi-vowel /r/ in final and preconsonantal positions is another prominent point of diversity between the dialects. Standard British is an *r*-less dialect: the *r*-curl, a raising of the tip of the tongue toward the alveolar ridge, does not occur except before vowels. The American dialects along the Atlantic seaboard, except for Middle Atlantic, are also *r*-less, but Standard American has the *r*-curl in all positions. The words *lord* and *laud* are homophones (/lɔd/) in British, but not in Standard American. In T. S. Eliot's lines in *The Waste Land*:

> O the moon shone bright on Mrs. Porter
> And on her daughter
> They wash their feet in soda water

Porter rhymes with *daughter* and *water* in Standard British

pronunciation. Standard British has a variety of /r/ when it
occurs between vowels that is called "flapped" *r*. The speaker
touches the tip of the tongue to the alveolar ridge in the manner of forming /d/. In recording this variety of British speech
very is written "veddy," *sorry*, "soddy," *American*, "Amed-
dican," *carry*, "keddy." Not all Standard British speakers use
this "flap," but it is heard often enough to be noticed.

Another consonantal difference that is readily sensed is the
tendency in the American dialect to voice /t/, making a lenis
/d/ of it, after a stressed vowel. Thus, *latter* and *ladder* are homophones (/lædɚ/), as are *traitor* and *trader* and *atom* and
Adam. In Standard British the /t/ remains unvoiced. This
may account for the observation sometimes made that British
English sounds "snippy." T. S. Eliot's lines in "The Love Song
of J. Alfred Prufrock," "That is not it at all, That is not what I
meant, at all." do indeed sound "snippier" with British fortis
/t/ than with the lenis American /d/.

Another pronunciation feature which is noticed with some
frequency is the British elision of the third syllable in four-
syllabled words ending in *-ary*, like *necessary*, which the British pronounce /nɛsəsrɬ/. So, too, with *military*, *secretary*, *dictionary*, and other words in this pattern. Some Americans say
/dɪkšənrɬ/, apparently thinking this the "better" or "correct"
pronunciation, without realizing that they are conforming to
a British practice. American practice normally puts a secondary stress on the third syllable: /díkšənèrɬ/.

Words ending in *-ile*—*futile*, *hostile*, *sterile*, *virile*, and others—end in /aɪl/ in British, but /əl/ in American. /aɪl/ is sometimes heard in American speech, because of uncertainty as to
which pronunciation is "correct."

A few words with an *-er* spelling vary between the dialects.
Clerk is pronounced /klɑk/ in Standard British, but /klɚk/ in
Standard American, and so with the names Derby and
Berkeley. The American pronunciation was probably affected
by respect for the spelling. Noah Webster wished that New
Englanders would stop saying *marcy* for *mercy*, and so they
did. Curiously, *sergeant* escaped a similar conformity to spell-
ing and is still /sɑɚǰɪnt/ in American speech.

In addition to these groups of words, some instances of divergent pronunciations of individual words occur. For example, British dialect pronounces *been* as "bean," the American, as "bin." The pronunciations /fɪgə/ and /ɛt/ for *figure* and *ate* are acceptable in the prestige dialect of British but are considered substandard by speakers of prestige American.

A subtle, not yet scientifically measured, difference between the dialects lies in what can be called the "music" of language. In this music, change in pitch is an important factor. Unlike tonal languages, like Chinese, pitch is not essential in conveying meaning in Indo-European. We can speak English sentences in a dead monotone and still be readily understood. Pitch variation is incidental in Indo-European, but it is also normal. English spoken without it sounds abnormal. It has often been observed that pitch variation occurs more frequently in British than in American, and the conclusion is then drawn that British speech is more "musical," and therefore pleasanter to the ear, than American, a relatively monotonous dialect. Another feature of linguistic music is rhythm and the speed of utterance. Americans who are not accustomed to the British dialect conclude that British speech is faster than their own, but such a conclusion is the result of mere unfamiliarity. A strange dialect, like a strange language, sounds fast. It is universal to believe that foreigners talk with astounding rapidity; it is incredible that they can understand one another. In fact, however, speaking speed varies with individuals, not with dialects or languages.

The stress patterning of foreign words varies occasionally between the dialects. The British are more prone to anglicize by stressing the first syllable of a two-syllable foreign word. Both dialects agree on /pǽrɪs/ for Paris (the Germans, incidentally, say /parís/), but only the British call Calais /kǽlɪs/ and Boulogne /búlən/. The British have long rhymed Seville with devil, as in Tennyson's line in "The Revenge": "Let us hang these dogs of Seville, the children of the Devil," and place primary stress on the first syllable in the French words *ballet, chateau, garage* /bǽle/, /šǽto/, /gɛ́ruž/. In time, American practice will probably agree with the British.

All in all, the phonological differences of British and American are sufficiently gross to identify either dialect immediately. No tourist in the other dialect's area can hope to conceal the fact of his origin for the duration of a sentence. But these differences are not important. It is a remarkable fact that standard English has minor variations in phonology but is universally understood. The schooled English speaker, whatever his origin, may travel anywhere with ease, understand what he hears, and have what he says understood. He may be eyed askance for a while in Alice Springs, or Cape Town, or Glasgow, but linguistically he is not really foreign among other schooled speakers of the common tongue. Speakers of nonstandard varieties of English are another matter. If an Alabama cotton picker, a Kentucky miner, a Maine lumberjack, a Cornish fisherman, a Glasgow shipyard hand, an Australian sheepherder, assuming all of them innocent of schooling, were thrown together, they would probably be equally confounded by the speech of all the others. But no schooled American listening to his television set can seriously say that he does not understand the voice of Sir Lawrence Olivier or that of the Prime Minister.

Vocabulary differences.   In the stock of words, the dialects vary more importantly than they do in phonology. Collections of words peculiar to either dialect can be impressively large, as H. L. Mencken intended them to be in his study, *The American Language.* But words gathered out of context and arrayed in clusters do not ordinarily occur frequently in spoken or written discourse. Conversations and books can go on for extended periods without a word turning up that is unfamiliar to a speaker of either dialect. Furthermore, the literate and linguistically sophisticated easily pick up new vocabulary items; no great effort is required to learn that *lift* means *elevator*, and that the *cinema* is a *movie* theater. British readers can grasp the sense of *foothills* and *canyon* from context and realize that *cookie* and *hot dog* are food items, even if the precise referent is not fully understood. The curious can, and do, resort to dictionaries.

A language has as many words as its speakers need. When words for objects new to experience are needed, speakers find them. English speakers in the New World needed words immediately to name the terrain features in their neighborhood and found it often convenient to adopt existing Indian names for such features, which accounts for the many American geographical names that are linguistically alien to English: Massachusetts, Michigan, Susquehanna, Rappahannock, Mississippi, Chicago, Watonga, and hundreds more. Flora and fauna new to European settlers were referred to by Indian names, often modified to suit European mouths: *potato*, *tomato*, *tobacco*, *squash*, *skunk*, *muskrat*.

Some American terrain terms were acquired from early French or Spanish settlers, terms like *bayou* and *levee* in Louisiana, or *prairie* to describe the Great Plains; in the Far West, Spanish contributed terms like *canyon* and *arroyo*. Americans began early to call a steep river bank a *bluff* and coined the odd word *gulch*. To the British reader or traveler, such words are initially mysterious and therefore annoying, but they can be learned.

Travelers in the other dialect area inevitably encounter differences in transportation terminology. Railroading was developed independently in Britain and America in the 1830s. No one foresaw a convenience in common terms, so consequently the terms differ. The American *engineer*, *conductor*, *freight train*, *cow catcher*, *tie* have British equivalents in *driver*, *guard*, *goods train*, *plough*, and *sleeper*. Independent development of the automobile around the turn of the twentieth century accounts for differences in terminology. American *hood*, *windshield*, *truck*, *gasoline* are British *bonnet*, *windscreen*, *lorry*, and *petrol*.

The millions of foreign speakers who settled in the United States contributed clusters of words from their languages to American English that remain alien to the British. German settlers were numerous and influential in American history before 1914. Cities like Cincinnati, "the American Rhineland," Chicago, Milwaukee, and St. Louis were outposts of German

Kultur. The prominence of German names in the brewing business attests to this, names like Pabst, Budweiser, Schlitz, Anheuser-Busch. The words *hinterland, kindergarten* (children's garden) and *delicatessen* (delicate eating) are in general use in American English, as are a number of food terms: *sauerkraut, pretzel, wurst, wiener, frankfurter, hamburger.* The proximity of Mexico accounts for a number of Spanish contributions to the American word list. After the Mexican War of the 1840s, "Anglos" swarmed into the Southwest, and there they found a flourishing cattle-raising industry that was equipped with a useful set of Spanish terms. The terms were taken over with the cattle: *ranch, rodeo, lariat* (from *la reata*), *corral.* Food terms were also borrowed such as *chili, tamale, frito, taco, enchilada.* Some Italian food terms are widely known: *chianti, spaghetti, lasagna, ravioli, pizza.*

After the Revolutionary War enough American print was scanned by British readers to notice words that were not current in British English. It grew fashionable to call such words Americanisms and to denounce them as provincial barbarisms. Thomas Jefferson was rebuked for using the verb *belittle* in his *Notes on the State of Virginia.* The poet Coleridge was disturbed by the word *talented,* and in the 1830s he and his fellow poet Southey attacked Americanisms with acerbity. Alarm was expressed that crude American neologisms would find their way into the English tongue and corrupt its purity. Lists of Americanisms were occasionally printed with the intention of warning those who aspired to gentility to avoid them. The adjectives *presidential* and *gubernatorial* were pointed to as examples of hideous coinage, as were terms like *reliable, influential* and *lengthy.* Attacks on American words continued well into the twentieth century. Woodrow Wilson's stay in Europe during the Versailles Peace Conference provided a fresh opportunity for attack. Wilson annoyed Clemenceau with his Fourteen Points, since even God had only ten, but he annoyed the British even more with his word choice. The London *Times* reported in 1927 that George Bernard Shaw remembered being shocked to hear Wilson use *obligate* in place of *oblige*. Shaw had gone on to say that a man could become president in spite of that, but never the king of England.

The brothers Fowler, H. W. and F. G., who were considered arbiters of good English at the turn of the century, wrote in *The King's English*: "Americanisms are foreign words, and should be so treated." The Fowlers recognized that the interchange of literature would lead to contamination. As they put it: "The English and the American language and literature are both good things; but they are better apart than mixed." They complained of Kipling that "he and his school are americanizing us" and remarked that "every one knows an Americanism, at present, when he sees it; how long that will be true is a more anxious question." They urged that "A very firm stand ought to be made against *placate*, *transpire*, and *antagonize*, all of which have English patrons." What the Fowlers feared has come to pass. Words fly freely in both directions across the ocean; what is new to one's practice is often attractive because of mere novelty and is borrowed inadvertently, without realizing its dialectal origin.

It was sometimes said in defense of Americanisms that some of them were not barbarous coinages but merely old-fashioned English. *Guess* in the sense of "suppose" ("I guess that's so") was thought of as crudely American until Chaucer's frequent use of "I gesse" was pointed out. The Fowlers, however, reminded their readers that what was good old English was not necessarily good new English and that a Britisher who currently used *guess* was not following Chaucer but the Yankees. The Fowlers conceded that *fall*, an American archaism, is preferable, with its homely Saxon clarity, to the British *autumn*, which is a Latin word. *Mad* in British is limited to the sense "insane," but in American can mean "angry," a sense used by Shakespeare. The verb form *gotten* dropped out of British English in the eighteenth century, but is preserved in the American dialect. These and a few other terms are not enough, however, to mark Standard American as notably archaic. Rural dialects in both countries have archaic features, like the Southern Mountain *holp* for *helped*, that are not found in the standard dialects of either country.

Spelling and grammar.   British and American differ slightly and unimportantly in some instances of spelling and grammar. Noah Webster, through his *American Spelling Book*, of which millions of copies were printed and religiously studied by generations of Americans who aspired to a blameless life, induced a number of useful spelling reforms that were generally accepted in American practice. Webster dropped the functionless *u* in words like *honour, labour, colour, favour*. The British stubbornly retain the *u*, sometimes acknowledging with wry wit that they would probably have dropped it on their own, had not the Americans done so first. Webster reduced the double consonant in *waggon* and *traveller* (*wagon, traveler*) and dropped the first *e* in *judgement*. He dropped the *u* in *mould*, the *e* in *axe*, preferred *s* to *c* in *offense, defense*, and spelled *-er* rather than *-re* in *theatre* and *centre*. Other reformed spellings urged by Webster, such as dropping unnecessary letters in words like *give, have, head* (*giv, hav, hed*) were not adopted, and, indeed, aroused resistance not only in Britain but also at home. Reformed spellings, however sweetly reasonable and advantageous they may be, meet emotional resistance among the literate. The traditional forms of the written language are apparently felt to be sacred; to change them is to desecrate a shrine.

American practice has lopped off the silent symbols *-ue* in *catalogue* and *-me* in *programme*, symbols the British prefer to retain. The British spell *tyre* (noun), *kerb* (noun), *plough*, and *storey* (floor) for the American *tire, curb, plow, story*. Editions of books printed for sale on the other side of the ocean sometimes adjust the dialect spellings to avoid offending the sensibilities of paying customers, but growing toleration of variants will probably make this practice unnecessary. Americans often see and appear not to mind the *u* in *saviour* and *glamour*, and commercial enterprises sometimes use *theatre* and *centre* in titles, presumably with an eye to elegance. British publishing practice now and then adopts an American spelling, and ultimately the number of variants that need to be tolerated will diminish to a barely noticeable level.

In points of grammar, differences between British and American usage are neither numerous nor obstacles to comprehension. The *shall-will* system is British. Dialogue like "Shall you play tennis today?" "I should like to." is at once perceived by an American to be strange to his practice. Non-obligational first person *should* occurs not infrequently in American business correspondence: "I should be pleased to hear from you," but probably few who write such sentences are aware that they are using an un-American idiom.

In British English, collective nouns are plural: "Parliament are sitting"; "The government are considering a reply"; "The audience are aware of what will happen"; "The crew are dissatisfied"; "The team are determined to do their best." According to Winston Churchill, "Politics are almost as exciting as war." American usage requires singular verbs with these nouns.

The American use of *gotten* as a past participle has long struck the British as a curiosity. The American idiom has both *got* and *gotten*, sometimes with differences of meaning. "I've got a job" and "I've gotten a job" are not the same thing, the difference lying in the time of possessing or acquiring. This subtlety sometimes eludes British fiction writers when they invent an American who says, "Have you gotten a match?"

In British English the use of *woken* as the past participle of *wake* is frequent, but it is rare, if not unknown, to American speakers.

The two major dialects of English today are the British and the American. Canadian English is a variety of American because of Canada's proximity to the United States and the strong influence on Canadians of the powerful polity to the south of them. South African and Australian English are minor dialects. Until recently there was no doubt that standard English from the international point of view was the British variety. European schools taught British to their pupils, and still do, both as a matter of custom and because of the prox-

imity of Britain to Europe. But it is no longer possible to re-
gard American English as a provincial and inferior variety of
the language, and disdain for the other dialect is now seldom
exchanged across the Atlantic. The British have assumed a
modest posture, and Americans feel they can afford to be
magnanimous. Linguistic authority, like other kinds, is conferred by power; schools in Europe and the Orient are beginning to attend to some of the peculiarities of the American
idiom, which is achieving the preeminence that John Adams
foresaw two hundred years ago, when, in proposing an academy to standardize American English, he wrote: "England
will never more have any honor, excepting now and then that
of imitating the Americans. . . . The population and commerce of America will force their language into general use."
This was brave talk in 1780, but is now not far from the fact.

Regional dialects of the United States.   American English
retains today the relative uniformity that elicited wonder in
the colonial period. The United States, like any large landmass, is divided into regions, each of which has some dialectal peculiarities. These peculiarities, however, are not so
pronounced that they inhibit ready understanding among
Americans from different regions. This uniformity is accounted for in various ways: for one thing, English has been spoken
in America for less than four hundred years, too short a span
for sharply differentiated dialects to develop without severe
isolation from one another. In Britain, regional dialects have
had 1,500 years to evolve in the quiet of rural isolation. The
mobility that has always been characteristic of Americans
is also cited as a factor in rubbing off dialectal corners. Another influence tending toward standardization is concern for
schooling and the ideal of universal literacy. The itinerant
Yankee school teacher was a conspicuous figure on the nineteenth-century scene. He was not very well paid, and he may
have been at times a bit ridiculous, but he was there. The unschooled are still found in America but, outside of northern
Europe, exist in smaller numbers than one finds in most parts
of the world. The written language is inevitably a standard-

ized form, and speakers who learn to read are inevitably affected by it. Audible communication on a national level—since 1920 with radio, and later in the form of talking motion pictures and television—may help to standardize the spoken language even further than is at present true.

The uniformity of American English is relative, not absolute. Everyone speaks a regional dialect, the dialect he learned to speak as a child, although this dialect may be "contaminated" if he moves into another region. Families that move some distance from home are sometimes distressed to hear the children quickly assume features of the new dialect. Furthermore, everyone has individual speech characteristics. We realize this when we observe our ability to recognize friends' voices over the telephone. There is, however, a standard American dialect. A term for this dialect is General American, a term that is not entirely satisfactory, but, since no better one has been devised, it can be said to serve. General American covers about two-thirds of the area of the United States and is spoken by more than two-thirds of the population. It is found north of the Ohio River and reaches from west of Pittsburgh to the Pacific Coast. Another, not unapt, term for standard American is "network English." This is the dialect, with minor, generally unnoticed, variations, that is heard on the national radio and television networks and in the theater and motion pictures. Unlike Britain, France, and Spain, where the standard dialect is determined by the capital city of the country—London, Paris, or Madrid—the United States does not observe a standard set by Washington, D.C. Our national capital is a polydialectal area, since politicians like Presidents Kennedy, Johnson, and Carter, for example, bring their "accents" with them. But most speakers who are attracted to the political power center arrive with General American and leave with their dialect intact. Before the Civil War, the urban seaports—Boston, New York, Philadelphia, and Charleston—enjoyed commercial, cultural, and some degree of dialectal superiority, but after 1870 the weight of population and industry shifted to the North Central states, to Ohio and the states west of it. Consequently, the Atlantic sea-

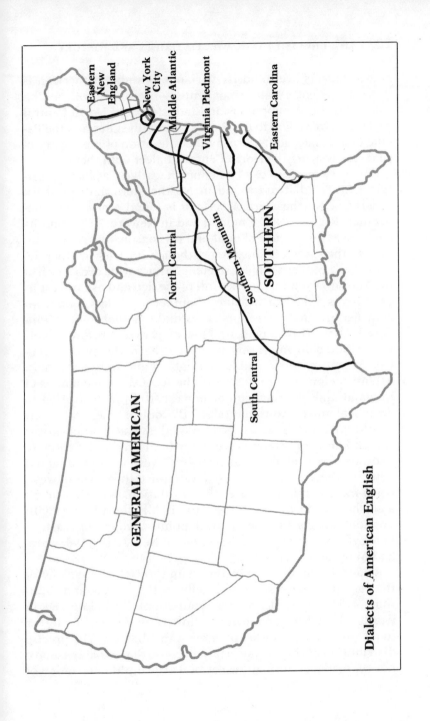

Dialects of American English

board dialects are minority variants. Standard American is determined not by an urban center—not by Detroit or Chicago—but by the populous and industrialized North Central region. Its extension to the Rocky Mountain states and the Pacific Coast is accounted for by the migration of a majority of speakers bearing the North Central dialect with them.

General American can be defined negatively as lacking certain features that are found in Northeastern and Southern American. Northeastern American is found east of the Connecticut River in New England and in New York City and its environs. The absence of final and preconsonantal /r/ is common to the speech of this area, although it varies in other details. The Southern dialect stretches over a wide area south of the Mason-Dixon line to the Gulf of Mexico and as far west as East Texas. Like Northeastern, Southern is "*r*-less," a prominent feature that these American dialects share with Standard British. This coincidental loss of /r/ except before vowels is attributed to migration patterns: the majority of seventeenth-century settlers in New England and in the Southern Atlantic colonies migrated from the southeastern counties of England and like their kin at home had a predisposition to drop final and preconsonantal /r/. By contrast, General American retains the /r/ in all positions; this is attributed to the speech habits of migrants from northern England, Scotland, and northern Ireland, who settled in western New England and elsewhere in the colonies and supplied the waves of westward-moving migrants after the Revolution. One Atlantic dialect has /r/ in all positions. This is Middle Atlantic, with Philadelphia as an urban focal point, comprising eastern Pennsylvania and adjoining sections of New Jersey, Delaware, and Maryland.

Aside from final and preconsonantal /r/, the phonology of the regional dialects varies chiefly in the vowels and diphthongs. The incidence of the semi-vowel /h/ before /w/ in words like *where* and *which*—/hwɛɚ/ or /wɛɚ/, /hwɪč/ or /wɪč/—is found sporadically among the dialects. The precise distribution of /hw/ is uncertain because dialectologists have not yet made a thorough survey of it. The diphthongization of

/u/ as /ɪu/ in words like *news*, *Tuesday*, *duke*—/nɪuz/, /tɪuzdɫ/, /dɪuk/ as against /nuz/, /tuzdɫ/, /duk/—is also sporadic. /ɪu/ is general in the Southern dialect, but it is heard also in General American speech. Those who feel concern for good English sometimes argue heatedly over /hw/ and /ɪu/, or whether *either* is to be pronounced /iðɚ/ or /aɪðɚ/, or whether *advertisement* should be stressed on the second syllable or the third. These variations are regional ones, not a matter of the level of cultivation of the speaker. Northeastern and Southern are not "standard" American because their speakers are outnumbered by the speakers of General American, but there is nothing "wrong" with minor pronunciation or vocabulary variants in the practice of equally cultivated speakers. A general toleration of such variants would make interdialectal social encounters more agreeable.

Visitors to large cities in various regions may be surprised to observe that regional characteristics are not necessarily heard. Not everyone who is encountered in Boston or New York City speaks Northeastern, and what is heard in New Orleans is not Southern in every detail. A metropolis, of course, attracts migrants from other regions, who bring their dialects with them. Regional dialects are best observed in small towns that have least traffic with "outsiders" and in the speech of its least educated residents. Schooled, traveled, cultivated, sophisticated speakers in every region tend to conform largely, if not entirely, to the detail of standard American; the speech of the unschooled, lifelong resident of an isolated village will exhibit the greatest deviance from that standard.

Eastern New England. This dialect coincides in some phonological detail with Standard British: /ɑ/ in words like *last*, /ɒ/ before /p/, /t/, /k/, and in *r*-lessness: President Kennedy in 1960 urged citizens to "move forward with vigor" (/muv fɔwəd wɪð vɪgə/). In this dialect an intrusive /r/ occurs between vowels: Cuba in "Cuba is an island" becomes /kɪubɚ/; when Ralph Waldo Emerson married Lydia Jackson she became Lydier Emerson, a change that displeased the lady enough to induce her to inform her acquaintances that her name was Lydian. The vowel /ʊ/ in *room*, *broom* is not uncommonly heard in this dialect.

New York City.   The dialect of New York City and its environs shares the *r*-lessness of Eastern New England, but does not use /ɑ/ in words of the *last* group, nor /ɒ/ in *top*, *pot*, *stock*. The sound /ɝ/, as in *early* /ɝlɨ/ is replaced by /ʌɪ/—/ʌɪlɨ/, a sound conventionally represented in roman characters by *oi*: "De oily boid gets de woim." /ɔɪ/ is replaced by /ʒ/: *join* is /jʒn/. Fiction writers representing the dialect spell *join* "jern," but there is, of course, no *r*-curl. These vowel and diphthong variants are not always heard in the speech of native New Yorkers who have a college education or its equivalent in social and linguistic experience, but they are common enough in what dialectologists call "folk-speech," the language of the uneducated. Outsiders find these New York sounds interesting, as when the North Carolina novelist Thomas Wolfe, in "Only the Dead Know Brooklyn," recorded "Bensonhoist" and "Greenpernt" as the names of sections of Brooklyn and cited foreignized /d/ and /t/ for /ð/ and /θ/: "Dere's no guy livin' dat knows Brooklyn t'roo an' t'roo." Another foreignized sound, associated with Yiddish speakers, is intrusive /g/ in "Long Island" /lɔngaɪlənd/. Another folk-speech phenomenon is the replacing of /t/ by the glottal stop /ʔ/ before /l/, as in *little bottle* /lɪʔəl baʔəl/. /a/ rather than /ɔ/ is heard in words like *orange*, *forest*, *fog* (though not in *dog*). The /a/, /ɔ/ alternation is rather sporadically distributed, incidentally. /skɔč ɔn ðə rɔks/ in Pittsburgh is /skač ɑn ðə rɑks/ in Cleveland and Detroit.

Middle Atlantic.   The dialect of Philadelphia, eastern Pennsylvania, southern New Jersey, Delaware, and northern Maryland differs little from General American. /r/ is heard in all positions. /ɪu/ occurs in *new*, *due*, /u/ in *roof*, and there is some tendency to vary between /ɔɝ/ and /oɝ/ in words like *board*.

Southern.   Southern American covers so large an area, from

Virginia to Florida and west to East Texas, that several sub-dialectal variations have been observed. Eastern Virginia and coastal Carolina have some distinctive phonological details, notably the diphthong /ʌu/ before voiceless consonants, as in *out*, *house*, and *south*—/ʌut/, /hʌus/, /sʌuθ/. (This diphthong is also heard, coincidentally, in the speech of Ontario.) Before voiced stops, like /d/, /au/ is used—/laud/. Sophisticated residents of Charleston find it amusing that in their dialect "Wretched" is a boy's name.

Southern Mountain extends through the Appalachian-Ozark range, from Kentucky to Arkansas. The dialect has long been used as a source of humor by cartoonists as a substandard variety of English spoken by shoeless consumers of homemade whisky, illiterate but not ill-natured. The diphthong /æu/ replaces /au/ in words like *out loud*—/æut læud/. The higher tense vowel /e/ is heard in place of /æ/ in *can't*—/kent/. This word is transcribed *cain't* by fiction writers to rhyme with *ain't* and *paint*. The second-person plural pronoun *you uns* (you ones) is general in this dialect and in unstressed position is pronounced /jʌns/ in some areas of the Ozarks. Archaic forms like *holp* for *helped*, *hit* for *it* and *axed* for *asked* have long been noted by observers, who sometimes conclude that dwellers in isolated valleys speak "Elizabethan English." Southern Mountain features are heard north of the Ohio River in the coalfields of southern Ohio, Indiana, and Illinois, brought by job-seeking migrants from across the river.

The Southern dialect is generally *r*-less, although some speakers in this broad area have /r/ in final and preconsonantal positions. Another prominent feature of the dialect is the tendency not to complete the diphthong /aɪ/, the speaker failing to bring the mandible up to the high, front position of the off-glide /ɪ/. Some speakers produce a mid-central off-glide /aə/, but in the speech of others only the monophthong /a/ is heard. Fiction writing that records the dialect transcribes the pronoun *I* as *ah*. There is a tendency to monophthongize the diphthong /ɔɪ/ to /ɔ/, making *oil* a homophone with *all* and *boil* with *ball*. The tendency to monophthongize diphthongs might seem economic and sensible, but, by contrast, Southern speakers tend to diphthongize front vowels, as in *paper* and *class*—peɪpə/, /klæɪs/.

Southern has voiced /z/ in *grease*, *greasy*, and *hussy*, whereas General American has /s/. Consonant clusters are sometimes reduced, as when /l/ is elided before /p/ in *help*—/hɛp/.

One of the most widely noted features of Southern is the second-person plural form *you all* (pronounced /jɔl/ in unstressed position). This useful form, distinguishing the plural from the singular *you*, is accepted on all social levels in the South, unlike the form *yous*, which is considered substandard in those regions where it is heard. It could be argued that *you all* should be universally adopted by English speakers to fill a dire need for a distinctive plural pronoun, but as yet speakers outside the Southern area are showing no inclination to use it.

The South Central states—Oklahoma, Texas, and Arkansas—share some features of Southern, but not all. *You all* is in common employment, but /r/ is generally heard in all positions. It is a cliché in "Western" fiction that cowboys call a horse a *hoss*, but the r-curl in /hɔɚs/ or /hoɚs/ is not uncommon. Monophthongized /aɪ/ and /ɔɪ/ as /ɑ/ and /ɔ/ are heard in this area, as is the assimilation of /ɛ/ to /ɪ/ before /n/, pronouncing *pen* as /pɪn/ and *ten cents* as /tɪn sɪns/. A dissimilated /æ/ in place of /ɪ/ before /ŋ/, pronouncing *thing* as /θæŋ/ is also sometimes heard. These last two vowel features have been observed as far east as Georgia, but their precise distribution is uncertain. The collection of dialect data is tedious and expensive, and much still needs to be learned.

General American can be defined as the dialect that lacks the features that define Northeastern and Southern. General American has /æ/ in *last*, /r/ in all positions, /aɪ/ and /ɔɪ/ with a definite high, front off-glide, /ɛ/ in *pen*, /ɪ/ in *thing*, and does not employ *you all* or *you uns*.

Aside from the phonological and morphological data cited, regional dialects vary somewhat in vocabulary. A "soft drink" is a "tonic" in Boston, a baby carriage is a baby coach in Philadelphia, people tell time variously as a quarter till, to, or of ten, they live in or on a street, they use various calls to hogs or chickens, they say pail or bucket, and frying pan, skillet, or spider, and an infant either crawls or creeps, depending on the region. These variations may momentarily startle a traveler, but they are no serious hindrance to communication.

One feature of American English that was not anticipated is that, apart from vocabulary, foreign influence is not discernible. It sometimes occurred to British observers in the nineteenth century that American English would eventually diverge significantly from the British variety because so many Americans were of some linguistic stock other than English. But no such effect took place. Certainly, foreign speech habits had no effect on native English pronunciation. The "broken English" of immigrants was mimicked for purposes of humor, but would hardly be imitated seriously, even subconsciously. The numbers and prestige of the established, native English-speaking community protect its language from phonological "mixing." So, too, with syntactic structures. Foreign patterns translated into English are perceived as unidiomatic. Examples turn up in print for humor's sake, like the Pennsylvania Dutch "The butter is all," the Swedish "cook coffee," or the urban Yiddishisms: "Drop dead yet," "You should live so long," or "So all right already," but such patterns are not incorporated into the native system.

Thus, a limited number of vocabulary items aside, the American whirlpool has swallowed many foreign languages without being affected by them. The process is still going on, inexorably working and inevitably to end in a society that is monolingual in English. Children born to foreign parents who share streets and playgrounds with English-speaking children learn perfect English from their peers. They instinctively know better than to imitate the imperfect English of their parents. In large, mixed communities the third generation prefers to know nothing of the grandparents' Polish, Hungarian, or Italian. Foreign languages survive longer in communities that successfully maintain isolation from the American mainstream, like the prosperous Pennsylvania Dutch farming area, the Cajun French area in Louisiana, or the French communities in New England along the Canadian border. Compulsory schooling, the attraction of television, the lure of the automobile and the freeway are making isolation improbable and are assimilating the non-English rivals of the dominant tongue. The presence of large numbers of recent Spanish-speaking migrants from Mexico, Cuba, and Puerto Rico provides a current social problem, but it is not likely that California, Miami, and New York will become effectively bilingual on the pattern of Quebec or Belgium, where only the intense chauvinism of the French or Flemish will maintain a bilingualism that is a severe inconvenience.

Regional and social variations, however, can be expected to survive throughout the English-speaking world despite forced schooling, mobility, and electronic communication. British, South African, Australian, and American will always be a little different, and some regional variants will always exist in the United States, as will nonstandard features like *knowed* and *blowed*, *seen* and *done* as preterits, and *went* as a past participle. Man is a conforming animal, but is never perfectly so.

NOTES AND BIBLIOGRAPHY

Krapp, George P. *The English Language in America*. 2 vols. New York, 1925. John Adams' opinions are found in a letter to Edmund Jenings, Sept. 30, 1780, that is cited in volume 1, page 7, of this work. It also contains a good deal of detail that is not at all obsolete.

Mencken, H. L. *The American Language*. 4th ed., New York: Alfred A. Knopf, 1946. Like everything of Mencken's, this book is lively and stimulating. It is the result of the author's lifelong interest in language. The title, and the thesis that "American" is not "English," stem from Mencken's Anglophobia, one of the prejudices he was pleased to entertain.

For American dialect study, the *Linguistic Atlas* has produced three significant volumes, all published by the University of Michigan Press at Ann Arbor: Hans Kurath, *A Word Geography of the Eastern United States*, 1949; E. Bagby Atwood, *A Survey of Verb Forms in the Eastern United States*, 1953; Hans Kurath and Raven I. McDavid, Jr., *The Pronunciation of English in the Atlantic States*, 1961.

The notable journal *American Speech*, a quarterly, includes dialect material. It is published by the University of Alabama Press under the sponsorship of the American Dialect Society.

The American Dialect Society publishes monographs through the University of Alabama Press on a variety of dialect topics at irregular intervals.

Select Bibliography

Abbott, Edwin A. *A Shakespearian Grammar*. London: Macmillan and Co., 1929.

Atwood, Elmer B. *A Survey of Verb Forms in the Eastern United States*. Ann Arbor: University of Michigan Press, 1953.

Baugh, Albert C. and Cable, Thomas. *A History of the English Language*. 3d ed. Englewood Cliffs, N.J.: Prentice-Hall, 1978.

Blair, Peter Hunter. *An Introduction to Anglo-Saxon England*. Cambridge: At the University Press, 1966.

Bloomfield, Leonard. *Language*. New York: Henry Holt, 1933.

Brunner, Karl. *Altenglische Grammatik, nach der angelsächsischen Grammatik von Eduard Sievers*. 3d ed. Tübingen, 1965.

Campbell, Alistair. *Old English Grammar*. Oxford: At the University Press, 1959.

Campbell, George. *The Philosophy of Rhetoric*. Edited by L. F. Bitzer. Carbondale: Southern Illinois University Press, 1963.

Curme, George O. *Syntax*. Boston: D. C. Heath, 1931.

Ekwall, Eilert. *Concise Oxford Dictionary of English Place Names*. 4th ed. Oxford: At the University Press, 1960.

Fowler, Henry W. and F. G. *The King's English*. 3d ed. Oxford, 1931.

Franz, Wilhelm. *Shakespeare-Grammatik.* 4th ed. Halle/ Saale: Max Niemeyer Verlag, 1939.

Fries, Charles C. *The Structure of English.* New York: Harcourt, Brace and Co., 1952.

———. *American English Grammar.* National Council of Teachers of English, English Monograph Series, no. 10. New York and London: Appleton-Century-Crofts, 1940.

Hockett, Charles F. *A Course in Modern Linguistics.* New York: Macmillan Co., 1958.

Hulbert, James R. *Dictionaries, British and American.* Revised ed. London: Deutsch, 1968.

Jespersen, Otto. *Growth and Structure of the English Language.* 9th ed. Oxford: Basil Blackwell, 1948.

———. *A Modern English Grammar on Historical Principles.* 7 vols. Heidelberg and Copenhagen, 1909–1949.

Jones, Richard F. *The Triumph of the English Language.* Stanford, Calif: Stanford University Press, 1953.

Jonson, Ben. *The English Grammar.* Vol. 8. Edited by C. H. Herford, et al. 11 vols. Oxford: At the University Press, 1925–1952.

Kenyon, John S. *American Pronunciation.* 10th ed. Ann Arbor, Mich.: George Wahr, 1951.

Krapp, George P. *The English Language in America.* 2 vols. New York, 1925.

Kökeritz, Helge. *Shakespeare's Pronunciation.* New Haven: Yale University Press, 1953.

Kurath, Hans. *A Word Geography of the Eastern United States.* Ann Arbor: University of Michigan Press, 1949.

——— and McDavid, Raven I., Jr. *The Pronunciation of English in the Atlantic States.* Ann Arbor: University of Michigan Press, 1961.

Leonard, Sterling A. *The Doctrine of Correctness in English Usage, 1700–1800.* University of Wisconsin Studies in Language and Literature, no. 25. Madison: University of Wisconsin Press, 1929.

McKnight, George H. *English Words and their Background.* New York and London: D. Appleton-Century Co., 1923.

Mencken, Henry L. *The American Language*. 4th ed. New York: Alfred A. Knopf, 1946.

Middle English Dictionary. Edited by H. Kurath, S. M. Kuhn, and J. Reidy. Ann Arbor: University of Michigan Press, 1952–.

Moore, Samuel. *Historical Outlines of English Sounds and Inflections*. Revised by Albert H. Marckwardt. Ann Arbor: University of Michigan Press, 1951.

Onions, Charles T. *A Shakespeare Glossary*. Oxford, 1911.

Partridge, A. C. *The Accidence of Ben Jonson's Plays, Masques, and Entertainments*. Cambridge: Bowes and Bowes, 1953.

Partridge, Eric. *Slang Today and Yesterday*. 3d ed. New York: Macmillan Co., 1950.

Pyles, Thomas. *The Origins and Development of the English Language*. 2d ed. New York: Harcourt Brace Jovanovich, 1971.

————. *Words and Ways of American English*. New York: Random House, 1952.

Serjeantson, Mary S. *A History of Foreign Words in English*. London, 1935.

Starnes, D. W. T. and Noyes, Gertrude E. *The English Dictionary from Cawdrey to Johnson*. Chapel Hill: University of North Carolina Press, 1946.

Sturtevant, E. H. *Linguistic Change*. New York: G. E. Stechert, 1942.

Thomas, Charles K. *An Introduction to the Phonetics of American English*. 2d ed. New York: Ronald Press, 1958.

Warfel, Harry R. *Noah Webster, Schoolmaster to America*. New York, 1936.

Williams, Joseph M. *Origins of the English Language*. New York: Free Press, 1975.

Wyld, Henry C. *A History of Modern Colloquial English*. London: T. Fisher Unwin, 1920.

Zandvoort, Reinard W. *A Handbook of English Grammar*. 3d ed. Englewood Cliffs, N.J.: Prentice-Hall, 1966.

Index

Abbott, E. A.: 159
Accademia della Crusca: 169, 189
Accidence of Ben Jonson's Plays, Masques and Entertainments, The: 156
Accusative case: 62
Adams, John: 219
Addison, Joseph: 155, 171–72
Adjective: 64–65
AElfric: 85
Aeolic: 23
Africa: 133
Afrikaans: 30
Agricola: 57
Albanian: 23
Alcuin: 59
Alfred, King: 31, 84
American Language, The: 213
Anatolian: 20
Andersen, Hans Christian: 30
Angles: 28, 58

Anglic spelling: 54
Anglicizing: 108–10
Anglo-Norman: 98, 107–108
Anglo-Saxon: 30
Anglo-Saxon Chronicle: 57
Antony and Cleopatra: 174
Arabic: 4, 22
Arcadian-Cyprian: 23
Armenian: 22
Arnold, Matthew: 22
Article, definite: 65
Aryan: 17
Ascham, Roger: 138, 142
Ash, John: 170
Aspiration: 41, 43
Assimilation: 52
Attic: 23
Avestan: 21–22

Bacon, Sir Francis: 5
Bailey, Nathaniel: 144, 187
Baker, Robert: 171
Baltic: 14, 25
Balto-Slavonic: 24
Bantu: 4

Barbour, John: 122
Barnes, William: 127
Barzun, Jacques: 186
Basque: 35
Baugh, Albert C.: 104
Bayley, Anselm: 196
Bengali: 21
Beowulf: 59–60, 99
Biglow Papers, The: 195–96
Black Death: 97
Bloomfield, Leonard: 43
Blount, Thomas: 139, 144
Boswell, James: 188, 190, 193
Breton: 26, 27
Britannic Celtic: 26
British dialect: 45, 50
Browning, Robert: 134
Bruce, The: 122
Buchanan, James: 194
Bulgarian: 26
Bullokar, John: 146
Bullokar, William: 144
Burns, Robert: 90, 127
Byzantine empire: 21, 23

"Cajun": 24, 227
Campbell, George: 171, 176, 181–83
Canadian English: 218
Canadian French: 24
Canterbury Tales: 62, 101, 176
Cawdrey, Robert: 144
Caxton, William: 146
Celtic: 26
Central French: 97, 107–108
Centum-satem: 34
Chaucer, Geoffrey: 62, 98, 111, 119, 176

Cheke, Sir John: 135, 138, 146
Chesterfield, Earl of: 189
Chinese: 4
Churchill, Winston: 174, 186
Clarke, John: 172
Cockeram, Henry: 144
Coleridge, Samuel Taylor: 198, 215
Collection of the History of England, The: 153
Cornish: 27
Croat: 26
Curme, George O.: 155, 173
Czecho-Slovak: 25

Daniel, Samuel: 138, 153
Danish: 4, 29
Dante Alighieri: 119, 133
Defence of Rhyme: 138
Deffence et Illustration de la Langue Francoyse: 133
Defoe, Daniel: 139
Deutsche Grammatik: 33
De Vulgari Eloquentia: 119
Dialects, American: 219–28
Dictionaries, early: 143–44
Dissertations on the English Language: 172, 208
Divine Comedy, The: 133
Doric: 23
Dramatic Poetry of the Last Age, The: 163
Dravidian: 21
Dryden, John: 139, 162–64, 172–73
Du Bellay, Joachim: 133
Dubliners: 185
Dutch: 31, 207

Easiest Introduction to Dr. Lowth's English Grammar, The: 170
Eastern Carolina dialect: 47
Eastern New England dialect: 45, 223–24
Eastern Virginia dialect: 47
East Greek: 23
East Midland dialect: 119
Eliot, Thomas S.: 210–11
Elphinston, James: 194
Elyot, Sir Thomas: 138
English Dictionarie: 144
English Expositor, An: 144
English Grammar: 171
English Grammar, The: 153, 156, 178, 182
Erasmus: 5
Essay of Dramatic Poesy, An: 163
Essay on Projects, An: 139
Estonian: 35
Etruscan: 24

Fielding, Henry: 127
Finnish: 35
Finno-Ugric: 14
First Part of the Elementarie, The: 146
Flemish: 30
Fowler, H. W., and F. G.: 179–80, 216
Frankish: 59
Franklin, Ben: 207–208
Franz, Wilhelm: 151–52, 159
Frederick the Great: 5
French: 4, 6, 30
French Academy, The: 166, 169

Frisian: 30, 31
Fuller, Thomas: 137

Gaelic: 27
Galsworthy, John: 173
Garrick, David: 187
Gaulish: 26
General American dialect: 50, 222–23
German: 4, 6, 25, 51
Germania: 28
Germanic: 28, 33
Glides: 49
Glossographia: 144
Goropius Becanus: 29
Gothic: 28
Governour, The: 138
Grammatica Linguae Anglicanae: 178
Gray, Thomas: 176
Great Russian: 25
Great Vowel Shift: 148–51
Greek: 4, 23, 51
Grimm, Jacob: 32, 33
Growth and Structure of the English Language: 141
Gypsies: 21

Hamlet: 140, 152, 158
Hart, John: 146
Hebrew: 16
High West Germanic: 30
Hindi: 4, 49
History of the English Language, A: 104
Hittite: 20
Hochdeutsch: 30
Holofernes: 140, 145
Horace: 170
Housman, A. E.: 110

Humber, River: 58, 112
Hundred Years' War: 97, 132

Iberians: 26
Ibsen, Henryk: 30
Icelandic: 29
Indian: 20, 21
Indo-European: 15, 20, 32
International Phonetic Alphabet (IPA): 44
Ionian: 23
Iranian: 21
Ireland: 27
Irish: 27
Italian: 4
Italic: 24

Jefferson, Thomas: 215
Jesperson, Otto: 141, 152, 155, 180
John of Trevisa: 97
Johnson, Samuel: 35, 53, 144, 169–70, 193
Johnson's *Dictionary*: 170, 197–92
Jonson, Ben: 50, 135, 137, 139, 153, 156, 163–64, 178, 182
Joseph Andrews: 127
Joyce, James: 27, 185
Julius Caesar: 156
Jutes: 28, 58

Kalidasa: 21
Kenrick, William: 194, 196
Kentish dialect: 120
King James Bible: 151, 157, 172
King Lear: 127, 141, 152, 156

King's English, The: 179
Krim-Gothic: 29

Language: 43
Larynx: 40
Latin: 5, 15, 24
Lawman's *Brut*: 98
Lettish: 25
Lithuanian: 25
Little Russian: 25
Love's Labour's Lost: 140, 145
Love Song of J. Alfred Prufrock, The: 211
Lowell, James Russell: 195–96
Low German: 30
Lowth, Robert: 170–78, 187
Low West Germanic: 31

MacArthur, General Douglas: 177
Mahratti: 21
Malayalam: 21
Manx: 27
Marlowe, Christopher: 141
Marston, John: 135
Measure for Measure: 141
Mencken, Henry L.: 213
Merchant of Venice, The: 152, 186
Middle Atlantic dialect: 224
Middle English: 46, 92
Midland dialect: 124
Miller's Tale, The: 99
Milton, John: 5, 139, 174
Modern English Grammar, A: 152
Modern High German: 61
More, Sir Thomas: 5

Morphological change: 114–18, 151–54
Mulcaster, Richard: 134, 146
Murray, Lindley: 171, 176

New words: 200–201
New World of English Words, The: 144
New York City dialect: 224
Nominative case: 62
Norman Conquest: 93–96
Normandy: 94, 96
Norman French: 98
Northeast Midland dialect: 128
Northern British dialect: 119, 121–22
North Germanic: 29
Norwegian: 29
Notes on the State of Virginia: 215

Ode to the West Wind: 174
Old Church Bulgarian: 26
Old English: 30, 31, 46, 56
Old Frisian: 30
Old Low Franconian: 30
Old Norse: 49
Old Saxon: 30
Omar Khayyam: 22
Orthoëpy: 192–96
Orthographie, An: 146
Oscan: 24
Overseas words: 142–43
Owl and the Nightingale, The: 98

Partridge, A. C.: 156
Petrarch: 133
Phillips, Edward: 144

Philosophy of Rhetoric, The: 171
Phoneme: 42
Phonological change: 147–51, 209–13
Plattdeutsch: 30, 31
Pocket Dictionary, A: 178
Poetaster, The: 156
Polish: 25
Pope, Alexander: 171–72, 196
Portuguese: 4, 24
Prakrits: 21
Priestley, Joseph: 170, 181
Prior, Matthew: 174
Pronoun, personal: 66–71
Pronouncing Dictionary, A: 194
Proposal for Correcting, Improving and Ascertaining the English Tongue, A: 165
Proto-Germanic: 31, 32
Prussian: 25
Punjabi: 21
Pygmalion: 185

Quintilian: 170

Ramayana: 20
Rape of the Lock, The: 196
Reeve's Tale, The: 122
Reflections on the English Language: 171
Rime of the Ancient Mariner, The: 198
Roman alphabet: 43, 44
Romansch: 24
Rudiments of English Grammar, The: 170
Russian: 4, 6, 25, 201

Sabines: 24
Sakuntala: 21
Sanskrit: 15, 21, 25, 34
Saxons: 28
School for Scandal: 172
Scots: 27, 57
Scots English: 50, 51
Scott, Sir Walter: 90, 104
Semantic change: 196–200
Semitic: 14
Semi-vowels: 49
Serbo-Croat: 26
Shahnamah: 22
Shakespeare, William: 39, 140, 156, 174   186
Shakespeare-Grammatik: 151–52, 159
Shall-Will: 177–81
Shaw, George Bernard: 27, 185, 215–16
Shelley, Percy B.: 174
Shepherd's Calendar, The: 136
Sheridan, Richard B.: 172
Sheridan, Thomas: 194
Short Introduction or guiding to print, write and reade Inglish Speech: 146
Short Introduction to English Grammar, A: 170, 187
Sidney, Sir Phillip: 134, 137, 188
Sir Gawain and the Green Knight: 90
Slang: 201–204
Slovak: 25
Slovenian: 26
Slavonic: 23, 25
Smith, Sir Thomas: 146
Smith, Sydney: 209

Sohrab and Rustum: 22
Sorbian: 25, 26
South Central American dialect: 119
Southeast Midland dialect: 119
Southern American dialect: 45, 224–26
Southern British dialect: 122–24
Southern Mountain dialect: 225
South Slavonic: 26
Spanish: 4, 24
Spectator, The: 173
Spelling as a problem: 144
Spelling change: 113, 217–18
Spelling reform: 53
Spenser, Edmund: 134, 136–37, 152
Standard American: 211, 220
Standard British: 124–26, 210–11
Steele, Sir Richard: 168, 173
Swedish: 29
Swift, Jonathan: 53, 165–68, 174
Syntax, 154–60, 173

Table Alphabeticall, A: 144
Tacitus: 28, 57
Tagore, Rabindranath: 21
Tamil: 21
Tatler, The: 168
Telugu: 21
Tennyson, Alfred: 110, 128, 212
Tetrachordon: 140

Thackeray, William M.: 192
Tibeto-Chinese: 14
Tocharian: 20
Tom Jones: 127
Transposition: 52
Troilus and Criseyde: 119
Turkish: 4, 35

Ulfilas: 28
Umbrian: 24
Umlaut, 63–64

Vanity Fair: 192
Vedic: 20
Verb: 71–74
View of the Present State of Ireland, A: 152
Vocabulary, contributions to, from: Celtic, 76–78; Latin, 78–85; Scandinavian, 85–90; French, 100–110
Volscians: 24
Voltaire: 5

Walker, John: 194–95
Waller, Edmund: 165
Wallis, John: 178
Walloon: 24
Waste Land, The: 210
Webster, Noah: 172, 208, 211
Webster's Third New International Dictionary: 191
Welsh: 26, 27
West Germanic: 30
West Greek: 23
West Midland dialect: 120
West Slavonic: 25
White Russian: 25
William the Conqueror: 94–96

Yeats, William Butler: 27

Zachrisson, Robert: 54

DATE DUE

GAYLORD			PRINTED IN U.S.A.